Sustainability in the Scottish Highlands

Scotland's Land
Series editor: Dr Annie Tindley

This series presents the latest scholarly work to academic and public readers on Scotland's land issues. Predominantly focusing on the history of Scotland's economic, political, and social and cultural relationships to land, landscape, country houses and landed estates, it also brings in cutting-edge approaches to explore new methodologies and perspectives around this politically contentious but stimulating issue. As an interdisciplinary series, it will necessarily contain a wide range of approaches, including history, law, economics and economic history, philosophy, environment/landscape studies, and human/cultural geography. The aim of the series is to bring together and publish the best work on land issues across a wide range of disciplines for a diverse set of audiences.

Published titles

The Land Agent: 1700–1920
Annie Tindley, Lowri Ann Rees and Ciarán Reilly (eds)

Scotland's Foreshore: Public Rights, Private Rights and the Crown 1840–2017
John MacAskill

Land Reform in Scotland: History, Law and Policy
Malcom Combe, Jayne Glass and Annie Tindley (eds)

Land Reform in the British and Irish Isles since 1800
Shaun Evans, Tony Mc Carthy and Annie Tindley (eds)

Town and Country Planning in the Scottish Borders, 1946–1996
Douglas G. Hope

The Estate and the Country House in Scotland, circa 1700: A Case Study of Sir William Bruce's Hopetoun House
Charlotte Abney Bassett

Sustainability in the Scottish Highlands: A Critical Ethnography of a Community Biosphere
Zoe Malcolm

edinburghuniversitypress.com/series/slf

Sustainability in the Scottish Highlands

A Critical Ethnography of a Community Biosphere

Zoe Malcolm

EDINBURGH
University Press

Edinburgh University Press is one of the leading university presses in the UK. Publishing new research in the arts and humanities, EUP connects people and ideas to inspire creative thinking, open new perspectives and shape the world we live in. For more information, visit www.edinburghuniversitypress.com.

Cover image: Plockton in Wester Ross Biosphere. Photo by Louise Pearson.
Cover design: Workhaus Designs

Edinburgh University Press Ltd
13 Infirmary Street, Edinburgh EH1 1LT

Typeset in 10.5/13pt Sabon by
Cheshire Typesetting Ltd, Cuddington, Cheshire
Printed and bound by CPI Group (UK) Ltd, Croydon, CR0 4YY

A CIP record for this book is available from the British Library

ISBN 978 1 3995 5652 1 (hardback)
ISBN 978 1 3995 5653 8 (webready PDF)
ISBN 978 1 3995 5654 5 (epub)

MIX
Paper | Supporting responsible forestry
FSC www.fsc.org FSC® C013604

This book is printed using paper from well-managed forests, recycling and other controlled sources

Contents

Figures

Abbreviations

ACC	Applecross Community Company
BCH	Biocultural Heritage
BCHT	Biocultural Heritage Territory
BR	Biosphere Reserve
GDO	Gaelic Development Officer
GME	Gaelic Medium Education
GSA	Galloway and Southern Ayrshire
HES	Historic Environment Scotland
HIE	Highlands and Islands Enterprise
MAB	Man and Biosphere Programme
MU	Manicouagan Uapishka
NTS	National Trust for Scotland
RLUP	Regional Land Use Partnership
SCF	Scottish Crofting Federation
SDGs	Sustainable Development Goals
SLC	Scottish Land Commission
SSE	South of Scotland Enterprise
UHI	University of the Highlands and Islands
UNESCO	United Nations Educational, Scientific and Cultural Organization
WNBR	World Network of Biosphere Reserves
WRB	Wester Ross Biosphere

Acknowledgements

I would like to dedicate this book to my research participants at the Wester Ross Biosphere. Their dedication to sustainability in difficult times is an inspiration. Many individuals have extended great hospitality to me over the years of working together and to them I am grateful. I have also benefited from the support and friendship of my doctoral supervisors and peers, my colleagues, my family and my husband. The book would not have been possible without their ongoing encouragement and support.

1

Introduction: A Critical Ethnography of a Community Biosphere

In the North-West Highlands of Scotland, since 2016, residents of Wester Ross and Lochalsh have been living in and managing a Biosphere Reserve (BR), or 'Biosphere'.[1] Scotland has two of the UK's seven Biospheres, which are part of a growing global network containing over 785 sites in 142 countries acting as 'places to provide local solutions to global challenges'.[2] BRs are a United Nations Educational, Scientific and Cultural Organisation (UNESCO) designation using participatory governance to adapt to regional conditions and foster collaborative action for sustainability among diverse stakeholders. In Wester Ross the Biosphere is community-led, representing a fairly unique approach in the World Network of Biosphere Reserves (WNBR). Whilst community participation in BRs has been somewhat researched,[3] such work is rarely driven by critical theory and this book is the first to explore what a community Biosphere means for sustainability in the Scottish Highlands. Importantly, community initiatives help to shift focus from individualised neoliberal responses to sustainability towards societal transformations that address the systemic nature of contemporary crises.[4] Thus, a community Biosphere might help us think and enact futures beyond the 'capitalist, growth-obsessed and ecocidal civilisation' of the present.[5] As places to foster positive connections between people and their environments,[6] BRs can also overcome the nature–culture dichotomy. This is a core focus of the book, alongside explaining the community Biosphere in Wester Ross as a rhizome – an assemblage of horizontal relations that opens up diverse, culturally specific sustainability trajectories, negotiated at the local–global nexus.

The book addresses four specific questions. First, what does the community Biosphere in Wester Ross mean in discourse and practice according to local actors? Second, how do actors involved in the community Biosphere negotiate nature–culture relations? Third, how are these relations shaped by the politics of scale, governance and land ownership? And finally, to what extent does the community Biosphere represent an alternative for more just and sustainable futures? Answering these brings together an array of complex and interwoven issues which are often siloed across academic disciplines, research fields and policy contexts. I adopt an interdisciplinary lens by working across critical heritage studies, environmental sociology, political ecology and human geography and utilise a critical theory approach to move beyond the 'common sense' of nature–culture dichotomies and neoliberal capitalist ideologies. After outlining this approach, I discuss the critical literatures that inspired the book across three themes: nature and heritage conservation, BRs in theory and practice, and nature–culture relations in the Scottish Highlands. The chapter concludes with an outline of the critical ethnographic methodology and the eleven remaining chapters.

THEORISING ALTERNATIVES TO COMMON SENSE

In order to imagine and enact more sustainable futures, we must move beyond what Antonio Gramsci called 'common sense'. Common sense is an 'uncritical and largely unconscious way of perceiving and understanding the world that becomes "common" in any given epoch'.[7] Common-sense discourses are naturalised ways of knowing that reflect elite ideologies and provide consent for the status quo of capitalist hegemony in everyday life.[8] The separation of nature and culture is common sense. It is a central ontology of Western modernity[9] and neoliberal societies.[10] The nature–culture dichotomy is embedded in common-sense capitalist and colonial ideologies which are themselves hegemonic, underpinning mainstream approaches to nature conservation.[11] Common senses and hegemonies are never fixed; they are challenged when we recognise that 'there are many alternatives'.[12] For example, alternatives can be found in the diverse ways of knowing and being among indigenous and colonised peoples that often challenge unsustainable thought and action.[13] Moreover, there are a 'sea of alternatives' to mainstream nature conservation, including convivial conservation, which is about ways of living better with each other and with nature.[14] Herein, I frame Wester Ross BR as an alternative to common sense; a case of culturally specific community action for more just and sustainable futures.

In moving beyond common sense I also draw on wider critical theories. I see value in adopting a 'both/and' approach,[15] bringing Gramsci's hegemonic politics together with the non-hegemonic politics of assemblage theory and anarchism. Wester Ross as a community Biosphere and rhizome is a case that centres the radical potential of BRs for more just and sustainable futures – theorised critically through (non) hegemonic politics. This perspective on BRs is sorely lacking, perhaps due to the historic dominance of the natural sciences in UNESCO's Man and Biosphere (MAB) programme and a disconnect between critical theory and mainstream sustainable development. Additionally, whilst BRs could encourage innovation and experimentation for radical socio-ecological transformation, this is not always occurring in practice.[16]

Finally, moving beyond common sense involves dissolving intellectual boundaries between nature and culture, and also heritage and sustainability. This is achieved through relational approaches working across nature and heritage conservation settings and positioning heritage within sustainability and nature–culture relations.[17] As future-focused concepts, both heritage and sustainability are invoked in different processes, values and visions of the future from business as usual to the socioecological transformation of capitalism.[18] A heritage sensibility recognises how the present is future-oriented and bound up with the past.[19] Indeed, we enact alternative futures through the ways that we engage with the past in the present.[20] My approach is fundamental to avoiding ahistorical analyses of contemporary environmental issues[21] – a critique levelled at Scottish environmental policies.[22] Understanding nature–culture relations in the Scottish Highlands today requires an appreciation of the regions' difficult pasts and their legacies.[23]

Heritage and nature conservation

Although heritage and nature conservation have largely evolved as separate areas of research, in both domains, critical scholars challenge the nature–culture dichotomy. This dichotomy represents the idea of fixed boundaries between 'spaces of nature and spaces of culture'.[24] For instance, 'the environment' is an 'abstraction' that represents naturalness and the absence of humans.[25] This is problematic conceptually and empirically, not least because 'the idea of naturalness is often the philosophical underpinning for waging a real war against indigenous peoples and local communities way of living and existing'.[26]

The nature–culture dichotomy is central to mainstream nature conservation and the heavily critiqued fortress model of protected areas that defines humans as a threat to nature.[27] US national parks, founded on narratives of 'wilderness', physically and ideologically erased indigenous peoples and cultures from the landscape.[28] Today, colonial narratives around protecting wildness continue to imply 'terra nullis' in landscapes that have always been inhabited[29] and the call to decolonise conservation is as relevant as ever.[30] In heritage conservation, the nature–culture dichotomy manifests in the separation of natural and cultural, tangible and intangible heritage in both policy and practice.[31] These are colonial constructs that reflect a Eurocentric bias in mainstream heritage designations, policies and practices.[32] Focusing on 'universal' value, mainstream approaches often neglect the interrelation of scales (local–global) and everyday heritage practices.[33] World Heritage Sites, for example, can displace local communities' heritage and worldviews[34] and we must better value diverse ways of knowing and doing heritage.[35]

In both nature and heritage conservation contexts there is a tendency to obscure relational, embodied ways of knowing and being in indigenous communities.[36] Arguably, this occurs through power relations that shape the production of common sense in service of hegemonic capitalist and colonial interests. Capitalist approaches to nature conservation have only intensified in recent years, with new markets and commodities from nature and the dominance of concepts like ecosystems services and natural capital.[37] Ultimately, 'saving nature' is about 'entraining nature to capitalism',[38] an approach supported by powerful global actors and processes like the UN Convention on Biological Diversity.[39] This involves elite land and resource grabs,[40] and ongoing processes of accumulation by dispossession, including violent enclosures for the creation of protected areas.[41]

In heritage conservation, power relations produce an 'authorised heritage discourse' – heritage defined and managed according to a narrow set of elite interests.[42] Therein, common-sense assumptions about the nature and meanings of heritage are tied to nationhood, professional values and material objects.[43] In contrast, critical scholars recognise heritage as a social construct and a practice or living process that can be produced 'from below' and in 'everyday' contexts.[44] Radical alternatives also draw inspiration from anarchist and decolonial thinking to challenge the legitimacy of state and private property models in favour of heritage as commons.[45] Key to this is resisting enclosures of common values by powerful actors through the commodification of heritage and creating more ethical models for working with communities and indigenous peoples' heritage.[46] Similarly, in nature conservation, alternative models suggest moving beyond hegemonic protected areas to 'promoted areas' and from privatised expert technocracies to common democratic engagement.[47] Critical approaches to nature and heritage conservation reinforce the need to transcend the nature–culture dichotomy and to challenge capitalist and colonial power relations. This means moving beyond common sense and finding ways to better value and recognise the diversity of alternatives, such as a community Biosphere in the Scottish Highlands.

Biosphere Reserves in theory and practice

BRs are not officially protected areas – they use soft law and do not bring new land use restrictions, nor does management come with its own legal mandate.[48] A BR is layered onto existing protected areas to create three new zones (core, buffer and transition) which align with the functions of conservation, logistic support and economic development (Figure 1.1). BRs emerged from the MAB programme in the 1970s, evolving over time with wider conservation logics.[49] Importantly, the Seville Strategy 1995 and the Lima Action Plan 2016 solidified the requirement for communities to be living in BRs to deliver sustainable development and participatory governance.[50] BRs not meeting this criteria were delisted or expanded,[51] nonetheless, there remains a concept–reality gap. This occurs where, for example, BRs are more conservation rather than development focused and use monocentric, top-down governance.[52] BRs can be places to demonstrate local solutions to global challenges but only where the concept is fully implemented.[53] Governance of BRs should be participatory, reconciling conservation and development alongside integrating scientific and traditional ecological knowledges.[54] BRs should foster collaborative approaches across multiple scales and sectors and between diverse actors regionally.[55] Thus, BRs often act as 'facilitators' of new sustainability networks.[56]

BRs also embody the local–global nexus. Globally, MAB philosophy emphasises discourses of sustainable development[57] and an 'endangerment sensibility' around biodiversity,[58] with individual BRs considered sites to translate such agendas into local/regional practice. Viewed critically, this remit and the BR designation can produce diverse outcomes across the WNBR. For example, in Guatemala, UNESCO's universalising logics problematically displaced local imaginaries,[59] whilst in Canada BRs are said to produce multi-scalar good governance.[60] Further research on local–global relations and socioecological transformations in different BRs and across the WNBR helps to enhance our understanding of MAB as a global, transdisciplinary learning network for sustainability.[61]

I focus here on BRs as a model for overcoming the nature–culture dichotomy; which they do by recognising multiplicity, relationality,[62]

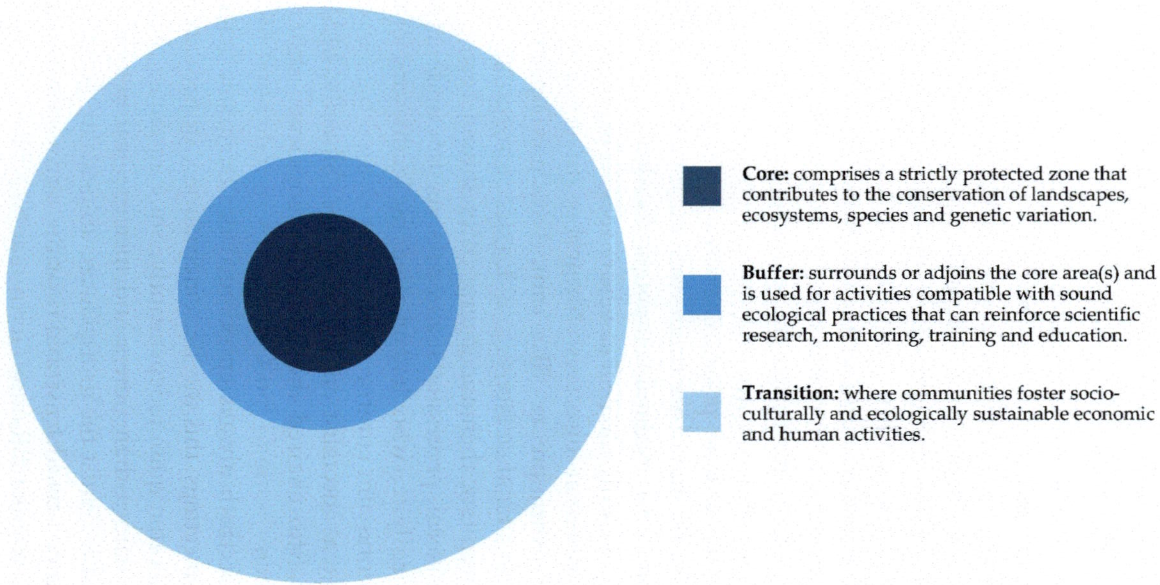

Figure 1.1 UNESCO BR zonation model.

and working at the human-environment interface.[63] BRs, for example San Pedro de Atacama in Chile, represent a 'complex system of resources and actors giving rise to specific types of nature–culture interactions' over time.[64] Additionally, BRs can be seen as biocultural models. Biocultural approaches address sustainability challenges through a plurality of human–nature interactions and worldviews.[65] Research of BRs emphasises how they support biocultural diversity,[66] produce relational understandings of sustainability and overcome socioenvironmental conflicts.[67] Importantly, BRs recognise the role played by indigenous peoples and local communities in stewardship of biocultural diversity and that traditional knowledges can inform place-based solutions for sustainability.[68] However, biocultural approaches are only valuable if they can account for power relations in the face of hegemonic cultural, political and economic forces and challenge the loss of distinct cultural practices, languages, knowledges, values and governance systems.[69]

Following a heritage sensibility, I therefore centre biocultural heritage (BCH) which embodies 'the culture, values and heritage of diverse peoples and their relationship with land'.[70] Although relevant to all societies, BCH is currently marginalised in cultures where the human–nature relationship is less acknowledged and in mainstream policy such as the Sustainable Development Goals.[71] BCH models emphasise the need to transcend conservation and development siloes,[72] and more radically centre land rights in decolonial governance through Biocultural Heritage Territories (BCHTs). As in-situ conservation, BCHTs, such as Parque de la Papa in Peru, allow communities to manage lands in accordance with their traditional knowledge, customary systems and cultural values, creating bottom-up resilient food systems.[73] Therein, *Sumaq Kawsay* (the holistic wellbeing of people and nature) serves as an alternative model of development.[74] So far BCH has received limited attention in BR contexts. One exception is research in Portugal's twelve BRs where BCH was argued as key to connecting people and nature, strengthening community identity and resilience and providing 'actionable pathways for addressing contemporary environmental challenges'.[75] Given the decolonial and community emphasis of BCH, it is highly valuable for exploring nature–culture relations in a community Biosphere and thinking beyond capitalist approaches to development and sustainability in the Global North.

Nature–culture relations in the Scottish Highlands

My interest in heritage and sustainability in the Scottish Highlands began several years ago when I conducted a discourse analysis of Scotland's nature conservation designations. Whilst reviewing documents on the creation of Wild Land Areas, I found examples of crofting organisations challenging common-sense discourses of wildness.[76] Crofting is an agricultural practice and form of land tenure that covers 25 per cent of the land of the Highlands and Islands.[77] Both the Crofting Commission and the Scottish Crofting Federation had argued against seeing the proposed areas as 'wild' given they were in crofting counties and crofting commons which had been worked by people for generations. Both suggested wildness contradicts the Gaelic concept of *dùthchas* – man's intimate relationship with and knowledge of land. These conflicting perspectives reflect contemporary challenges for more sustainable nature–culture relations in the Scottish Highlands and bring to the fore longstanding tensions around land throughout the regions' history.

The Highland Clearances of the eighteenth and nineteenth centuries fundamentally shaped communities and remain in local consciousness today.[78] The Clearances saw Highland landlords dispossess people from land to make way for capitalist 'improvement', namely large-scale sheep farming.[79] They formed the crofting system as a land tenure that ensured crofter's survival was dependent on selling their labour, such as in kelp harvesting industries.[80] Following 'improvement', the ideology of 'romance' created the 'Myth of the Highlands' – a cultural construct in which landscapes (seemingly absent of people or culture) were seen positively as natural.[81] This remains hegemonic common sense today, evident in the proliferation of Wild Land Areas, ahistorical constructions of landscape emptiness[82] and reoccurring accounts of 'lone, enraptured, males' seeking wild places.[83] Challenging this myth means recognising that Highland landscapes are not natural but cultural,[84] and their 'unpopulated character' is as much symbolic of the 'eradication of human communities' as it is 'wild nature'.[85] Additionally, it is argued that many Highland landscapes that appear wild are in fact degraded and require restoration.[86] From the mid-1940s, Frank Fraser Darling's work on the West Highland Survey led him to conclude the Highlands were a 'devastated countryside' and a 'wet desert' caused by deforestation, private property and the market economy.[87] His analysis offered an attempt at solving the 'Highland Problem' – namely economic decline and depopulation.[88] Thus, as much as the Highlands have been romanticised, they are also constructed as a 'problem'; a region economically and socially underdeveloped from the perspective of the British state.[89] The construction of the region as a 'special policy area' from the late 1800s to more recently has had both negative and positive connotations encompassing new crofting legislation and notions that governments and their agencies should support the Highlands and Islands in light of past injustices like the Clearances.[90]

Crucial context for this book is the recognition that the Highlands have been, and continue to be shaped by power relations in which the interests of traditional estate owners and state-led conservation solidify hegemonic capitalist and colonial relations.[91] Thus, I consider a critical and decolonising frame as necessary in the Scottish context as much as elsewhere globally. In particular, the *Gàidhealtachd* (emphasising Gaels in the Highlands) suffered historic colonisation with consequences for nature–culture relations. This includes radical change in land and natural resource governance associated with the Clearances and ongoing relations of domination between an imperial power and a marginalised Gaelic population.[92] The physical enclosure of commons accompanied the erasure of cultural relations with land, such as *dùthchas*, which was prevalent in Gaelic society pre-Clearances.[93] Gaelic culture and communities were equally eroded through the Myth of the Highlands and attempts by the British state to 'civilise' Gaels who were deemed backward and a barrier to capitalist 'progress'.[94]

This historical context is crucial for contextualising contemporary debates on conservation and development of the Highlands, including tensions between repeopling and rewilding. Repeopling is about responding to the history of Clearances and addressing contemporary demographic challenges linked to rural depopulation. It is also about reviving Highland communities and culture, drawing on concepts like *dùthchas* as part of creating 'a cultural, ethical and reciprocal relationship with place'.[95] Arguably this is part of a narrative in which crofters and local communities in the *Gàidhealtachd* are seen as the rightful stewards of Highland landscapes.[96] A focus on 'repopulating' landscapes also challenges notions of emptiness and wildness, offering alternatives by using productive pasts to inspire more diverse futures.[97] In contrast, rewilding is about making space for nature in a context of regional landscape degradation and amidst a global biodiversity crisis. Whilst this is important, rewilding is mostly driven by conservation elites, excludes communities[98] and reproduces power relations in land through the rise of green lairds.[99] This is perhaps unsurprising given that in Scotland, as elsewhere, nature conservation goes hand in hand with neoliberal capitalism. As such, it is the norm for corporate investors and elites to control large areas to produce commodities from land with little involvement of, or respect for, the rights of people living there.[100] Additionally, mainstream conservation reproduces a nature–culture divide, failing to recognise that ecological loss in the Highlands is 'deeply entwined with cultural loss' including Gaelic, place-based knowledges and traditional land practices.[101] Thus, both the nature–culture dichotomy and power relations associated with neoliberalism, land and nature must be challenged.

Currently there is a monopoly of private land ownership in rural Scotland.[102] This is despite an ongoing national policy and legislative agenda for land reform which has increasingly centred community empowerment and community land ownership for sustainable development.[103] Whilst there are positive accounts of communities challenging neoliberal property norms and the nature–culture dichotomy, such as on the Isle of Harris,[104] Wester Ross remains under extensive private ownership with large sporting estates. The colonial nature of land in Scotland is also increasingly evident, for example, estate ownership in the North-West Highlands is linked to profits from slavery.[105] As such, Scotland and the Highlands must be understood as both colonised and coloniser.[106] We can take seriously the colonial treatment of Gaels and their culture, whilst also recognising the role of Highlanders in systems of slavery,[107] 'New World' land grabs and settler colonialism.[108] This is not just about land but about recognising that contemporary sustainability transitions are shaped by colonial modernity.[109] Exploitative relations between the Global North and South include reliance on extraction of natural resources and cheap labour, as well as the framing of western ontologies and ideologies as superior to those of indigenous communities. Herein, I adopt a decolonial lens by rejecting this perceived superiority and bringing learning about sustainable nature–culture relations from Global South communities together with an ethnographic analysis of a community Biosphere in the Highlands.

A CRITICAL ETHNOGRAPHY IN WESTER ROSS

Wester Ross is a region rich in biodiversity and cultural heritage. It is a highly designated area for nature, containing many protected sites and special natures such as the ancient Caledonian woodlands at Beinn Eighe. There is strong Gaelic heritage and Norse influence as evident in place names, like *Ceann Loch Iù* (Kinlochewe) and Slattadale, alongside oral traditions and cultural practices. The region is one of the most sparsely populated areas of Europe and the Scottish Government's urban–rural classification system deems it a 'very remote rural' area based on population and accessibility of services.[110] There are around 8000 residents living in four main settlements of Wester Ross: Gairloch, Kyle of Lochalsh, Lochcarron and Ullapool as well as many smaller villages. A UNESCO BR was originally designated in 1976 covering only the area of Beinn Eighe National Nature Reserve. In 2015, the BR was expanded to over a hundred times this size, a process necessary to meet the new criteria that BRs should include living communities (Figure 1.2).

This newly designated area and the community organisation set up to manage it were the focus of a critical ethnography for my doctoral research. Critical ethnography is shaped by critical theory. Methodologically it is about 'what is' and 'what could be', recognising a desire not just to understand the world, but to change it for the better.[111] Thus, in my research with Wester Ross BR, I not only observed, but became active

Figure 1.2 Wester Ross Biosphere in North-West Scotland. © OS Base Map and NatureScot data (Open Licence v3).

as a volunteer and critical friend – a relationship which continues today. The book, however, is based on fieldwork conducted between 2019 and 2022, involving participant observation, interviewing and documentary analysis carried out in-person and online during the Covid-19 pandemic. When living in and visiting the area before and after the pandemic, I was predominantly based in Gairloch, Kinlochewe and Applecross, and thereafter Ullapool, Coigach, Kyle of Lochalsh and Garve (Figure 1.3). I adopted a multi-sited ethnographic approach to 'follow people, connections, associations and relationships across space'[112] and time. This helped to avoid seeing Wester Ross as a naturally given, homogenous area, recognising that it comprises a set of complex cultural and place-based relationships. Administratively, the BR region is part of the much larger Highland Council local authority area, as well as being served at a local level by seventeen community councils and numerous community development companies. As aforementioned there is widespread private land ownership, with around eighty different owners, including some national conservation charities and public bodies. Development and conservation are governed by wider national or regional bodies, such as

Figure 1.3 Sites of ethnographic fieldwork in Wester Ross. © OS Base Map.

Highlands and Islands Enterprise, NatureScot and Historic Environment Scotland. In my fieldwork, I explored relationships within and between such actors, whilst focused on the BR organisation. I participated in BR community work, governance meetings and had individual interactions with those involved, collecting rich qualitative data in the form of ethnographic fieldnotes, interview and meeting transcripts, as well as images and organisational documents.

One of the main ethical issues to navigate throughout the fieldwork was the nature of small communities where people are easily identifiable by their attributes, such as being chairperson of a community council or local development trust, and likewise with those working in specific roles for the BR. Throughout the book I use pseudonyms to protect identities as far as possible, providing some contextual details for participants who were most directly involved and gave consent for me to do so (see Appendix). With participants I negotiated conditions of anonymity individually, within the wider premise of naming the Biosphere organisation given it would be impossible to anonymise the Highlands only BR. My activist positionality also required an everyday ethics in which I continually negotiated consent as part of building relationships with participants.

An element of critical ethnography is creating relations of solidarity with participants, and I did this with key individuals involved in the BR. First and foremost, this was about offering my time, expertise and capacity to an under-resourced community organisation. Over the years I supported their work through simple acts like hosting online meetings and more complex ones like co-designing projects, writing funding applications and chairing the BR's education and research group. I have been a critical friend seeking to tell the story of the Biosphere on its own terms and create dialogue about new possibilities and directions. For example, encouraging the BR to take action on areas like climate change and Gaelic development, creating new local relationships between local actors, and bringing funding through new research collaborations. Over time, I built trusting personal relationships and friendships with key participants which further strengthened capacity for collaboration. Through critical ethnography research can be both a process of knowledge generation and an act of care. Key participants, and later close friends, often faced emotional challenges whether related to the BR or in their personal lives. Although I do not discuss these in the book, providing moral and practical support to others in difficult and emotive times was a fundamental part of my approach to research ethics.

CHAPTER OUTLINES

I unpack the story of Wester Ross BR across ten ethnographic chapters, followed by a theoretical synthesis chapter and a conclusion. Chapter 2 introduces the BR as a UNESCO designation and a community organisation, based on the perspectives of those involved. It explains why the BR was supported locally, and the process of zoning that established it. It also explains the organisational structure, roles and responsibilities of the BR organisation and perceptions of what the BR means for the area. Chapter 3 follows on from this by introducing the idea of the BR as placemaking, beginning with the creation of regional identity in a context of community fragmentation and local politics, before discussing key regional challenges related to sustaining fragile rural communities and places. The chapter offers an in-depth case study of the BR's sustainable tourism work which illustrates how the BR responds to, and is shaped by conditions not of their own making.

Chapter 4 addresses the theme of regional (un)sustainability and nature–culture relations. It outlines how BR actors further problematise regional conditions and unpacks contestations that shape BR identity and the pursuit of culturally specific sustainability action. It explains the BR's position on the integration of natural and cultural heritage and on cases like rewilding, which illuminate how actors negotiate and overcome the nature–culture dichotomy. Chapter 5 focuses on how BR actors approach conservation and management of cultural heritage, with examples linked to the region's loss of traditional knowledge and skills, as well as people, places and stories. It evidences the BR's biocultural approach where conservation occurs not for its own sake, but to support rural communities and livelihoods.

Chapters 6 and 7 offer in-depth analyses of the pasts, presents and futures of crofting and Gaelic in the BR. Chapter 6 unpacks how crofting is understood as heritage in Wester Ross, and the challenges surrounding the death of crofting communities. It also discusses crofting as a sustainable land use practice and livelihood, both within the BR and in a wider Scottish context. It concludes with a discussion about the BR's role in creating new crofting futures. Chapter 7 similarly explains Gaelic as heritage, drawing out the loss of Gaelic over time and the devaluation of Gaelic through the lived experiences of local people in Wester Ross. It then explains perceptions of Gaelic revival to show where Gaelic is valued as part of contemporary communities and how the BR became an actor for Gaelic development. Predominantly this includes valuing the language and culture as part of nature–culture relations, bringing to the fore Gaelic worldviews as part of local ecological and place-based knowledges.

Chapter 8 explores how the BR negotiates the local–global nexus, drawing on concepts of planetary consciousness and explaining relations of solidarity and inequality between actors in Wester Ross and the wider WNBR. It considers the issue of regional spatial justice in relation to common-sense narratives and practices of development in Scotland, and relations between the BR and Highlands and Islands Enterprise. It concludes with a case of food futures as an example of scalar politics associated with European (Brexit) and global contexts (Covid-19). Chapter 9 continues the focus on the politics of scale in the context of nature conservation in Scotland. It unpacks tensions around local–national interests and the responsibility of different actors (communities, third sector and the state) for managing nature. Alongside explaining how the BR works with NatureScot, the chapter compares approaches of national actors and the BR to outline possibilities for multi-scalar, biocultural conservation; articulating what is unique about the community Biosphere and how to move beyond mainstream conservation.

Chapter 10 considers how actors interpret the role of the BR in relation to the regions' land use and ownership. It draws on perspectives of BR actors, landowners and communities as part of explaining the challenges and opportunities for more sustainable and engaged relations with land. It presents the case study of Applecross where a local community development trust has been actively pursuing community land and asset ownership on a peninsula almost entirely privately owned. The case illustrates key tensions and difficulties for local communities to self-determine their futures in Wester Ross.

Chapter 11 is about the BR as an alternative for just and sustainable futures. It syntheses examples from previous chapters to critically theorise the many alternatives of a community Biosphere in relation to hegemonic politics. Subsequently, it draws on anarchist praxis, biocultural heritage and planetary thinking, drawing out the book's main themes to articulate what it means to move beyond common-sense nature–culture relations. Chapter 12 concludes the book with a focus on two final themes of importance: the need for critical approaches to sustainability challenges, especially those involving communities; and the need to value the community Biosphere and BRs generally as part of creating more just and sustainable futures.

CONCLUSION

This book tells the story of a community Biosphere in the Scottish Highlands – a case chosen for its potential to overcome the nature–culture dichotomy and to challenge unsustainable capitalist, colonial relations. This chapter introduced the main context for the book, explaining my inspiration to move beyond common-sense approaches in Scotland and beyond. As an interdisciplinary, critical ethnography, the book asks what a community Biosphere means to local actors and how they negotiate nature–culture relations in discourse and practice. It situates the community Biosphere in scalar politics, power relations and governance contexts and unpacks many alternatives for sustainability. In so doing, it aims to generate new thinking and practice for more just and sustainable futures in both the Scottish Highlands and globally.

NOTES

1. Martin F. Price, 'The Evolution of the Biosphere Reserve Network in the United Kingdom,' in *UNESCO Biosphere Reserves: Supporting Biocultural Diversity, Sustainability and Society*, ed. M. Reed and M. Price (Routledge, 2020), 89–101.
2. 'What are Biosphere Reserves?' UNESCO, accessed 11 June 2025, https://en.unesco.org/biosphere/about.
3. Ana Filipa Ferreira et al., 'Biosphere Reserves' Management Effectiveness – A Systematic Literature Review and a Research Agenda,' *Sustainability* 12, no. 14 (2020): 5497; Susanne Stoll-Kleemann, Anne Cristina De La Vega-Leinert and Lisen Schultz, 'The Role of Community Participation in the Effectiveness of UNESCO Biosphere Reserve Management: Evidence and Reflections From Two Parallel Global Surveys,' *Environmental Conservation* 37, no. 3 (2010): 227–38.
4. Benedikt Schmid, Thomas S. J. Smith and Gerald Taylor Aiken, 'Governing Through Community: Transformative Geographies From the Bottom Up,' *Environmental Policy and Governance* 31, no. 3 (2021): 155–8.
5. Martin Savransky, 'Ecological Uncivilisation: Precarious World-Making after Progress,' *Sociological Review* 70, no. 2 (2022): 369.
6. 'About the Man and the Biosphere (MAB) Programme,' UNESCO, accessed 11 June 2025, https://www.unesco.org/en/mab/about?hub=66369.
7. Antonio Gramsci, *Selections From the Prison Notebooks*, trans. Quinton Hoare and Geoffrey Nowell-Smith (Lawrence and Wishart, 1998), 322.
8. Stuart Hall and Alan O'Shea, 'Common Sense Neoliberalism,' in *After Neoliberalism? The Kilburn Manifesto*, ed. S. Hall, D. Massey and M. Rustin (Soundings, 2015).

9. Dennis Byrne, Sally Brockwell and Sue O'Connor, 'Introduction: Engaging Culture and Nature,' in *Transcending the Culture–Nature Divide in Cultural Heritage Views From the Asia-Pacific Region* (ANU E Press, 2013).
10. Jeanne Bogert et al., 'Reviewing the Relationship between Neoliberal Societies and Nature: Implications of the Industrialized Dominant Social Paradigm for a Sustainable Future,' *Ecology and Society* 27, no. 2 (2022): 7.
11. Bram Büscher and Robert Fletcher, *The Conservation Revolution: Ideas For Saving Nature Beyond the Anthropocene* (Verso, 2020).
12. Christa Wichterich, 'Contesting Green Growth: Connecting Care, Commons and Enough, in *Practising Feminist Political Ecologies: Moving Beyond the Green Economy*, ed. W. Harcourt and I. Nelson (Zed Books, 2015), 83.
13. Iain MacKinnon, Lewis Williams and Arianna Waller, 'The Re-Indigenization of Humanity to Mother Earth: A Learning Platform For Cultivating Social-Ecological Resilience to Challenge the Anthropocene,' *Journal of Sustainability Education*, 16 (2018), http://www.susted.com/wordpress/content/the-re-indigenization-of-humanity-to-mother-earth-a-learning-platform-to-cultivate-social-ecological-resilience-and-challenge-the-anthropocene_2018_01/.
14. Büscher and Fletcher, *The Conservation Revolution*.
15. Mark Purcell, 'Gramsci is Not Dead: For a "Both/And" Approach to Radical Geography,' *ACME: An International E-Journal for Critical Geographies* 11, no. 3 (2012): 512–24.
16. Markus Leibenath et al., 'Biosphere Reserves as Landscape Laboratories for Sustainability Transitions,' *Landscape Research* 50, no. 3 (2025): 491–504.
17. Rodney Harrison, *Heritage: Critical Approaches* (Routledge, 2013).
18. Frank Adloff, 'Sustainability,' in *Critical Terms in Futures Studies*, ed. P. Heike (Springer International Publishing, 2019).
19. David C. Harvey, 'Heritage and Scale: Settings, Boundaries and Relations,' *International Journal of Heritage Studies* 21, no. 6 (2015): 577–93.
20. Rodney Harrison, Caitlin DeSilvey, Cornelius Holtorf et al., eds. *Heritage Futures: Comparative Approaches to Natural and Cultural Heritage Practices* (UCL Press, 2020); Harvey, 'Heritage and Scale,' 577–93; Colin Sterling and Rodney Harrison, 'Introduction: of Territories and Temporalities,' in *Deterritorializing the Future: Heritage in, of and after the Anthropocene*, ed. R. Harrison and C. Sterling (Open Humanities Press, 2020), 19–55.
21. Raphaël Mathevet et al., 'Using Historical Political Ecology to Understand the Present: Water, Reeds, and Biodiversity in the Camargue Biosphere Reserve, Southern France,' *Ecology and Society* 20, no. 4 (2015): 17.
22. Rebecca Main et al., 'Scotland's Environmental Histories: Mapping a Way Forward,' *Scottish Historical Review* 104, no. 2 (2025): 155–73.

23. S. Karly Kehoe and Chris Dalglish, 'History, Heritage and Sustainable Development: A Position Statement on the Scottish Highlands,' *Northern Scotland* 9, no. 1 (2018): 1–16.
24. Cormac Walsh, 'Landscape Imaginaries and the Protection of Dynamic Nature at the Wadden Sea,' *Rural Landscapes: Society, Environment, History* 7, no. 1 (2020): 1–20.
25. Tim Ingold, 'Globes and Spheres: The Topology of Environmentalism,' in *The Perception of the Environment: Essays on Livelihood, Dwelling and Skill* (Routledge, 2021), 209–18; Marcelo Lopes De Souza, 'Whose Environment? Epistemic-Political Disputes over a Concept and its Uses,' in *Undoing Human Supremacy: Anarchist Political Ecology in the Face of Anthroparchy*, ed. S. Springer et al. (Rowman and Littlefield, 2021), 119–40.
26. Charles R. Clement et al., 'Naturalness is in the Eye of the Beholder,' *Frontiers in Forests and Global Change* 4, no. 800294 (2021), 3.
27. Büscher and Fletcher, *The Conservation Revolution*; Bram Büscher, 'Reassessing Fortress Conservation? New Media and the Politics of Distinction in Kruger National Park,' *Annals of the American Association of Geographers* 106, no. 1 (2016): 114–29.
28. William Cronon, 'The Trouble with Wilderness: Or Getting Back to the Wrong Nature,' *Environmental History* 1, no. 1 (1996): 7–28.
29. Jenny Pickerill, 'From Wilderness to WildCountry: the Power of Language in Environmental Campaigns in Australia,' *Environmental Politics* 17, no. 1 (2008): 95–104.
30. William M. Adams and Martin Mulligan, 'Introduction,' in *Decolonizing Nature: Strategies for Conservation in a Post-Colonial Era*, ed. W. M. Adams and M. Mulligan (Earthscan Publications, 2003), 1–15.
31. Harrison, *Critical Approaches*.
32. Laurajane Smith, *Uses of Heritage* (Routledge, 2006).
33. Tracey Ireland et al., 'Engaging the Everyday: The Concept and Practice of "Everyday Heritage",' *International Journal of Heritage Studies* 31, no. 2 (2025): 192–215.
34. Lisa Breglia, *Monumental Ambivalence: the Politics of Heritage* (University of Texas Press, 2006); Michelle Cocks, Susanne Vetter and K. Freerk Wiersum, 'From Universal to Local: Perspectives on Cultural Landscape Heritage in South Africa,' *International Journal of Heritage Studies* 24, no. 1 (2018): 35–52; Graeme MacRae, 'Universal Heritage Meets Local Livelihoods: "Awkward Engagements" at the World Cultural Heritage Listing in Bali,' *International Journal of Heritage Studies* 23, no. 9 (2017): 846–59.
35. Tim Winter, 'Clarifying the Critical in Critical Heritage Studies,' *International Journal of Heritage Studies* 19, no. 6 (2013): 532–45.
36. Leane Makey, '"Thinking With Kaipara": A Decolonising Methodological Strategy to Illuminate Social Heterogenous Nature–culture Relations in Place,' *Nature and Space* 0 (2022): 1–29.

37. Büscher and Fletcher, *The Conservation Revolution.*
38. Bram Büscher et al., 'Towards a Synthesized Critique of Neoliberal Biodiversity Conservation,' *Capitalism Nature Socialism* 23, no. 2 (2012): 7.
39. Catherine Corson and Kenneth Iain MacDonald, 'Enclosing the Global Commons: The Convention on Biological Diversity and Green Grabbing,' *Journal of Peasant Studies* 39, no. 2 (2012): 263–83.
40. Evangelia Apostolopoulou and William M. Adams, 'Neoliberal Capitalism and Conservation in the Post-Crisis Era: the Dialectics of "Green" and "Un-Green" Grabbing in Greece and the UK,' *Antipode* 47, no. 1 (2015): 15–35; Wendy W. Wolford et al., 'Global Land Deals: What Has Been Done, What Has Changed, and What's Next?," *Journal of Peasant Studies* 0, no. 0 (2024): 1–38.
41. David Harvey, 'The "New" Imperialism: Accumulation by Dispossession,' *The Socialist Register* (2004): 63–87; Alice B. Kelly, 'Conservation Practice as Primitive Accumulation,' *Journal of Peasant Studies* 38, no. 4 (2011): 683–701.
42. Smith, *Uses of Heritage.*
43. Smith, *Uses of Heritage*; Breglia, *Monumental Ambivalence.*
44. Breglia, *Monumental Ambivalence*; Kehoe and Dalglish, 'History, Heritage and Sustainable Development,' 11.; Iain J. M. Robertson, 'Introduction: Heritage from Below,' in *Heritage from Below*, ed. I. J. M. Robertson (Routledge, 2016).; Iain J. M Robertson, 'Afterword,' in *After Heritage: Critical Perspectives From Below*, ed. H. Muzzaini and C. Minca (Elgar, 2018), 169–180; Ireland et al., 'Everyday Heritage,' 192–215.
45. Colleen Morgan, 'Save The Date for Future Mourning: Prefiguration and Heritage,' *Forum Kritische Archäologie* 10 (2021): 1–5; Zoe Russell, 'An Anarchist Imagination for Critical Heritage Studies: Prefiguring Equitable and Sustainable Futures in Crofting and Beyond,' in *The Routledge International Handbook of Heritage and Politics*, ed. Gönül Bozoğlu, Gary Campbell, Laurajane Smith and Christopher Whitehead (Routledge, 2024); Pablo Alonso Gonzalez, 'From a Given to a Construct: Heritage as a Commons,' *Cultural Studies* 28, no. 3 (2013): 359–90.
46. James L. Flexner, 'Doing Archaeology in Non-State Space,' *Journal of Contemporary Archaeology* 5, no. 2 (2018): 254–9; Edward Gonzalez-Tennant, 'Anarchism, Decolonization, and Collaborative Archaeology,' *Journal of Contemporary Archaeology* 5, no. 2 (2018): 238–44; Helen Graham, 'Publics and Commons: The Problem of Inclusion for Participation,' *ARKEN Bulletin* 7, (2017): 150–68; Helen Graham, 'Horizontality: Tactical Politics for Participation and Museums,' in *Engaging Heritage: Engaging Communities. Heritage Matters*, ed. B. Onciul, M. L Stefano and S. Hawke (Boydell and Brewer, 2017), 73–90; David Pacifico, 'Beyond the Property Paradigm: Fragments for an Anarchist Approach to Archaeological Heritage,' *Journal of Contemporary Archaeology* 5, no. 2 (2018): 283–302.

47. Büscher and Fletcher, *The Conservation Revolution*.
48. Marc Hockings, Ian Lilley, Diane Matar et al., 'Integrating Science and Local Knowledge to Strengthen Biosphere Reserve Management,' in *UNESCO Biosphere Reserves: Supporting Biocultural Diversity, Sustainability and Society*, ed. M. Reed and M. Price (Routledge, 2020), 241–54.
49. Stefan Bargheer, 'Conserving the Future: UNESCO Biosphere Reserves as Laboratories For Sustainable Development,' in *Endangerment, Biodiversity and Culture*, ed. F. Vidal and N. Dias (Routledge, 2015), 115–33; Desirée Fiske, 'Towards an Anthropocene Narrative and a New Philosophy of Governance: Evolution of Global Environmental Discourse in the Man and the Biosphere Programme,' *Journal of Environmental Policy & Planning* 24, no. 1 (2022): 109–22.
50. Maureen Reed, 'Conceptual Origins and First-Generation Biosphere Reserves,' in *UNESCO Biosphere Reserves: Supporting Biocultural Diversity, Sustainability and Society*, ed. M. Reed and M. Price (Routledge, 2020), 13–28; Martin F. Price, 'The Re-Territorialisation of Biosphere Reserves: The Case of Wester Ross, Northwest Scotland,' *Environmental Science & Policy* 72 (2017): 30–40.
51. Martin F. Price, 'The Evolution of the Biosphere Reserve Network in the United Kingdom,' in *UNESCO Biosphere Reserves: Supporting Biocultural Diversity, Sustainability and Society*, ed. M. Reed and M. Price (Routledge, 2020), 89–101.
52. Mario Torralba, Maria Garcia-Martin and Cristina Quintas-Soriano et al., 'Implementation of Social-Ecological Management Approaches in Biosphere Reserves in the Mediterranean Basin,' in *UNESCO Biosphere Reserves: Supporting Biocultural Diversity, Sustainability and Society*, ed. M. Reed and M. Price (Routledge, 2020), 281–96; Klara Johanna Winkler, 'The Implementation of the Conceptual Shift in Conservation: Pathways of Three German UNESCO Biosphere Reserves,' *Ecosystems and People*, 15, no. 1 (2019): 173–180.
53. Tania Moreno-Ramos and Eduard Müller, 'Biosphere Reserves, Ideal Sites to Implement Holistic Approaches in Regenerative Development,' in *UNESCO Biosphere Reserves: Supporting Biocultural Diversity, Sustainability and Society*, ed. M. Reed and M. Price (Routledge, 2020), 254–69.
54. Hockings et al., 'Integrating Science,' 241–54.
55. Maureen Reed and Martin F. Price, 'Unfinished Business: The Present and Future Contributions of Biosphere Reserves to Sustainability Science,' in *UNESCO Biosphere Reserves: Supporting Biocultural Diversity, Sustainability and Society*, ed. M. Reed and M. Price (Routledge, 2020), 321–32; Heike Walk, Vera Luthhardt and Benjamin Nölting, 'Participatory Learning For Transdisciplinary Science in Biosphere Reserves: A Modified Role For Universities,' in *UNESCO Biosphere Reserves: Supporting Biocultural Diversity, Sustainability and Society*, ed. M. Reed and M. Price (Routledge, 2020), 297–309.

56. Julia Baird et al., 'Integrating Conservation and Sustainable Development Through Adaptive Co-management in UNESCO Biosphere Reserves,' *Conservation and Society* 16, no. 4 (2018): 409–19; Julia Baumgartner et al., 'Biosphere Reserves as Drivers of Regional Governance? Communication Challenges Within the UNESCO Biosphere Reserves Engiadina Val Müstair (Switzerland) and Schwäbische Alb (Germany),' *eco.mont Journal on Protected Mountain Areas Research* 15 (2022): 4–10.
57. Fiske, 'Towards an Anthropocene Narrative.'
58. Bargheer, 'Conserving the Future.'
59. Silvia Posocco, 'Zoning: Environmental Cosmopolitics in and Around the Maya Biosphere Reserve, Petén, Guatemala,' *Nature and Culture* 3, no. 2 (2008): 209.
60. Johanna Wilkes, 'Reconnecting with Nature through Good Governance: Inclusive Policy across Scales,' *Agriculture* 12, no. 3 (2022): 3.
61. Leibenath et al., 'Biosphere Reserves as Landscape Laboratories.'
62. Uta Berghoefer, Ricardo Rozzi and Kurt Jax, 'Many Eyes on Nature: Diverse Perspectives in the Cape Horn Biosphere Reserve and their Relevance for Conservation,' *Ecology and Society* 15, no. 1 (2010), 18.
63. Erik Aschenbrand and Thomas Michler, 'Why Do UNESCO Biosphere Reserves Get Less Recognition than National Parks? A Landscape Research Perspective on Protected Area Narratives in Germany,' *Sustainability* 13, no. 24 (2021): 13647; Johanna Wilkes, 'Reconnecting with Nature through Good Governance: Inclusive Policy across Scales,' *Agriculture* 12, no. 3 (2022): 3.
64. Constanza Parra and Frank Moulaert, 'The Governance of the Nature–Culture Nexus: Lessons Learned from the San Pedro de Atacama Case Study,' *Nature and Culture* 11, no. 3 (2016): 245.
65. Jan Hanspach et al., 'Biocultural Approaches to Sustainability: A Systematic Review of the Scientific Literature,' *People and Nature* 2, no. 3 (2020): 643–59.
66. Peter Bridgewater, 'Biosphere Reserves: Special Places for People and Nature,' *Environmental Science and Policy* 5, no. 1 (2002): 9–12; Maureen Reed and Martin F. Price, eds., *UNESCO Biosphere Reserves: Supporting Biocultural Diversity, Sustainability and Society* (Routledge, 2020); Peter Bridgewater and Ian D. Rotherham, 'A Critical Perspective on the Concept of Biocultural Diversity and its Emerging Role in Nature and Heritage Conservation,' *People and Nature* 1, no. 3 (2019): 291–304.
67. Alicia D. Barraclough et al., 'Global Knowledge–Action Networks at the Frontlines of Sustainability: Insights from Five Decades of Science for Action in UNESCO's World Network of Biosphere Reserves,' *People and Nature* 5, no. 3 (2023): 1430–44.
68. Hockings et al., 'Integrating Science,' 241–54.

69. Juliana Merçon et al., 'From Local Landscapes to International Policy: Contributions of the Biocultural Paradigm to Global Sustainability,' *Global Sustainability* 2, no. e7 (2019): 1–11.
70. Alexandria K. Poole, 'Where Is Goal 18? The Need for Biocultural Heritage in the Sustainable Development Goals,' *Environmental Values* 27, no. 1 (2018): 57.
71. Michelle L. Cocks, 'Biocultural Diversity: Moving Beyond the Realm of "Indigenous" and "Local" People,' *Human Ecology* 34, no. 2 (2006): 185–200; Poole, 'Goal 18', 55–80.
72. Anneli Ekblom et al., 'Conservation Through Biocultural Heritage – Examples from Sub-Saharan Africa,' *Land* 8, no. 1 (2019): 1–15; Karl-Johan Lindholm and Anneli Ekblom, 'A Framework for Exploring and Managing Biocultural Heritage,' *Anthropocene* 25 (March 2019): 1–11.
73. Krystyna Swiderska and Alejandro Argumedo, 'What is Biocultural Heritage?' *International Institute for Environment and Development*, 2017, https://pubs.iied.org/g04151; Krystyna Swiderska et al., 'Indigenous Peoples' Food Systems and Biocultural Heritage: Addressing Indigenous Priorities Using Decolonial and Interdisciplinary Research Approaches,' *Sustainability* 14, no. 18 (2022): 11311.
74. Sammi Bennett and Krystyna Swiderska, 'Sumaq Kawsay: Alternative Development Rooted in the Wellbeing of Humans and Nature' (2023), https://biocultural.iied.org/sumaq-kawsay-alternative-development-rooted-wellbeing-humans-and-nature.
75. Maria F. Rollo, 'Interconnected Nature and People: Biosphere Reserves and the Power of Memory and Oral Histories as Biocultural Heritage for a Sustainable Future,' *Sustainability* 17, no. 9 (2025): 1–33.
76. Zoe Russell, 'Common Sense Discourses of Nature: A Gramscian Analysis of Conservation Designations in the Scottish Highlands,' in *Heritage and Environment* (ICC, 2021), 47–66.
77. 'Frequently Asked Questions,' Scottish Crofting Federation, accessed 11 June 2025, https://www.crofting.org/about-scf/frequently-asked-questions/.
78. Siân Jones, '"Thrown Like Chaff in the Wind": Excavation, Memory and the Negotiation of Loss in the Scottish Highlands,' *International Journal of Historical Archaeology* 16, no. 2 (2012): 346–66; Magnus Course, 'Houses of Uist: Memory and Dwelling in the Outer Hebrides: Houses of Uist,' *Journal of the Royal Anthropological Institute* 25, no. 1 (2018): 1.
79. Peter Womack, *Improvement and Romance: Constructing the Myth of the Highlands* (Macmillan, 1989), 2.
80. James Hunter, *The Making of the Crofting Community* (Birlinn, 2000).
81. Womack, *Improvement and Romance.*
82. Main et al., 'Scotland's Environmental Histories'; Edward Stewart, 'Wicked Wild Wastes? Challenging Wildness through Repopulating Approaches

to Archaeological Narratives in Scottish Highland Landscapes,' *Scottish Historical Review* 104, no. 2 (2025): 249–77.

83. Kathleen Jamie, 'A Lone Enraptured Male', review of *The Wild Places*, by Robert Macfarlane, Psychology and Anthropology, *London Review of Books*, 6 March 2008, https://www.lrb.co.uk/the-paper/v30/n05/kathleen-jamie/a-lone-enraptured-male.
84. Patricia Macdonald and Angus Macdonald, 'Marginal Lands? An Overview of the Environmental Contexts of Cultural Landscapes in the Highlands and Islands of Scotland,' *International Journal of Heritage Studies* 15, no. 2–3 (2009): 108–41.
85. James Hunter, *On the Other Side of Sorrow: People and Nature in the Highlands* (Birlinn, 2014).
86. Hunter, *Other Side of Sorrow*.
87. Frank Fraser Darling, *Natural History in the Highlands and Islands* (London, 1947); Frank Fraser Darling, ed., *West Highland Survey: An Essay in Human Ecology* (London, 1955).
88. M. S. Brokaw, 'Solving the "Highland Problem": Frank Fraser Darling and the West Highland Survey, 1943–1955' (unpublished MPhil thesis, University of St Andrews: 2004).
89. Katie Louise McCullough, 'Resolving the "Highland Problem": The Highlands and Islands of Scotland and the European Union,' *Local Economy* 33, no. 4 (2018): 421–37; Gillian Munro and Keith Hart, '"The Highland Problem": State and Community in Local Development,' Arkleton Centre for Rural Development Research (2000), 49.
90. Ewen A. Cameron, 'The Scottish Highlands as a Special Policy Area, 1886 to 1965,' *Rural History* 8, no. 2 (1997): 195–215.
91. Mark Toogood, 'Decolonizing Highland Conservation,' in *Decolonizing Nature: Strategies for Conservation in a Post-Colonial Era*, ed. W. M Adams and M. Mulligan (Earthscan Publications, 2003), 152–71.
92. Iain MacKinnon, 'Colonialism and the Highland Clearances,' *Northern Scotland* 8, no. 1 (2017): 22–48; Iain MacKinnon, '"Decommonising the Mind": Historical Impacts of British Imperialism on Indigenous Tenure Systems and Self-Understanding in the Highlands and Islands of Scotland,' *International Journal of the Commons* 12, no. 1 (2018): 278–300; Iain MacKinnon, 'The Invention of the Crofting Community: Scottish History's Elision of Indigenous Identity, Ideology and Agency in Accounts of Land Struggle in the Modern Gàidhealtachd,' *Scottish Historical Review* 98, no. 1 (2019): 71–102; Iain MacKinnon, 'Recognising and Reconstituting Gàidheil Ethnicity,' *Scottish Affairs* 30, no. 2 (2021): 212–30.
93. MacKinnon, 'Decommonising the Mind,' 278–300.
94. Tom Devine, *Clanship to Crofters' War: The Social Transformation of the Scottish Highlands* (Manchester University Press, 1994).
95. Mairi McFadyen and Raghnaid Sandilands, 'On "Cultural Darning and

Mending": Creative Responses to *Ceist An Fhearainn* / The Land Question in the *Gàidhealtachd*,' *Scottish Affairs* 30, no. 2 (2021): 173.

96. Toogood, 'Decolonizing Highland Conservation,' 153.
97. Stewart, 'Wicked Wild Wastes?'
98. Alison Martin et al., 'Who Decides? The Governance of Rewilding in Scotland "between the Cracks": Community Participation, Public Engagement, and Partnerships,' *Journal of Rural Studies* 98 (February 2023): 80–91.
99. Fraser Macdonald, 'Wild Beasts,' *London Review of Books* 43, no. 18 (2021): 44–5.
100. Matias E. Margulis, Nora McKeon and Saturnino M. Borras, 'Land Grabbing and Global Governance: Critical Perspectives,' *Globalizations* 10, no. 1 (2013): 1–23.
101. Mairi McFadyen et al., *Integrating Intangible Cultural Heritage in Nature Recovery: A Place-Sensitive Approach in the Scottish Highlands* (British Academy, 2025), https://www.thebritishacademy.ac.uk/documents/5971/00012_Nature_Recovery_Paper_7_-_McFadyen_Final.pdf.
102. Andy Wightman, 'Who Owns Scotland?' (2025), https://andywightman.scot/wp-content/uploads/2025/03/WOS_2024.pdf.
103. Malcolm Combe, Jayne Glass and Annie Tindley, *Land Reform in Scotland: History, Law and Policy* (Edinburgh University Press, 2020); Andrea Ross, 'The Evolution of Sustainable Development in Scotland – A Case Study of Community Right-To-Buy Law and Policy 2003–2018,' *Sustainability* 11, no. 1 (2019): 1–18.
104. Fiona Mackenzie, *Places of Possibility: Property, Nature and Community Land Ownership* (John Wiley Sons, 2013).
105. Iain MacKinnon and Andrew Mackillop, *Plantation Slavery and Landownership in the West Highlands and Islands: Legacies and Lessons*, Community Land Scotland (2020), https://www.communitylandscotland.org.uk/wp-content/uploads/2020/11/Plantation-slavery-and-landownership-in-the-west-Highlands-and-Islands-legacies-and-lessons.pdf.
106. Toogood, 'Decolonizing Highland Conservation.'
107. David Alston, *Slaves and Highlanders: Silenced Histories of Scotland and the Caribbean* (Edinburgh University Press, 2021).
108. John C. Weaver, *Great Land Rush and the Making of the Modern World, 1650*–1900 (McGill-Queen's University Press, 2003).
109. Saurabh Arora and Andy Stirling, 'Colonial Modernity and Sustainability Transitions: A Conceptualisation in Six Dimensions,' *Environmental Innovation and Societal Transitions* 48, (2023): 100733.
110. Urban-Rural Classification 2020, Scottish Government, accessed 11 June 2025, https://www.gov.scot/publications/scottish-government-urban-rural-classification-2020/pages/2/.

111. Jim Thomas, *Doing Critical Ethnography* (Sage, 1993), 4; Soyini Madison, *Critical Ethnography: Method, Ethics, and Performance* (Sage, 2005).
112. Mark-Anthony Falzon, 'Introduction: Multi-Sited Ethnography: Theory, Praxis and Locality in Contemporary Research,' in *Multi-Sited Ethnography: Theory, Praxis and Locality in Contemporary Research*, ed. M. A. Falzon (Routledge, 2009), 2.

2

The Wester Ross Biosphere: Designation and Organisation

THE CONCEPT–REALITY GAP REFLECTS the difference between the ideal of the Biosphere Reserve (BR) model in theory and its implementation in practice (see Chapter 1). No two BRs are the same globally, each establishing unique approaches to participatory governance that are adapted to regional circumstances. This chapter introduces how the BR has been interpreted and applied in Wester Ross, in the North-West Scottish Highlands. It unpacks the regional conditions surrounding the creation of the designation and the organisation that was set up to manage it, focusing on what these mean for communities, heritage and sustainability according to local actors.

The first half of the chapter discusses perceptions of the BR around the time of its redesignation, derived from consultation documents and local actors who were involved. It also considers the BR's zoning process and the implications of this for ordering nature–culture relations in association with state conservation logics. The second half of the chapter introduces the community organisation Wester Ross Biosphere (WRB). It explains key characteristics and interests of the individuals involved and their reasons for participating in this UNESCO sustainability initiative. Additionally, it outlines key organisational practices, decision-making structures and wider organisational strategies, such as thematic working groups and WRB's (2018–23) strategic plan. It offers insight into how those involved perceive the workings of the organisation in the first instance, including challenges associated with being an underfunded and misunderstood community Biosphere.

THE BIOSPHERE AS DESIGNATION

Following consultation of communities across Wester Ross and Lochalsh about the possibility of expanding the existing Beinn Eighe BR, a Highland Council report concluded there was: 'a strong community desire to progress with the process of redesignation'. From consultation documents, and discussions with local actors, I ascertained that this support was largely because the UNESCO BR was interpreted as different to the kinds of conservation that had come before.

Not another designation

Early into my fieldwork, I gained insight into perceptions of the BR designation and consultation process from local people who had been involved. Alison was one such person, a Wester Ross resident who moved into the area to raise her family and work for NatureScot at Beinn Eighe National Nature Reserve. Although she is now retired, at the time she shared valuable local knowledge when we met in her offices and home to discuss the Wester Ross BR. She explained that initially NatureScot's position was that they were unlikely to push forward the UNESCO nomination themselves, but, 'if communities wanted it, we would support it'. She described how it was ultimately a few passionate advocates that moved things forward, whilst everyone else was simply not opposed to the idea of the BR. For her, the lack of opposition was because, unlike other conservation designations, the BR has a soft boundary. For example, landowners knew that it was 'not going to change anything'. Indeed, the Highland Council report on the BR describes the benefits of designation and states clearly it 'does not create new protected areas nor any new regulations and does not restrict economic development or the rights of landowners or the public'.

Alison situated local views about the BR in regional context by arguing that in Wester Ross, more so than elsewhere, 'people have a healthy disrespect for designations'. This was based on her past experience of consultations for the Wester Ross National Scenic Area where there were tensions and a feeling of 'not another designation'. She described that local people dislike top-down statutory conservation, which is evident in historic opposition to a National Park for Wester Ross (see also Chapter 9). Thus, for Alison, the BR's lack of statutory enforcement is what 'sold it' to people. The dislike of interference in land management she attributed to distrust of authority held by bodies like NatureScot. She reflected on occasions where they had 'got it wrong', such as how the designation of Inverasdale as a Site of Special Scientific Interest created 'uproar' by failing to consider the crofting landscape. One landowner also conveyed their scepticism of conservation, telling me how a Wild Land Area had created 'artificial boundaries' on their estate, 'slamming a line' down the middle to deem certain parts special and others not. Alison's view of conservation boundaries was also somewhat critical, in that lines are only drawn exactly around the features for which there is 'strong scientific evidence'. Whilst this is key to conveying values associated with national, European or international importance, for her this is only effective at protecting small areas and tends to ignore landscape scale. Hence, the BR was seen by her as a positive regional designation that could emphasise wider ecosystem functioning and sustainability.

In consultation documents, the regional focus of the BR was also valued by communities in association with international UNESCO status as a 'label to bring visibility' and 'put Wester Ross on the map'. This was tied to economic and social development opportunities for the region and fears about losing the positive connotation of UNESCO designation. Robert, a long-serving local Highland councillor who was also involved in the BR redesignation process, described that there was a desire to 'get recognition for Wester Ross', because despite its rich natural and cultural heritage it is lesser known compared with its neighbour the Isle of Skye. Additionally, there was a feeling that the BR would foster a 'bottom-up approach' that could 'empower communities', in contrast with years of 'top-down approaches'. Such feelings partly explain why the BR was implemented through a community-led governance model, as an alternative to state-led conservation. The empowerment of communities and working from the bottom-up represent the desire for new ways of doing conservation and development that arguably can open up space for a more 'nuanced, relational, place-based and situated perspective on nature and nature conservation practices'.[1]

BR zoning in practice

The criteria for BR zoning include biophysical, political and societal arguments, reflecting different conceptions of boundaries. Figure 2.1 shows the current Wester Ross BR zonation which is 96 per cent transition zone, 3 per cent buffer zones and 1 per cent core zones. A collaborative consultation process shaped the outer boundaries ensuring that the BR was compliant with UNESCO criteria to include living communities. Geospatial mapping helped to create the core and buffer areas which are required to be under conservation management. This process was supported by Norman, a long-term resident of Wester Ross who works as an estate manager for the National Trust for Scotland (NTS) at one of their regional properties. When it became clear that these properties could be part of a new BR, Norman became involved.

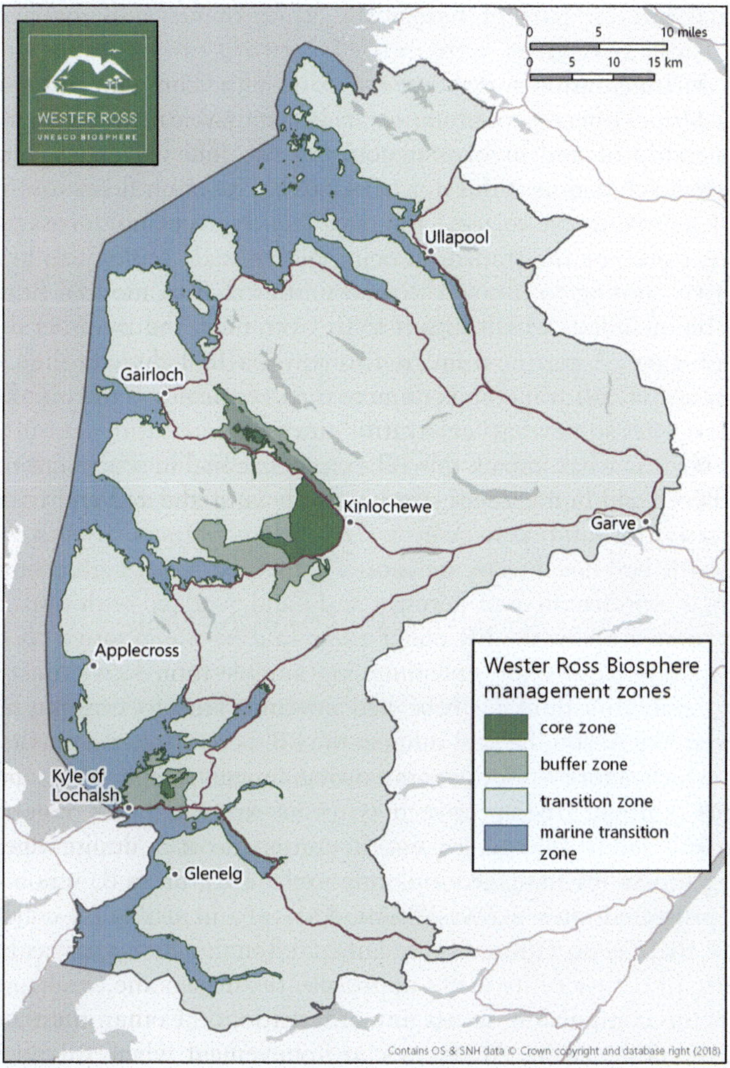

Figure 2.1 Wester Ross Biosphere zones. © Wester Ross Biosphere.

Drawing on his expertise, Norman was aptly placed to carry out what he called the 'objective assessment' of possibilities for the core and buffer zones of the BR. He explained that initially three possible core zones were identified. The first was Beinn Eighe, managed by NatureScot as a National Nature Reserve alongside the adjacent Loch Maree Islands that whilst privately owned are under a conservation management agreement. The second was *Collie Mhór* a Site of Special

Scientific Interest part of Balmacara estate owned and managed by NTS. These two areas were carried forward, and zoning working group documentation notes that inclusion of a core area in the south (*Collie Mhór*) offered communities in nearby Kyle of Lochalsh a sense of ownership of and involvement in the BR. The third possible core zone was excluded as it did not meet UNESCO criteria because it was part of a private estate used for deer stalking and not managed for conservation. For the transition zone, Norman described this as more subjective, aiming to allow all communities that wanted to be in the BR to be included, which meant that 'over time, the boundaries kept getting bigger'. A marine transition zone was also included to reflect the importance of cultural connections to the sea, although the biophysical boundary was somewhat 'arbitrarily' drawn.

It is unclear what impact this BR zoning has had in practice, as newly created core and buffer zones seem not to have stimulated any change in conservation or land management. This was confirmed by Alison, who said the BR had not directly influenced activity at Beinn Eighe. Similarly, Callum, a representative of Forestry and Land Scotland with responsibility for some areas in the BR buffer zone, said he was positive about the designation but it was not yet 'influencing' conservation decisions. Overall, he felt, 'nobody's thinking how can we contribute to this Biosphere?' However, like Alison, he saw value in the BR as a 'blanket' over the area, within which actors work towards existing designations' legal obligations.

From Norman's perspective it is unsurprising that BR zones have not directly led to change, because in conservation, a 'designation does nothing unless it's managed and enforced'. This, he said, was why so many protected sites across Wester Ross are in degraded condition, because there is no enforcement. Thus, although BR status was largely supported because of its softer approach, this brings the challenge that there is 'no compulsion' to act any differently, other than the threat of losing the designation. After years of involvement in the BR, Norman conveyed to me a 'disconnect' between BR management and landowners/managers. On this basis we might ask, as others have done, whether BRs are effective mechanisms for action on sustainability or simply 'bureaucratic labels'.[2] Both views are likely to be found in a BR, because different actors involved can interpret the designation as either legitimising the status quo or as a way to motivate change.[3]

BR designation and zoning also (re)order nature–culture relations. For example, the designation of Maya BR in Guatemala acted as a technology of governance informed by UNESCO-MAB's 'environmental cosmopolitanism' which combined with an authoritarian state logic to create 'zones of exception' – areas where human settlement and specific human uses of land are not permitted.[4] In Wester Ross the situation differed because core areas chosen were already absent of people. Although not creating new exclusions, the BR did reproduce state conservation logics and the Myth of the Highlands (see Chapter 1) in the nomination form to UNESCO by describing core zones as 'uninhabited, remote and wild'. Whilst the first is true, the latter are subjective terms. Critics of the language of 'remoteness' attributed to parts of the Highlands and Islands ask, remote from what? From whom? Moreover, as discussed in Chapter 1, wildness is a social construct, defined according to urban dwellers, ahistorically and without consideration of the multi-layered cultural contexts of a landscape.[5] The Letterewe estate to the shores of Loch Maree, part of the BR core zone, is promoted for tourism as 'the Last Great Wilderness of Scotland' by its owners – a phrase that ignores past and present cultures and land uses. The conservation logic of Biosphere core zones as areas for protecting wild, unpeopled areas ought to be critiqued – and producing environmental histories of landscapes in those zones could help to better articulate and reframe their value beyond the trope of wildness. Although part of the UNESCO nomination form, narratives of wildness have importantly not been promoted by the BR community organisation which has more consistently characterised the region as positively shaped by people and culture.

THE BIOSPHERE AS ORGANISATION

In 2016, Wester Ross Biosphere (WRB) was set up as a community-led organisation for governing the BR designation. Legally it was a company limited by guarantee, before later becoming a registered charity. Elisabeth, WRB's chairperson, described their community-led governance as 'unusual for Biospheres'. This is because most involve a more formalised stakeholder partnership with local government, state agencies, charities and community groups. Elisabeth, a retired resident of Wester Ross, with experience working in Highland Council and local community groups told me that whilst community model was positive, it also reflected that when establishing the BR organisation, there was very limited interest, funding or support from public sector organisations or the Scottish Government. Hence, being community-led is both a consequence of local resistance to top-down state conservation and a lack of wider financial or political buy-in.

Residents assemble

WRB has a volunteer board of directors, comprising between twelve and fifteen community members. Living in the BR is the main eligibility criterion to become a director but in a sparsely populated rural area the organisation has not been inundated with volunteers. Residents of the BR can also sign up to free membership and receive regular updates through a WRB newsletter. The membership is small, yet growing, with around 120 members, representing less than 2 per cent of the area's population. Most community members who stand for election are successful and the board also co-opts two to three additional directors to bring in local residents that have advisory expertise as Highland Councillors, like Robert, or as a NatureScot representative, like Alison. The board selects a chairperson whose role it is to facilitate meetings, a position that has been held by Elisabeth and later Norman of NTS.

Directors have lived in communities across the region, participated for varying lengths of time, to varying degrees, and for different reasons. One long-standing contributor is Seumas, a retired resident, who moved to Wester Ross from elsewhere in Scotland to raise his family. A Gaelic speaker, passionate about Highland culture, he became involved in the BR consultations:

> I attended the meetings where we tried to formulate the ideas for why Wester Ross would be a good place to have a Biosphere. We were concerned about the status of Wester Ross, both its economy as well as its sustainability as an area. The name Wester Ross, it was a political name but without a boundary. It's a defined area now, with a population of 8000.

More recently, Coinneach, a middle-aged resident originally from Wester Ross but who left the area for work, became a director. He inherited a family croft and returned to live on it, whilst retaining employment elsewhere. Coinneach explained how he was approached by Norman to join WRB, given his valuable crofting and Gaelic knowledge. Coinneach said he had agreed because he felt the Biosphere represented that 'human beings are the essential bridge between not just the built environment and the natural environment but also between grassroots community politics, and large-scale politics'. Most WRB directors were active not only in the BR but in other local community groups, representing a breadth of distinct interests and experiences, spanning cultural heritage, Gaelic, crofting, tourism, planning and development, land management, nature conservation and education. Whilst WRB engaged a diverse range of residents on its board, especially in terms of gender and sectors, the consistent core group were mostly over fifty years old.

Running WRB operationally was long-term staff member Phoebe. Whilst originally from the US, she settled in Wester Ross after marrying into a local family and having a child. She was responsible for writing the BR's nomination form to UNESCO and was subsequently successful in applying to work as the BR coordinator. Her employment has varied from two to five days per week, dependent on NatureScot and other project funding. There has also at different times been between one and four additional staff members especially for funded tourism and Gaelic projects. Figure 2.2 and Figure 2.3 show the composition of WRB as an organisation during my fieldwork and at the present time, with different organisational roles highlighted.

The main responsibility of directors was to attend board and thematic working group meetings held in person across the BR and online (the latter prompted by the Covid-19 pandemic). Meetings were the main space where WRB actors come together to create a collective organisational identity as the BR had no physical infrastructure. Board meetings focus on core priorities such as funding and keeping WRB afloat, whilst thematic meetings were intended for project development and space to engage local people in BR activities. The thematic groups were the only internal structure to WRB, comprising six groups chaired by different directors: Natural Heritage, Cultural Heritage, Sustainable Development (Tourism), Education and Research, and Marketing and Finance (see Figure 2.4). Directors could participate in as many, or as few, thematic groups as they wished, allowing them to share place-based, professional and personal knowledges and interests. For example, Jane, who had chaired the Cultural Heritage Group, was a local museum curator; Brian, who chaired the Natural Heritage Group, was a specialist in fisheries and biodiversity conservation, and Mairi, who chaired the Education and Research Group, was a youth worker.

Whilst Elisabeth always encouraged the groups to bring more local people into meetings, this was extremely varied, and groups operated differently and often quite independently. Some meetings and groups were consistently larger than others and meetings varied in length, format and frequency. Whilst the groups were an attempt to operationalise the BR remit, they caused frustration for Phoebe who for a time attended all meetings to take minutes. Given many meetings lasted two to three hours and could lack structure or purpose, she described them as a 'waste of time'. Alison, expressed similar frustrations during an Education and

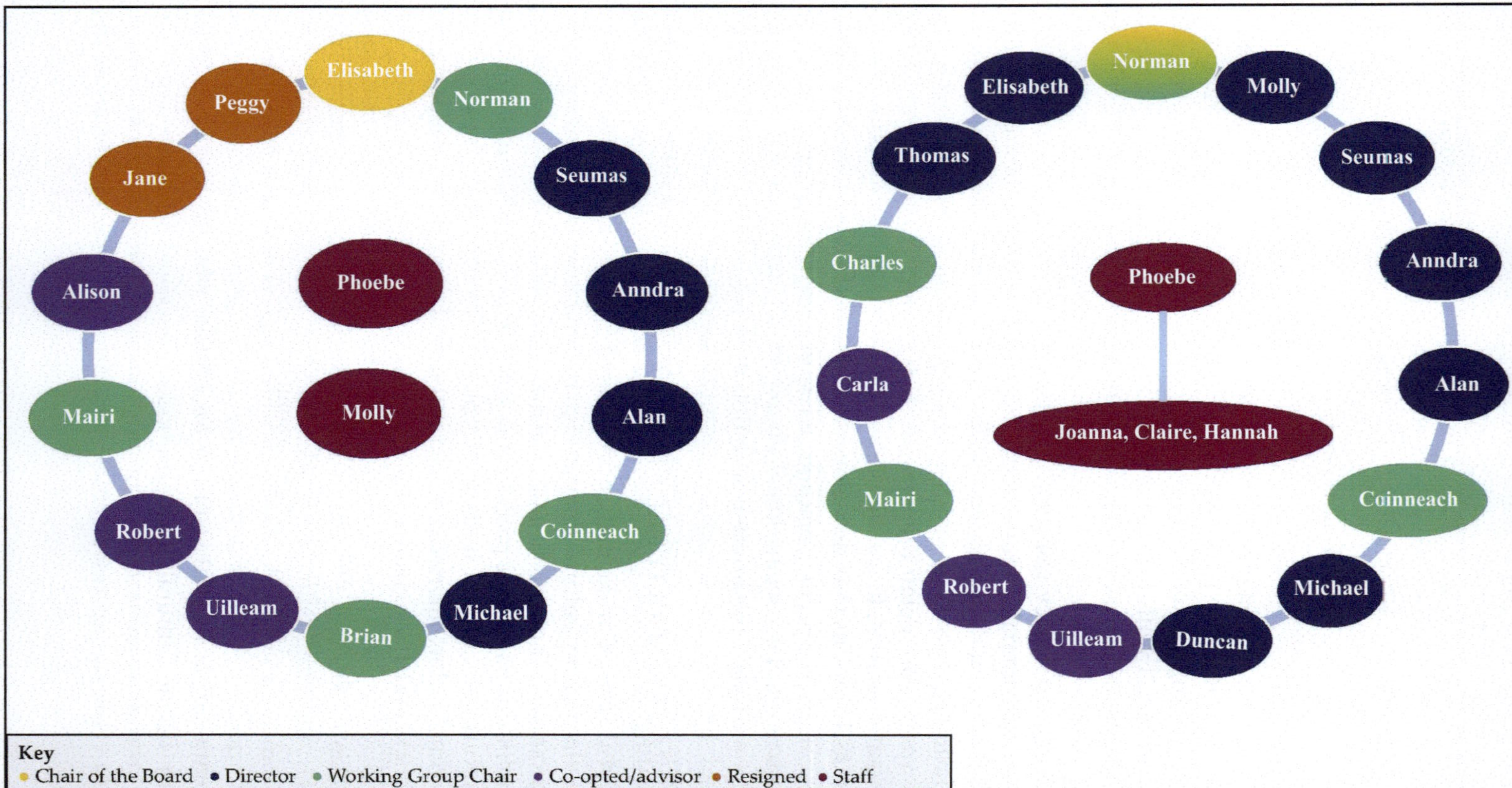

Figure 2.2 Wester Ross Biosphere 2019–22.

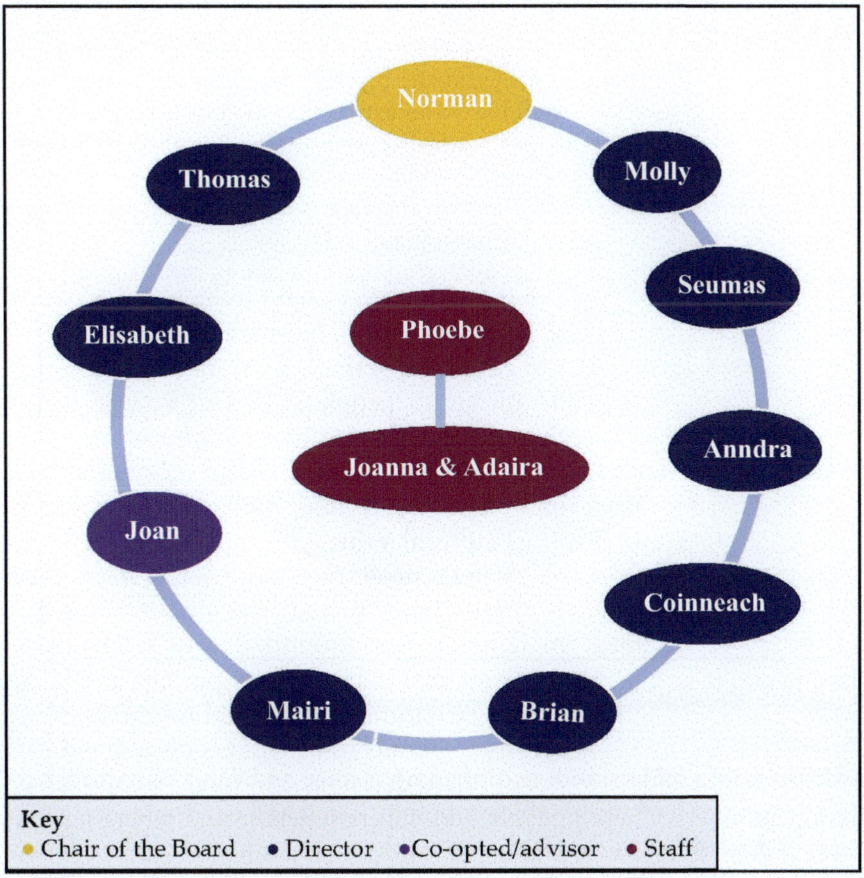

Figure 2.3 Wester Ross Biosphere 2025.

Research Group meeting where she said discussion was simply circling numerous talking points and not leading to any plans for action.

Deliberations

WRB's priorities for action were outlined in their first strategic plan covering the years 2018–23. A new plan is currently in development, tied to the BR's ten-year periodic review. The 2018–23 plan was produced by Phoebe from her research about the priorities of various local communities (often gleaned via community councils) and in accordance with the BR remit for conservation, sustainable development, knowledge sharing and communication. Specific aims and outcomes include: raised awareness of the BR and MAB across public, private and third sectors; increased community

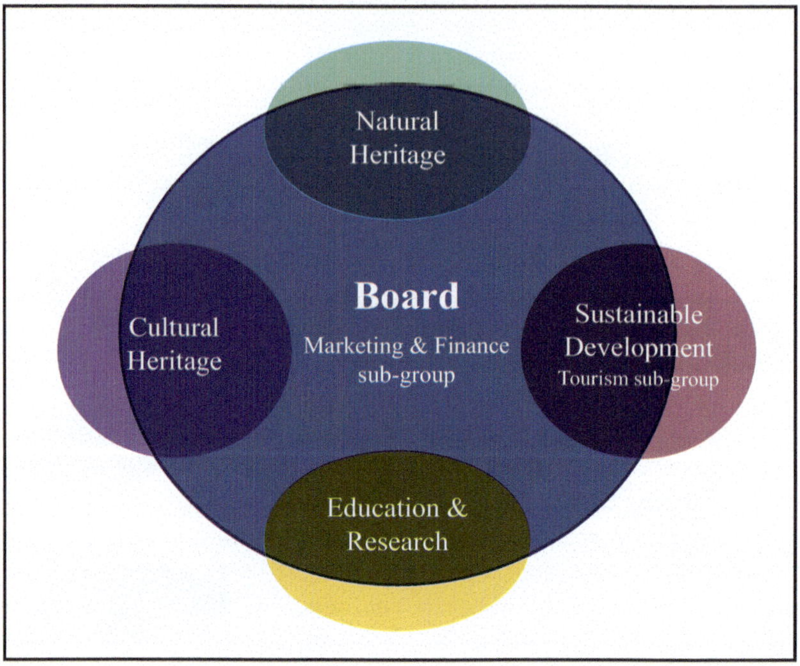

Figure 2.4 Wester Ross Biosphere thematic working groups.

awareness and understanding of the importance and value of natural heritage; promotion of sustainable economic, social and environmental practices; partnerships to develop sustainable tourism; knowledge exchange and networking with partners and other BRs. Each had a set of actions, with targets, timelines, suggested partners and resource implications. However, the plan was not always strategically utilised in thematic group discussions. The effectiveness of thematic groups was a regular source of debate among the board. Conceptual arguments included why WRB should have a separate Sustainable Development Group given this should underpin everything a BR does. Practical arguments for dissolution were that growing staff numbers created capacity for project development, allowing directors to focus on strategic issues. Deliberations continued until the decision to disband the thematic groups was made.

For WRB slow processes of deliberation have been central to organisational decision-making and social relations among actors. This reflects that what the BR means for communities, heritage and sustainability in Wester Ross is not given, but negotiated over time. Elisabeth explained how her role as chairperson meant encouraging people to put forward different ideas and for her to 'see both sides' of an argument.

Where deliberations were not always productive, Elisabeth, and later Norman, attempted to manage emotions and tensions among board members – with variable success. A desired outcome of WRB deliberations for Elizabeth was to be able to represent and reflect 'the needs of the area, thinking of what is for the greater good of the community as opposed to reflecting the thoughts and ideas of the board'. As I will show in this book, this required WRB actors to embrace the full complexity of articulating a culturally specific approach to sustainability and heritage in Wester Ross, inclusive of all residents.

The complexity of deliberations was sometimes made explicit at meetings, such as when Coinneach replied to a fellow director, 'everything you said I had thoughts and feelings about, and none of them are short conversations'. Often, Elisabeth or Norman would have to halt discussion without resolution or clear plans for action, usually suggesting future discussion was necessary. A former staff member and director once described a thematic group meeting thus: 'you just have like thirty people talking in all directions'. Such deliberations are arguably part of why some perceive WRB as a 'talking shop' and feel frustrated about overall progress. For example, Alison argued 'people have been talking about the Biosphere for about seven years now, and still nothing has happened'. Such feelings are tied to a strong appetite among many for significant and immediate action. Among the board, pace of change is seen as a problem and has caused tensions regarding WRB's financial fragility and organisational sustainability.

However, as participatory models BRs are not necessarily about rapid change; they require 'slowing down the pace'.[6] This is necessary for establishing meaningful processes of collaboration, creating inclusive and transparent communication, and trying to build trust and capacity among diverse communities and across cultures. Only by slowing down the pace can there be agreement on common actions and solutions to problems shaped by diverse interests. Whilst it may be frustrating for some, deliberations helped build inclusivity in WRB's place-based decision-making.

In the context of criticism against top-down approaches in Wester Ross, WRB as an organisation must build its legitimacy as a regional actor in a space where no such organisation has existed before. However, it is also true, as most WRB actors told me, that the organisation could have achieved more if they were adequately funded and resourced. Slowly over time WRB has sought to address this, first by becoming a registered charity to open up more funding opportunities, and thereafter by pursuing an entrepreneurial model, helping to support the BR's self-sufficiency through consultancy projects relevant to their expertise around regional sustainability.

'Biosphere, what's a Biosphere?'

Aside from keeping itself going financially, a major task for WRB, as for most BRs, is to raise awareness of a relatively misunderstood and unknown designation.[7] The perception that local communities and stakeholders are unfamiliar with BRs and WRB emerged frequently. During an international tourism project, Elisabeth welcomed partners from Norway and Iceland, providing some context that in the UK it is common to hear 'Biosphere, what's a Biosphere?' Whether known as a BR or a Biosphere – the designation is not well understood.[8] Lack of knowledge included those living in BRs, alongside governments and public bodies. Alison, for example, told me that NatureScot directors are unlikely to know what a Biosphere is. As suggested by a former WRB director and community development professional, the Biosphere concept does not instantly resonate with people, even if those people do care about the opportunities a BR brings. She argued that the BR must be translated into language that communities understand and see the benefits from. Thus, it makes sense that WRB had a strategic aim to develop 'a recognisable Wester Ross Biosphere identity'.

This involved communicating the BR as a UNESCO designation, and WRB's unique community-led approach. Their first communications leaflet addressed the former, explaining BRs 'do not belong to one organisation', but adopt a shared and participatory approach. They aim to 'foster sustainable development through cooperation between the public and private sector, within communities, and by bridging local knowledge with global awareness'. Regarding the latter, in an interview, WRB's Gaelic Development Officer, Adaira, suggested that over time, 'more people are becoming aware of who we are and what we do, and that it's community-led.' This has been a work in progress since redesignation, with Phoebe taking on a key role in communicating the community Biosphere to a range of audiences. Her approach was tailored towards what would resonate with people; for example, she suggested anything to do with zonation is 'for UNESCO', and not relevant to engaging with communities: 'we don't talk about the zones because it puts people off'. WRB's website also reframes BR functions of conservation, development and logistic support into pillars of 'living, learning and legacy'. It explains 'the new style Biosphere is a place where people live and actively learn about their surroundings to inspire a legacy rich in both natural and cultural heritage'. During a range of events, I also observed Phoebe tell audiences that WRB are not like other designations because the Biosphere 'does not draw a hard line between people and nature'.

However, it was clear from board meetings that the BR was often misunderstood locally. One example of this was WRB being asked by community members to oppose local developments. One occasion led Elisabeth to suggest to the board that people are 'thinking that we are representing them on behalf of the environment, which we are not'. The economic development role of the BR seemed lesser appreciated by communities and the board agreed they would not support or oppose developments on environmental grounds, as this is only one part of its remit. Robert, a Highland councillor advising the board, was frustrated that the BR was interpreted wrongly as a 'green lobby'. For him this was problematic because, 'whilst we are responsible for taking care of the nature, passing it on to the next generation, we've got to remember people live here. It's a living working area.'

This sentiment was shared among directors, who generally sought to balance all priorities of the designation – illustrating WRB as a new style BR that is not only conservation focused. Moreover, WRB embody the notion that sustainability is not a fixed outcome but an orientation. Phoebe told me, there is no 'blueprint of what sustainable development should look like' because 'we are not a top-down organisation' but exist to help 'facilitate a process'. However, the complexity of this was sometimes challenging for directors to communicate to others. As Coinneach put it, he felt it was a struggle to find an 'elevator pitch' for the Biosphere. To aid in this, a communications strategy was developed out of a participatory WRB workshop, including a new mission statement that aimed to provide a more coherent sense of organisational identity. Today, the organisation is explained as follows:

> Wester Ross Biosphere Ltd is the community-led charity that manages the UNESCO designation locally. Our team of Trustees, staff, members, supporters and volunteers aim to bring communities together to ensure the wellbeing of our natural and cultural landscape and our long-term economic future – to create a thriving Wester Ross for everyone. We aim to balance the interests of everyone who lives within our boundaries or visits us, including individuals, businesses and community organisations, to ensure sustainable development for all.

This description appeared on WRB's website on a page titled 'finding the balance between conservation and development is at the heart of what we do'. It also sat alongside a set of organisational principles such as: 'community led by people who live and work in the Biosphere' and 'problem solving to promote sustainable economic, social and environmental practices'. During my work, I also discussed with Phoebe how the BR might be explained as threefold: designation, organisation and approach to place-making. Finding accessible ways to communicate WRB's identity is important, and breaking down the BR concept into its components and nature–culture relations also avoids reifying BRs.

From a more theoretical standpoint, I see WRB as organisationally like a rhizome. This is a type of root structure that expands from multiple points horizontally, and a way to theorise multiplicity and overcome dichotomous thinking.[9] WRB, like rhizomes, are a non-hierarchical assemblage that is always in a state of becoming.[10] WRB's emergent collective identity continually evolves, shaped by social relations and negotiations of the UNESCO remit in the culturally specific context of Wester Ross. This will become clear in later chapters of the book, and readers may wish to bear in mind the notion of WRB as a rhizome to help understand its multiplicity and resist attributing to it a fixed organisational identity.

CONCLUSION

BRs differ in how they are implemented, adapting to regional conditions within a common UNESCO framework. In this chapter I explained how the BR has been applied and interpreted locally over time in Wester Ross as a designation and a community organisation. As a designation, the BR has been perceived as different to other kinds of conservation models, given its softer boundaries, regional focus and bottom-up approach to sustainability. However, what the designation actually changes, especially through the creation of zones, is ambiguous. There was no obvious impact from the introduction of the designation on conservation or land management. This is in some ways unsurprising because BRs generally have no specific powers to compel change, and because people in Wester Ross supported the BR for this very reason.

Nonetheless, change was sought at a regional scale through the newly created community-led organisation WRB, set up in 2016. I introduced WRB as an organisation of local community members with a diverse set of interests and skills but a shared desire to use the BR to encourage regional action for sustainability. Most recognise that such action has been at times elusive, which is not only an issue of funding, but related to the slower pace of building inclusive and culturally appropriate collective action over time.

The chapter importantly set out how local actors most involved interpret what a community Biosphere means for the region. The need to balance multiple objectives rather than act as a green lobby, conveys the holistic approach of new style BRs. However, the complexity of addressing all aspects of regional sustainability makes the BR challenging to communicate and it was at times misunderstood. This necessitates more accessible ways of communicating WRB to different audiences, especially local communities and other stakeholders. However, I also argued that the community Biosphere is an example of a rhizome, horizontal and non-hierarchical in its relations. The Biosphere has an emergent identity that is open and flexible and this is fundamental to how actors negotiate nature–culture relations. I illustrate this in further chapters, turning now to the BR as place-making.

NOTES

1. Cormac Walsh, 'Landscape Imaginaries and the Protection of Dynamic Nature at the Wadden Sea,' *Rural Landscapes: Society, Environment, History* 7, no. 1 (2020): 1–20.
2. Kaera Coetzer, Edward Witkowski and Barend Erasmus, 'Reviewing Biosphere Reserves Globally: Effective Conservation Action or Bureaucratic Label?,' *Biological Reviews of the Cambridge Philosophical Society* 89, no. 1 (2014): 82–104.
3. Zoe Russell, 'The Isle of Man Biosphere Reserve: An Entire Nation Approach to Sustainable Development,' *Environmental Policy and Planning* 25, no. 3 (2022): 273–86.
4. Silvia Posocco, 'Zoning: Environmental Cosmopolitics in and Around the Maya Biosphere Reserve, Petén, Guatemala,' *Nature and Culture* 3, no. 2 (2008): 209.
5. Rebecca Main et al., 'Scotland's Environmental Histories: Mapping a Way Forward,' *Scottish Historical Review* 104, no. 2 (2025): 155–73; Edward Stewart, 'Wicked Wild Wastes? Challenging Wildness through Repopulating Approaches to Archaeological Narratives in Scottish Highland Landscapes,' *Scottish Historical Review* 104, no. 2 (2025): 249–77.
6. Liette Vasseur, 'Embracing Cultures in Ecosystem Governance in Biosphere Reserves: Slowing Down the Pace,' in *UNESCO Biosphere Reserves: Supporting Biocultural Diversity, Sustainability and Society*, ed. M. Reed and M. Price (Routledge, 2020), 309–20.
7. Reed and Price, 'UNESCO Biosphere Reserves,' 1–10.
8. Mathevet and Cibien, 'French Biosphere Reserves,' 114–24.
9. Jessica S. Gullion, 'Assemblages and Entanglements,' in *Diffractive Ethnography* (Routledge, 2018), 105–14.
10. Gilles Deleuze and Felix Guattari, *A Thousand Plateaus: Capitalism and Schizophrenia* (University of Minnesota Press, 1987).

3

The Biosphere as Regional Place-making

CONSERVATION DESIGNATIONS ARE EMBEDDED in places and part of place-making practice.[1] Whilst some designations may displace local landscape imaginaries of place,[2] Chapter 2 showed how the BR in Wester Ross was seen as a way to strengthen place-based regional identity. BRs generally are argued to support 'place-based innovations' by creating shared identities, sense of place, and new regional networks for collective action.[3] This chapter explains what this looks like in Wester Ross, focusing on the BR as place-making practice. I approach place-making as being about 'the construction of a regional identity, a bounded territory, and a relational network' which importantly 'all depend on stories we tell about ourselves, each other, and our places within larger sets of stories'.[4]

Moreover, how territories are perceived and reconfigured and the 'potentialities' of nature–culture entanglement are part of the ongoing transformation of place.[5] I begin with WRB actors' narratives about regional identity, highlighting issues of community fragmentation and place-based inequalities, and narratives of historic cultural identity. Next, I move on to wider interpretations of regional autonomy and themes of empowerment, planning and development within local community place-making. Finally, I unpack key issues for place-making both locally and regionally, drawing particularly on WRB's sustainable tourism work. I introduce narratives about community-led placemaking and structural barriers to culturally appropriate sustainability action. In so doing, I highlight WRB actors' awareness of the wider economic conditions that shape regional futures and their rejection of common sense place myths in favour of alternative place trajectories.

REGIONAL IDENTITY: BEYOND FRAGMENTATION

Wester Ross is often perceived by WRB actors as regionally fragmented, with communities in the north and south especially disconnected:

> In Wester Ross, it's very different. The communities in the Cairngorms, are all separate but they're all around the same mountain area. Here the communities are all separate and they're looking in different directions. If anything, Ullapool's looking up to the North towards the Geopark, Kyle and this area are looking to the South-West towards Skye … it is much less of a cohesive entity than in the Cairngorms. (Michael, WRB Director, formerly Cairngorms National Park ranger)

Similarly, Robert, who travels the region as a Highland councillor, told me that communities are insular: 'they don't want to know what's going on with each other'. Whilst BR designation brings multiple communities together spatially at a regional scale, socially, sense of place is much more localised, often defined by school catchments. According to Elisabeth, communities in the south (of which she is part) identify with Lochalsh rather than Wester Ross and 'dismiss' the Biosphere, thinking 'that's not us'. In that sense, she felt the BR could have been named Wester Ross and Lochalsh BR to create more cohesion across these areas and communities. This is part of the challenge when a BR is introduced in an area that does not already have a cohesive regional identity.[6] Community fragmentation is partly due to physical geography; mountainous landscapes and lochs create 'isolation, rather than communication'.[7] There are few reasons or opportunities for local communities across a sparsely populated rural area to connect and interact. The BR as regional scale place-making was thus a way to get communities 'all talking and working in one direction' (Robert).

Attempting to work across multiple places and communities regionally requires sensitivity to social difference and uneven development across the BR. For example, considering the neighbouring areas Aultbea and Gairloch, the former was perceived as a less desirable place to live and without the community infrastructure and wealth of the latter. This reflects how places are shaped by relations of class, power and inequality,[8] which ultimately feeds into local sense of place. Some Gairloch residents thought Aultbea was 'a shithole', describing this as both 'playful rivalry' but also indicating that Aultbea has more social housing whilst Gairloch has had a regeneration associated with the wealth of middle-class incomers. Relations within places are also important, for example in Gairloch residents have come into conflict around whether specific community groups are benefitting locals or incomers. Rural development, if it ignores internal power relations and class differences, can worsen existing inequalities and create new ones.[9] However, WRB actors, who are part of these communities, seemed well aware that community-led regional collaborative governance would require attention to difference and sensitivity to local politics. This is often tied to their own personal experiences; for example, Coinneach speaking as someone who grew up in Aultbea, left, and then returned in later life, said 'one can be local, local-local, or local-local-local', representing 'degrees of localness'.[10] Identity claims based on family ancestry are part of local–incomer tensions in many Wester Ross communities.[11] Anndra, originally from another area of Scotland, described past experiences as chairperson of the local development trust bidding for community ownership of a local asset. He explained, 'I was seen as an incomer, I don't know what the problem was, but there were people that were against the community ownership.' Across the region, tensions between incomers and locals often seemed to be fundamentally about who has legitimacy to define and speak for 'the community'. There were also differences in perceptions of place that urban-based incomers held compared with local views, such as in relation to the environment.[12] Tensions around place-making and community development also exist where two different community organisations are working towards their own visions for local futures.

WRB enables a new regional identity that tries to go beyond fragmentation, with BR community-led governance involving collective action across multiple community actors, from development trusts, to community councils and crofting communities – often in tension with one another. WRB actors are under no illusion that it can speak for these actors but rather must work directly with them, building collaborative action that is inclusive, and that accommodates differing cultural experiences and relations to place. Alongside narratives of contemporary fragmentation were also narratives of a historic shared cultural identity, based on the region's cultural heritage and past connectivity. Such narratives tended to emerge in response to the notion that the BR was too large an area to manage. Anndra, for example, knowledgeable about cultural heritage and Gaelic, said Wester Ross BR 'makes sense because there are cultural connections that go back a long way'. Similarly, Seumas described a north–south cohesiveness that is part of an east–west divide in Ross-shire, which conveys geographic, cultural and linguistic differences.[13] For example, local accents vary within and outwith the BR. Another aspect for Seumas was the area's shared cultural connection to the sea, which remains today as many communities live along the coast (see Figure 3.1).

Whilst youth activist groups like Ullapool Sea Savers illustrate the importance that local people still place on marine environments, historically connections to the sea were stronger. This was due to livelihoods from

Figure 3.1 Gairloch viewed from Achtercairn archaeology trail.

the sea and social relations via sea routes which have been replaced over time with longer journeys by road. Fionnlagh, a local resident born and living in Applecross told me how a decommissioned ferry route to Kyle took around twenty minutes, whilst today it is much longer via the mountain road the *Bealach Na Ba*. Whilst touring the Applecross peninsula Fionnlagh pointed out the adjacent islands, explaining that historically communities were socially connected via the short trip by sea. In terms of livelihoods, he also told me how he grew up on a fishing boat with his father, the same boat now rotting in the bay, symbolic of the decline of this once common, albeit challenging livelihood.[14] Hence, the idea of the BR creating a new regional sense of place also brings heritage to the fore, considering what places and communities looked like in the past, and using this in the present to inspire the future.

Finally, narratives about the need for a shared regional identity are also bound up with a desire for greater autonomy. Due to the sparsely populated nature of Wester Ross, Seumas described how the region is 'at the bottom of the queue' when it comes to the allocation of resources. Michael explained that the area has historically been 'bypassed' by development, whilst Robert said today it is 'overlooked' politically. Wester Ross's regional identity is constructed in relation to a perceived lack of self-determination and centralised political decision-making – whether in London, in Edinburgh, or even in Inverness. In the 1990s,

Anndra was involved with the Highlands and Islands Alliance, a political party which argued:

> If it [devolution] was going to come to Edinburgh, it shouldn't stop at Edinburgh. Devolution should spread across the Highlands and Islands, and communities would have empowerment. If it's something affecting Wester Ross, then the people of Wester Ross should have a say in it.

The desire for regional place-making is thus tied to a wider narrative about Wester Ross as lacking decision-making power. Many across the region have criticised that centralised governance has not adequately served the needs of the regions' rural communities. In discussions with WRB actors and local residents, examples of local governance working better elsewhere included Germany: 'a model of much more engaged local communities, more decision-making and resource held at the local level' (Chris, local resident, 30–40). Likewise, Michael suggested that in 'the Faroes and so on, the power starts with the community councils and the communities, then they get together if they want to share services'. Whilst pointing to a need for wider systems change, many communities in Wester Ross are working towards more local autonomy by engaging in processes of place-making and community-led development.

SUSTAINING LOCAL COMMUNITIES

A central theme of concern across Wester Ross and for WRB actors, was how to sustain the BR as a living and working area in the face of demographic challenges. When I asked Phoebe her views on community empowerment, she explained:

> Community empowerment comes by having communities. People are getting older, and people aren't coming back, there aren't houses. So, community empowerment means communities can keep, not even necessarily growing just sustaining themselves by making sure that there's still people there to do it. And those people need to have meaningful relationships with one another, not just based on that place. Not just a Disney World in the summer, retirement home kind of community. Community empowerment for me is the ability of communities to keep their young people there, and jobs and to be able to sustain themselves, go a step further and growth is fine but at this point it's about sustaining those communities.

These concerns were pertinent in all areas I visited in Wester Ross. In Applecross, a resident described 'a real danger in that a lot of communities will just kind of disappear and become these areas of just holiday homes ... sort of like an empty shell in a way'. Indeed, on my Applecross tour with Fionnlagh, I was surprised at how many houses he said were empty for most of the year. The issue of second homes and holiday homes is often problematised by local people; as a barrier to providing affordable local housing to keep young people in the area and attract new families.

Community groups across Wester Ross have been purchasing land and assets to engage in local place planning to deliver the infrastructure, like housing, that can sustain a local population. Many recognise that this is necessary because of the retreat of the state, with declining provision of public services. For example, Applecross Community Company state:

> Communities are being asked to step in where the public and private sector is unable or unwilling to operate. We are acutely aware of this having taken on the ownership and management of the petrol station in 2008, local public toilets in 2011, and ongoing service provision of broadband.

The manager of community-owned enterprise Gairloch and Loch Ewe Action Forum similarly described operating in the space of 'market failure'; where the public sector has stepped back or is inactive, and where it is not profitable for private business. This is a challenging space to be in alongside the many complexities of community planning and development. In Applecross, for example, a community vision and land use plan were produced, and key sites for development identified. However, they were later refused planning permission, showing misalignment with wider Highland Council plans. The local development officer expressed her frustration at the time, 'we're making so much effort, building our own houses, and yet there's endless hurdles to get through'. She criticised the lack of joined up approach in planning and minimal support for communities to navigate complex funding and legislative systems. WRB has sought to support communities in this work, and were recently contracted by Highland Council to facilitate a new Highland Plan that built on the priorities of local communities. Communities without a local place plan were supported to develop one, allowing WRB to combine multiple local plans into a coherent regional vision.

Whilst a useful example of what BR regional placemaking increasingly looks like, it has remained challenging for WRB to create this regional coordinating role. They often struggled to fund regional activities and were in competition with other community groups for limited resources. When finalising the budget for a regional sustainable tourism project, Phoebe expressed a concern to directors that WRB should not 'step on anyone's toes'. Despite having insecure finance, she felt they 'should not ask for too much' to avoid taking away from others, or be perceived as 'soaking up' all the funding. However, this was resisted by Alan, a director who consistently pushed for WRB to improve its financial situation. He argued, 'the Biosphere needs the resource in order to make this happen'. WRB has always existed in an austere funding environment which has been a major barrier to regional place-making. Phoebe's concerns reflect too that perceptions of WRB have been directly linked to funding. Staff have often told me they are questioned by local people, who ask critically, 'who is paying for your job?' Some might think that WRB is well-funded, and Adaira, WRB's Gaelic Development Officer, felt it was important people become aware of the BR, and that 'we don't get lots of government funding'. Sensitivity around funding community development is also tied to local politics. I heard, for example, in Applecross, how some people, usually politically conservative, are 'philosophically opposed' to public money being used to fund community groups because they unfairly compete with private businesses (Applecross Community Company Director). Wester Ross as an area is arguably dominated by private economic interests and this is a barrier to sustaining communities, engaging in community development and advancing a regional approach to sustainability. This becomes clearer when examining WRB's tourism work.

'Good places to visit must first be good places to live'

WRB were funded to participate in a European collaborative project with partners in Iceland and Norway to develop eco-tourism for rural areas. However, early community engagement caused a change in focus in Wester Ross. Molly, the appointed project officer, explained at the time how communities in Wester Ross 'do not want more tourism initiatives' whether 'eco' or otherwise, they want current tourism to be managed better. Locals felt visitor numbers have significantly increased in recent years, and so WRB sought evidence to assess this perception and the 'carrying capacity' of the region's communities and environments. This partly reflects a need to understand how tourism has been changing in Wester Ross as a result of the North Coast 500 (NC500) driving route. This private initiative, according to locals, has not only increased visitor numbers but changed visitor types, encouraging more transience – seeing multiple sites in a short space of time and rarely engaging with local culture or economies. I witnessed and heard about pressures on infrastructure (roads, toilets, waste disposal), especially around the pandemic and the volume of motorhomes in peak season. In light of negative commentary about tourism, WRB's project sought to evidence the nuance of social, environmental and economic perceptions among residents, visitors and businesses. Standout issues were that 64 per cent of residents are concerned about visitors' environmental responsibility, but the same number also value the contribution of tourism to the economy.

The project vision overall stated: 'Wester Ross will be a thriving sustainable tourism destination where the needs of the community, visitor, economy and environment are recognised, understood and planned for.' In bringing this to life, Molly, and WRB utilised a particular place-making narrative, that was seen as key to more sustainable tourism: 'good places to visit, must first be good places to live'. The notion of 'good places' seemed tied to addressing major infrastructural challenges across the BR and problematic visitor behaviours (blocking single track roads, littering, and damage caused by 'wild' camping). WRB worked especially with Visit Wester Ross and co-produced Scotland's first destination management plan, based on community priorities. The project came at time when the organisation was in early phases of building trust and legitimacy among local communities. As part of initial community work sense of place workshops were held in Kyle of Lochalsh and Garve, two of the region's lesser engaged communities. The workshops tried to elicit residents' notions of special local places to protect and places to redistribute tourists to resolve pressures around hotspots. They were also premised on using natural and cultural heritage as part of sense of place for more sustainable tourism. However, the events were poorly attended, and those that did attend were sceptical about the BR and how their information would be used. People were happy to complain about tourism, but reluctant to share details about local cultural heritage and their sense of place. After the first workshop Molly seemed disappointed and drained, feeling she was perceived as an 'outsider' and that communities do not yet understand or trust WRB. Trust issues are common in BRs,[15] and although WRB is 'community-led', this does not grant automatic legitimacy.

Alongside trying to work directly with local communities, the project involved a 'learning journey' with international project partners in Ullapool and a final conference in Gairloch to launch the destination management plan to a range of stakeholders. It was in these particular spaces that I observed WRB actors' narratives that many regional conditions were 'not of our own making'.[16] A range of social, political and economic conditions within and beyond Wester Ross were highlighted, namely: control for planning and governance; landownership; affordable housing; and dependency on tourism. I will discuss each in turn.

On the first morning of the learning journey, Molly explained to WRB directors and partners from Norway and Iceland that decision-making and resources for infrastructure and planning in Wester Ross are controlled by centralised authorities and not local communities. Alison, representing NatureScot at the time, countered this by asking if 'responsibility' was more appropriate than 'control'. Molly replied that as a local resident: 'I have no control over things that are being done, the council and public bodies hold all the power and authority'. This led on to her suggestion that WRB's participatory, community-led approach can only achieve so much without buy-in from more powerful stakeholders with resources at regional and national scales. She described the real difficulty 'engaging with higher up people with authority' and budgets for infrastructure for the project. Discussions led to comparing Scotland with Norway and Iceland, and WRB actors were critical of the former's more centralised power and weaker local government. Elisabeth also explained for international attendees that as a sparsely populated rural area in the larger Highland Council region, Wester Ross is not a priority even at 'local' government level and that statutory planning areas do not coincide with the BR boundaries.

On land ownership, during the learning journey, Molly said in Wester Ross it is 'difficult to find out information about who owns what', and 'who is responsible' for what areas of land. This is tied to absentee landowners and a lack of transparency with owners of sporting estates, as well as complexity around crofting. Norwegian and Icelandic partners had different experiences of land ownership as it is not legal for individuals to own large tracts of land. Such international comparisons seemed to solidify regional conditions as a product of the Scottish national context and 'the Highland Problem' (see Chapters 1 and 8). At the tourism conference, land ownership also emerged when Phoebe was asked by an attendee if the BR is doing anything to address the high concentration of private landownership in Wester Ross. They explained their concern that private landowners were able to make decisions about vast areas of land without any sustainability knowledge. Phoebe explained how WRB have struggled to work with landowners, with some distrust on both sides.

Lack of affordable housing also emerged at the conference, identified as an issue for both hospitality workers and local people. Phoebe argued that affordable housing is key to sustaining communities in the BR, and Norman criticised the prevalence of holiday homes and short-term tourism accommodation. These issues have only intensified following the surge in demand for rural property that was a consequence of the Covid-19 pandemic. It became clear during conference discussions that complex market and political conditions surrounding rural housing would be very challenging to tackle in practice as most were beyond the control of local or regional actors.

The final condition problematised was the region's economic dependency on tourism. Over time in communities in Wester Ross tourism has replaced livelihoods associated with land and sea. For example, Ullapool used to be one of the ten major fishing ports in the UK, established in 1788, but this once dominant industry has declined significantly.[17] Ullapool Community Trust note 'whilst the harbour is still active, tourism has come to play a vital role in the local economy'.[18] As such, Ullapool is now a 'tourist hotspot'[19] and across the BR many of the region's jobs are in tourism and hospitality. The conference to launch WRB's destination management plan brought conflicting narratives about the future of tourism to the fore, especially between WRB actors and private business interests.

As part of co-organising, Visit Wester Ross had invited some businesses on the east coast, national tourism organisations and representatives of the NC500 to speak at the event. Responding to the theme of sustainable tourism, the NC500 speaker said in his presentation: 'we may not be good at sustainable tourism, but neither is Visit Scotland or the Highland Council'. A seemingly frustrated attendee asked, 'but what are you going to do in the future, what are your actions for improving the sustainability of your approach?' The speaker replied, 'we want to make your business busier and make you busier'. This did not go down well in the room, and was clearly at odds with local feeling about overtourism in Wester Ross. Linking to the idea of sustainable tourism as three pillars, the speaker continued to explain that NC500 is 'focusing on the economy bit'. This implied the two other domains, 'respect for culture' and 'respect for environment', were not their responsibility. Here a neoliberal growth paradigm infuses the notion that tourism is promoted 'at any cost, with little space for alternative discourses'.[20] The NC500 mentality is thus an example of the wider problem in which tourism for private and elite profit-making occurs at the expense of subsistence, wellbeing and ecological sustainability, and ultimately disempowers local communities.[21]

In contrast, Phoebe, presenting for WRB, had argued 'economies should serve society' and evolve in a way that stays within the safe operating space of the planet. She argued BRs are places to create sustainable communities and livelihoods, complementing Molly's presentation that introduced the idea that 'good places to visit must first be good places to live'. These messages, whilst seeming to resonate with many residents, fell on deaf ears among the business representatives and some University of the Highlands and Islands academics. For example, Phoebe was met with comments like, the BR 'would be more successful if it could monetise its brand ... ultimately it's about the bottom line'. WRB staff and directors seemed frustrated about the failure to engage meaningfully with 'sustainable' tourism.

Later, in this context, Norman more directly challenged the idea of growth in a discussion session, arguing that 'most tourism is unsustainable' given it involves global air travel. He argued that Wester Ross needs a more diverse economy rather than relying only on tourism. A business representative stood up and responded angrily that tourism is 'essential' to the area. He said, 'what about my children, what will they do if there is no tourism? There are no other industries because forestry and fishing, these are hardly sustainable either.' The idea that 'there are no other industries' embodies the neoliberal mantra that 'there are no alternatives'. Here, we see how neoliberal place myths help justify continued capitalist accumulation.[22] This applies not only to tourism, but food too. A business owner with a large productive farm on the east coast told the conference the only choice for Wester Ross is fattening animals to send east, because 'you cannot grow anything on the land in the west coast'. Molly, at our group table said this was not true, because local communities across Wester Ross do grow food, including a variety of fruits and vegetables. The main difference she explained, is that they do it for self-sufficiency rather than industrial monocultural production for commodity export – the norm in capitalist agriculture. Hence, WRB actors publicly and privately challenge neoliberal place myths, seeming to use the community Biosphere as a vehicle to 'create alternative place-specific trajectories'.[23]

Following the European tourism project, WRB began to pursue sustainable tourism through funding from Highlands and Islands Enterprise to implement the destination management plan. This was WRB's first main independently funded project, with a value of around £300,000 which was used to employ three area officers for the BR (North, Mid and South) who could work with local communities and regionally through a new body, the Wester Ross Tourism Partnership. The partnership, set up during and following the pandemic, with representation from all local community areas, operated for around three years. It was valuable as a mechanism for collaborative working across local communities in response to ongoing challenges of: high domestic tourist numbers; irresponsible visitor behaviour; and lack of infrastructure. Whilst the partnership body (chaired by WRB) was disbanded due to a lack of funding, it did show how the BR facilitates new regional place-making; building relationships with and between local communities to collaboratively address regional challenges.

CONCLUSION

Place-making brings to the fore different narratives about a region's identity and its communities. Wester Ross is seen as a region that is culturally cohesive based on a shared historical connectivity and different from other parts of the Scottish Highlands. It is also seen as fragmented due to geography, and as having a more localised sense of place. It is important to consider contemporary dynamics of contestation and difference, given the multiplicity of communities and places in the BR region. Whilst in pursuit of a stronger regional identity, WRB actors are highly sensitive to local politics of place given they themselves experience this as residents. Wester Ross was also seen as a place lacking regional autonomy with WRB actors and local communities alike questioning current models of centralised governance. Importantly, as I have argued in the chapter, this was tied to concerns about the future of the area, namely, whether it will survive as a place of living, working communities. Many communities are trying to make this possible through local development and planning and WRB has begun to facilitate this and support regional scale activity. For WRB actors place-making was about creating a more sustainable regional community and economy, problematising wider sociopolitical systems and structures not of their own making. I focused here on WRB's tourism work, which has been shaped by a narrative that good places to visit must first be good places to live.

Such narratives have been a response to common-sense place myths, such as that the region should rely on the growth of tourism, despite how this fails to prioritise community needs or sustainability. In advocating for good places to live, WRB construct regional sustainability as requiring affordable housing, a diverse economy, more transparent landownership, decision-making power and adequate infrastructure. In practice, WRB have created new community-led mechanisms to identify and respond to regional needs through collective action. Whilst these have been somewhat useful, funding has been a key barrier to continuing this work longer term.

Together with Chapter 2, this chapter shows what the BR in Wester Ross means for local actors as a designation, an organisation, and for place-making. I next discuss how WRB actors negotiate the region's unsustainability and natural and cultural heritage in discourse and practice.

NOTES

1. Daniel R. Williams, 'Spacing Conservation Practice: Place-Making, Social Learning, and Adaptive Landscape Governance in Natural Resource Management,' in *The Sage Handbook of Nature*, ed. T. Marsden (Sage, 2018), 285–303.
2. Cormac Walsh, 'Landscape Imaginaries and the Protection of Dynamic Nature at the Wadden Sea,' *Rural Landscapes: Society, Environment, History* 7, no. 1 (2020): 1–20.
3. Caroline H. Dabard, Carsten Mann and Berta Martín-López, 'Biosphere Reserves as Catalysts for Sustainability Transformations: Five Strategies to Support Place-Based Innovation,' *Current Opinion in Environmental Sustainability* 73 (2025): 101508.
4. Theresa Warburton, 'What Looks like a Grave: Native and Anarchist Place-Making in New England,' *Studies in American Indian Literatures* 32, nos. 1–2 (2020): 1–2.
5. Nadia Bartolini, 'Fixing Naturecultures: Spatial and Temporal Strategies for Managing Heritage Transformation and Entanglement,' in *Heritage Futures: Comparative Approaches to Natural and Cultural Heritage Practices*, ed. R. Harrison, C. DeSilvey, C. Holtorf, S. MacDonald, N. Bartolini, H. Fredheim, A. Lyons, S. May, J. Morgan and S. Penrose (UCL Press, 2020), 375–95.
6. Raphaël Mathevet and Catherine Cibien, 'The French Biosphere Reserves: Looking for Ecological Solidarity and Stewardship,' in *UNESCO Biosphere Reserves: Supporting Biocultural Diversity, Sustainability and Society*, ed. M. Reed and M. F. Price (Routledge, 2020), 114–24.
7. Douglas Willis, 'Man and the Land: Physical Environment and Settlement in the North-West Highlands,' in *Peoples and Settlement in North-West Ross*, ed. J. Baldwin (Scottish Society for Northern Studies, 1994), 9.
8. Mark Shucksmith, 'Class, Power and Inequality in Rural Areas: Beyond Social Exclusion?,' *Sociologia Ruralis* 52, no. 4 (2012): 377–97.
9. Shucksmith, 'Class, Power and Inequality.'
10. Angus Macleod and Geoff Payne, 'Locals and Incomers: Social and Cultural Identity in Late Twentieth Century Coigach,' in *Peoples and Settlement in North-West Ross*, ed. J. Baldwin (Scottish Society for Northern Studies, 1994), 391–411.
11. Charles Jedrej and Mark Nuttall, *White Settlers: The Impact of Rural Repopulation on Scotland* (Harwood, 1996); Macleod and Payne, 'Locals

and Incomers'; Andrea Nightingale, 'Challenging the Romance with Resilience: Communities, Scale and Climate Change,' in *Practising Feminist Political Ecologies: Moving Beyond The Green Economy*, ed. W. Harcourt and I. Nelson (Zed Books, 2015), 182–208.

12. Jedrej and Nuttall, *White Settlers*.
13. Willis, 'Man and the Land.'
14. See Malcolm Gray, 'Crofting and Fishing in the North-West Highlands, 1890–1914,' *Northern Scotland* 1, no. 1 (1972): 89–114.
15. Heike Walk, Vera Luthhardt and Benjamin Nölting, 'Participatory Learning for Transdisciplinary Science in Biosphere Reserves: A Modified Role for Universities,' in *UNESCO Biosphere Reserves: Supporting Biocultural Diversity, Sustainability and Society*, ed. M. Reed and M. Price (Routledge, 2020), 297–309.
16. Benedikt Schmid, Thomas S. J. Smith and Gerald Taylor Aiken, 'Governing through Community: Transformative Geographies from the Bottom Up,' *Environmental Policy and Governance* 31, no. 3 (2021): 155–8.
17. Jean Munro, 'Ullapool and the British Fisheries Society,' in *Peoples and Settlement in North-West Ross*, ed. J. Baldwin (Scottish Society for Northern Studies, 1994), 245–70.
18. Ullapool Community Trust, Community Growth Plan 2017–2027, https://ullapoolcommunity.org/wp-content/uploads/2019/12/CGP-2017_Executive-Summary.pdf.
19. Eleanor White, Rianne van Melik and James Bendle, 'Perceived Impacts of Tourism on Community Identity: Perspectives of Two Scottish Highland Communities,' *Tourism Planning and Development* 21, no. 6 (2024): 917–39.
20. Stroma Cole, 'A Gendered Political Ecology of Tourism and Water,' in *Political Ecology of Tourism: Community, Power and the Environment*, ed. M. Mostafanezhad, R. Norum, E. Shelton and A. Thompson-Carr (Routledge, 2016), 32.
21. Ron Nicholls, Freya Higgins-Desbiolles and Grant Rigney, 'Ngarrindjeri Authority: A Sovereignty Approach to Tourism,' in *Political Ecology of Tourism: Community, Power and the Environment*, ed. M. Mostafanezhad, R. Norum, E. Shelton and A. Thompson-Carr (Routledge, 2016), 51.
22. Schmid et al., 'Governing Through Community'; Christa Wichterich, 'Contesting Green Growth: Connecting Care, Commons and Enough,' in *Practising Feminist Political Ecologies: Moving Beyond the Green Economy*, ed. W. Harcourt and I. Nelson (Zed Books, 2015), 67–100.
23. Schmid et al., 'Governing Through Community.'

4

(Un)Sustainability and Nature–Culture Relations

Building on earlier chapters which introduced the BR as designation, organisation and place-making, this chapter details WRB's approach to regional sustainability and nature–culture relations. I begin by outlining how WRB actors problematise regional conditions around historic and contemporary unsustainable practices and industries, and view balancing conservation and development as a central aim. Using examples of designing a business supporter scheme and discussions of green jobs, I show that sustainability in Wester Ross is a complex and contested issue. Debates among actors centre what kinds of action are desirable and by whom, in the creation of more sustainable regional futures.

Conservation practice is often shaped by a distinction between nature and culture – a central ontology of western thinking and the dominant social paradigm of neoliberal societies.[1] In the second half of the chapter I consider whether WRB overcomes this mentality in their work around conserving natural and cultural heritage. I start with the perspectives of directors on the separation of the natural and cultural into two thematic working groups. Subsequently, I consider their perceptions of natural and cultural as interwoven, using the example of the business supporter scheme and rewilding. This illustrates debates within WRB that shape their approach to nature–culture relations and their organisational identity.

TACKLING UNSUSTAINABILITY

BRs as model regions for sustainable development must often address complex issues such as unsustainable land use and conflicts over land.[2] In Wester Ross, whilst WRB actors recognise and celebrate the special qualities of BR landscapes, a prominent concern is that historically most landscapes have been exploited and degraded. Special landscapes of conservation and landscapes of degradation are often separated in conservation discourse and practice,[3] but the BR draws attention to both as part of a regional focus on sustainability. Michael, along with others in WRB, argued that Wester Ross is a 'wet desert': a deforested and overgrazed landscape tied to land management for sheep and deer. Popularised by Frank Fraser Darling, the 'wet desert' is a narrative that contests perceptions of Highland landscapes as 'natural'.[4] It draws attention to how in Wester Ross, as elsewhere, treeless landscapes may be appreciated by visitors but in fact symbolise historical degradation and the clearance of people.[5] For Seumas: 'Wester Ross has not been developed sustainably … commercial forestry, fish farming, and aspects of crofting, very little of it has been sustainable in the true sense of the word'. However, he also said that as 'unsustainable' as some practices and industries are, they provide much-needed jobs. In his local area, for instance, fish farms and Kishorn Port are large employers that have ensured the local community has rarely suffered from unemployment. As of 2025 this is only set to solidify, with the announcement of £24 million of investment in Kishorn by the Scottish Government.[6] For Seumas, when thinking about development in Wester Ross sustainability requires 'a degree of compromise' and 'finding balance' across industry, ecological restoration and provision of housing.

This perspective of 'finding balance' has also emerged centrally in narratives of stakeholders governing the Isle of Man BR.[7] However, in practice, balance can seem elusive. Wester Ross is a region dominated by land uses and industries that many consider unsustainable. In contrast to Seumas's view, one former WRB director, an estate gamekeeper, was highly critical of any continued support for fish farming and the role of national government in legitimising corporations whose practices threaten the conservation of wild salmon. He argued that although unsustainable industries like fish farms do provide employment, more and better livelihoods for local people could be created in alternative sustainable industries. Thus, for WRB, the route to regional sustainability and specifically what this means for rural livelihoods in practice is contested.

Greening jobs and industries

How, and whether, WRB should engage directly with unsustainable industries in the BR has been a point of debate among the board. During the sustainable tourism conference discussed in Chapter 3, Phoebe was asked by a resident of Wester Ross if WRB work with unsustainable businesses. She said that whilst WRB directors feel differently on the issue, for her, 'the Biosphere must keep the door open; we cannot refuse to talk to people because we decide they are unsustainable'. She continued, 'if Shell approached us and wanted to work to be greener, would that not be a good thing?' Similarly, Seumas has told the board of his view that WRB could play a role in 'converting non-green industries into greener industries'. Although Norman agreed it would a huge success for the BR to do this, he cautioned the board about difficulties in practice and that this is a 'political' issue.

Whilst WRB has been cautious so far in relation to regional industries, they have learned about what this has entailed in Manicouagan Uapishka (MU) BR in Canada. WRB has hosted MU for knowledge exchange workshops during which MU's manager, Pierre, explained their work with the industrial giant Alcoa – the world's sixth largest producer of aluminium and a key industry in their BR. In discussion, some WRB directors, such as Alan, were sceptical, asking how such relationships affect a BR's brand and integrity – a UNESCO organisation working with extractive industry. For Pierre, it is within the BR remit to support the greening of industries in their regions in any way they can – especially if the alternative would be ignoring them completely.

For WRB, however, their first steps in creating relationships with business were more directly influenced by Galloway and Southern Ayrshire BR. Particularly the decision to learn from and create their own version of a business supporter scheme. Planning the scheme, the Sustainable Development Group discussed the issue of who could participate and what this might mean for WRB. Seumas wondered what would happen if a fish farm tried to join and asked whether WRB would assess and decide which businesses were 'worthy' – or 'can anyone apply'? Phoebe's view, similar to her comments above, were that she would welcome any business seeking to improve their sustainability but doubted that any fish farms would try to join anyway. Norman felt WRB should not single out specific industries or employers, given that all development, such as wind farms can be opposed with difficulty in defining specific activities as inherently sustainable. He explained:

> It might be it doesn't matter how you do this, it's horrible, or it might be that a certain level is acceptable … extractive industries, estates that might poison and shoot birds of prey, where do you draw the line? I think we just have to be clear, set the criteria, and dodgy ones who apply won't get through. If we exclude certain industries, it would be too subjective.

Alan also felt that WRB should not 'discriminate against large employers'. Reflecting back on the example of Alcoa and MU BR, he said one does not have to approve of a company's practices to influence them to change. However, Alan and most others, felt that WRB's business scheme should be tailored towards smaller local businesses and groups. The resulting scheme comprises a supporter charter with a set of principles and is promoted online by WRB for 'businesses, schools, communities and groups who already demonstrate a commitment to sustainable development, as well as those who want to do so'. Since launching, the scheme has been growing with around fifty current supporters 'promoting and developing the sustainability of the region'. An interactive online map links to these supporters, allowing residents and visitors to engage with businesses like Ullapool Unpacked CIC, a zero-waste community shop, or Balnacra Arts and Pottery. Like WRB membership, it is free to sign up to the charter, and supporters can use a bespoke logo to show support for WRB and sustainability.

Given that this scheme was developed without funding, WRB actors have also sought out opportunities for investment in more sustainable rural livelihoods in the BR. Seumas advised the Sustainable Development Group that the Scottish Government planned to invest in 'green jobs', with a potential figure of £1 million for Highland Council. He argued this could be an opportunity for WRB to do more, despite admitting he was unclear what was meant by 'green jobs'. He told the group how he asked his MSP and Friends of the Earth Scotland and got responses 'straight out of Edinburgh … both came back with a load of jobs, which frankly were city jobs, urban jobs … not really relevant to Wester Ross'. This opened up discussion about whether WRB should define what a green job is, although it might also imply having to define 'non-green jobs', which is more contentious. Alan saw less of a role for WRB regarding green jobs because, 'if you ask most people what a green job is they'd be baffled, just like when you ask them what a Biosphere is'. He felt WRB ought to focus on 'something more concrete' than figuring out how to be relevant through green jobs. He argued, 'people here are just happy to have a job period. Whether it's green or not.'

Seumas, however, was keen to bring national funding to Wester Ross to address the region's many 'non-green jobs' and felt the Biosphere supporter scheme was a concrete starting point to promote existing green jobs in Wester Ross. At a later meeting, he then presented some researched green jobs relevant to Wester Ross, including: food sustainability, zero waste, crofting, climate change, renewable energy, improving local supply chains and 'blue jobs' like traditional boat building and marine conservation or small-scale fishing. Anndra felt that Wester Ross's cultural heritage was a clear inspiration for green jobs, such as vernacular crafts 'dry stane dyking, thatching'. Norman, chair of the group, saw overlap between green jobs and WRB priorities, citing the need for countryside rangers to help manage unsustainable tourism. This also prompted further debate about WRB's role in wider national context (see Chapter 9). Norman also suggested as a community-led BR, conversations about green jobs should now start happening with local communities 'from the bottom up'. The group therefore decided to host an online discussion event on the subject of green jobs. It was open to all in the BR and began with a presentation from Zero Waste Scotland about existing circular and sustainable economy initiatives. Discussions at the event brought out a feeling that rural areas need rural solutions. Indeed, one of Seumas's original arguments was that public money should be brought to Wester Ross, 'otherwise it will go to the big cities'. He felt that 'Wester Ross and it's rural and remote conditions should be flagged up'. Event attendees included Alison, now retired from NatureScot, but sharing her experience that many circular economy solutions do not work in rural areas like Wester Ross because there is no 'critical mass'. From my own observations, it did appear that the Zero Waste Scotland speaker, whilst focused on the Highland region, was not accounting for the specific conditions of sparsely populated rural regions like Wester Ross. This reflects the need for more place-based and community participatory approaches to just transitions and circular economies in rural Scotland.[8]

The need for regionally specific approaches also emerged as WRB actors debated how to respond to national narratives about just transitions in Scotland. Alan suggested to the board that WRB should sign up to support a Friends of the Earth pledge for a Green Recovery 'building back better from coronavirus' associated with the Scottish Government's Covid-19 recovery plans. Recognising WRB is not a campaign group, he qualified that it is not 'political' to align with the government's view, and support the initiative, because, 'it's directly affecting Wester Ross Biosphere whatever happens nationally in Scotland'. However, his proposal was not supported by the board. Norman felt WRB should take a more direct approach to the Scottish Government as a way to position the BR as a mechanism to develop 'these ways of being more sustainable as we move out of Covid'. He wanted to see the organisation taken seriously as a catalyst for practical solutions. Additionally, on Alan's suggestion that it would not 'hurt' to support the pledge, Coinneach disagreed. He said WRB might 'alienate more people by getting into Friends of the Earth's slipstream' and explained:

> Everything I'm trying to do; I'm trying to keep it on a ground level and trying to bring everybody with us. [...] With build back better, greener, these are very generic statements ... It's building our narrative and our dialogue – not to take opposition to Friends of the Earth or anybody – but our voice, when we're building our voice, it's coherent, and its uniquely ours.

Here Coinneach conveys the need for narratives about change that reflect the culturally specific conditions in Wester Ross and develop the unique identity of WRB, which must be inclusive of all residents. As a crofter and an offshore worker, he has direct experience of perspectives within industries that are being targeted in the transition. He felt WRB must acknowledge the historic struggle in Wester Ross to secure a livelihood, a legacy that has been inherited and results in some reliance on unsustainable industries. Thus, organisational narratives about transitions should not alienate individuals, such as local mechanics, who hold negative views of environmental campaign groups. This point captures in more detail the wider feeling among WRB actors, that the BR must be neutral. It also illustrates some of the complexities that arise in BR deliberations that slow down the pace in the name of formulating more culturally specific, place-based and participatory approaches to sustainability. This seems key to how WRB moves beyond commonsense approaches to nature–culture relations.

NATURAL AND CULTURAL HERITAGE

A central part of what makes BRs valuable is their potential to overcome the nature–culture dichotomy, moving beyond fortress models which 'separate humans from the environment'.[9] I turn now to what this means in discourse and practice for WRB, focusing on their approach to natural and cultural heritage. In organisational discourse, these are conceptualised as interwoven: 'natural and cultural heritage cannot be separated'. WRB's website explains:

> Biospheres do not draw a hard line between people and nature. Rather they consider that nature is always surrounded by people, and that people need nature to live. They explore how to connect people, nature and development in sustainable ways.

The nomination to UNESCO also recognised that 'biological diversity is part of the cultural heritage', indicating a 'biocultural' approach (see Chapter 1). In practice, however, WRB had two distinct groups for natural and cultural heritage. This separation was a point of discussion among WRB's board. Following an election, Elisabeth, as chairperson, raised the subject of thematic working groups, proposing a decision on whether all groups were needed and who would join each. She explained, 'there's crossovers' in the groups and that practically it makes sense to join only one or two. Alan, newly elected, asked, 'is there a big difference between Natural and Cultural Heritage?' Elisabeth and Seumas said 'yes' in unison, and continued:

Elisabeth: Natural Heritage tends to be about environment and Cultural Heritage is more into –
Alan: people?
Elisabeth: – the history type side and museums and things like that.
Seumas: I was going to say is Gaelic unnatural? I mean if you dispose of Cultural Heritage where does Gaelic go?
Michael: No, I don't think we can.
Elisabeth: I think Alan was thinking of amalgamating them, but that would be too wide a brief that one.

Amalgamation re-emerged a year and half later, during a discussion about whether the groups were fit for purpose. Elisabeth again felt that two separate groups should be maintained because the subject area created if they merged would be 'too big' and 'a lot of detail would be lost'. She felt out of all of the groups these two were the strongest and 'have different aims'. She said whilst there is overlap, both are currently 'working' in their own right; successfully meeting (including with people beyond the board), applying for project funding and developing events.

The idea that two separate groups are needed seemed to reflect less a nature–culture dichotomy and more a practical recognition that individuals have specific expertise and interests. Indeed, Jane, once chair of the Cultural Heritage Group and a museum curator, told me that in discussions of natural heritage she felt, 'I have nothing to contribute' and 'only input 10 per cent of the time'. Natural and cultural heritage domains, although often shaped by the same conservation logics do involve unique practices, forms of knowledge and management that operate fairly autonomously.[10] A typical Natural Heritage Group meeting might cover the minutiae of the Highland Biodiversity Plan or design an invasive species conference, whilst the Cultural Heritage Group discuss Gaelic language and museum archives. Although in discourse WRB describe natural and cultural heritage as inseparable, in practice, they created separate space for each as a way to explore a range and depth of subject matter. This approach seemed to enable each group to focus on project development for specific funding streams and stakeholders which rarely crossed over, reflecting a wider separation of nature and culture in the Scottish policy, practice and funding landscape.

However, one of the problems of separating natural and cultural heritage is that it may lead to overemphasis on one over the other. Jane, for example, previously felt that WRB often has 'more of a focus on the natural heritage side of things'. Similarly, in the Isle of Man, a cultural sector representative argued that in MAB natural science is seen as 'the real science' of Biospheres, whilst culture, arts and heritage are marginalised to fringe events. Indeed, historically MAB practitioners and BR managers are often trained in natural sciences.[11]

Despite Jane's comments, this has been less of a challenge for WRB, especially with Phoebe trained in cultural anthropology. She among most others holds conceptually holistic views of natural and cultural heritage. I observed this emerging in dialogue among each working group, where actors often transcend the nature–culture dichotomy through emphasising the importance and connectivity of people and place. For example, the Natural Heritage Group reviewed the draft Highland Biodiversity Plan to submit a WRB response and discussed the section titled 'people' where a key outcome was 'land-based, and tourism businesses thrive'. A group member from the Woodland Trust argued that a key problem is people are still leaving the area and thus the plan should also focus on population retention, which is 'such a big part of planning' and 'underpins any discussion about natural heritage, or tourism'. Brian, chair of the group, agreed, adding, 'lots of people depend on biodiversity and healthy environments' beyond land or tourism interests. This was one of many examples where a 'natural heritage' issue was situated by WRB actors in wider nature–culture relations. Similarly, the Cultural Heritage Group and WRB's projects usually emphasise people's cultural connection to nature and landscapes, such as work on Gaelic in the landscape (see Chapter 7). The relationality of nature–culture in most WRB actors' way of thinking has helped to avoid reproducing dichotomies whilst working in different practice contexts in the thematic working groups. Much of this seems tied to how the BR is a space for community-led decision-making, where local, place-based knowledge and experiences hold greater significance than professional domain expertise.

At the board level a more integrated approach to natural and cultural heritage becomes apparent, where it is tied closely to organisational identity and external communications. For example, WRB's business supporter scheme is based on a set of principles which Phoebe developed and presented to directors. Norman, commenting on the principles, argued:

> Where it says conserve the resources of natural, I would put natural and cultural and have them together at the top because that's the principles of Biospheres to me. That would leave an extra pillar to emphasise the local. I think some of my twitchiness about perceptions of the Biosphere, is because of the word bio people assume it's about the conservation of natural heritage, and so anything that blends the two together is a good thing. So, I would have that as the first principle, natural and cultural.

When Elisabeth suggested that perhaps they ought to have seven, rather than six principles to emphasise the cultural, Norman further reiterated, 'I think we need natural and cultural together'. As argued in Chapter 2, what the Biosphere is and means to people is tied to how it is perceived and narrated, with potential for misinterpretations. Alan had also highlighted links to UNESCO narratives about ecosystems and cultural values, stating 'they blend it together and that's what makes each Biosphere distinctive, its cultural value'. The idea of 'blending' is somewhat different to 'balancing', suggesting more integration compared with trading off. It speaks more to the 'biocultural' approach which although evident implicitly, is not currently part of WRB actors' discourse. The final scheme principles state that supporters of the BR 'help to conserve and promote the natural and cultural resources of the Biosphere area' and 'support the economy to benefit people and nature'. This, among other examples of board decisions, reinforces a consistency of approach in bringing people and nature together and seeing natural and cultural as interwoven.

However, this was not always well communicated to some external audiences, for example on social media. WRB had limited social media presence for most of its early years, focusing predominantly on Facebook and later becoming active on sites like Instagram and TikTok. The Facebook page was informally managed initially by a volunteer director without media training, who often shared posts of unpeopled landscapes absent of cultural heritage, communities and sustainability. A tendency to focus on nature is also evident beyond WRB – such as in European Marine World Heritage sites where it has been argued that using a more explicit biocultural heritage lens would help to centre people and culture.[12] Phoebe among others were rightly concerned about how WRB's Facebook might not fully represent the nuance about their identity as a community-led body and organisation for both nature and culture. As the BR developed, a communications strategy was therefore created, using the capacity of paid staff to create more diverse content conveying WRB's holistic approach to sustainability – and prioritising cultural heritage such as through Gaelic (see Chapter 7). As such things significantly improved over time with WRB able to communicate the organisation was for heritage, community and sustainability. However, the use of social media has remained challenging – it not only creates opportunities for positive engagement with communities, but can garner negative views as well. This is especially true around emotive topics, requiring careful management of the BR's organisational identity.

Supporting rewilding?

For WRB actors, the negotiation of nature–culture relations is inherently about the negotiation of the BR's identity as an organisation seeking culturally appropriate sustainability action. This becomes clear in the example of rewilding – an increasingly common, yet contested conservation strategy in Scotland. In the BR, the issue of rewilding emerged when one of the UK's largest-scale rewilding projects was announced encompassing Affric, in the south of the BR. Norman chairing a board meeting shortly after explained that fellow director Thomas had raised the question of WRB's 'role' in rewilding. He thus tabled discussion, especially because rewilding was 'growing arms and legs' and was previously contentious among the board. A former director and gamekeeper had been 'the most outspoken' on it and Norman suggested that the current board ought to 'decide if it's something we should be engaging with proactively'.

Alan, originally from the US but living near the rewilding project, felt that WRB should state their support because rewilding is part of limiting climate change. He argued, 'rather than reinvent the wheel, let's get on board, and add our support'. Coinneach was less supportive and said, 'rewilding is very nuanced'. He was critical of the actions of 'well-intentioned' landowning trusts, such as the John Muir Trust and Royal Society for the Protection of Birds, who in pursuing rewilding often reproduce underlying patterns of unequal land ownership. He felt as landowners, these trusts focus all their efforts around 'managing a resource', rather than on 'the people who are part of the land'. He suggested that for WRB to play a role means 'the communities who will be affected by the landscape scale change in management need to be involved. We need to support the people.' Uilleam, a Highland councillor originally from Uist, added that he was not 'against' rewilding 'if it was done right' but that a more important focus is 'encouraging young people to stay' in the Highlands. Norman tended to agree and was not convinced WRB should support rewilding, describing it as a 'very vague concept'. These concerns reflect academic arguments that rewilding is ambiguous and can be responsible for 'obscuring the long history of human involvement in the landscape' and solidifying landowner power.[13] However, there was some agreement among the board that WRB could 'enter the debate' on rewilding, especially where initiatives are proposed in Wester Ross and where they could ensure 'communities are engaged with' (Norman). This may prove challenging, given that participatory approaches in rewilding have so far been elusive because of a strong conservation imperative, concentrated ownership, power and control over land, and trading off community interests against a wider national public interest.[14]

Whilst WRB have yet to significantly engage with rewilding, there are ways that doing so could benefit both people and nature in the BR. The region is in need of ecological, social and economic regeneration; these are not mutually exclusive. Rewilding could thus be seen as part of a BR approach to regenerative development – a holistic model that empowers communities in the regeneration of landscapes, economies, societies and politics in BR territories.[15] WRB could also help overcome conflict around repeopling or rewilding by promoting the role of cultural heritage in ecological regeneration. What this might look like was articulated by local resident and historian Chris, son of Alison (NatureScot advisor to WRB's board). Although not directly involved with WRB, he saw a role for the BR in promoting sustainable landscapes based on traditional land use practices around cattle driving and transhumance to enhance biodiversity. It has also been argued that there is scope for a Gaelic approach to rewilding.[16] These examples challenge the notion that rewilding is only about enhancing biodiversity whilst overlooking traditional and cultural landscape practices.[17] Though rewilding can 'paradoxically reassert nature–culture boundaries',[18] WRB as an actor is well placed to avoid this dichotomous thinking and support culturally appropriate, participatory approaches in practice.

CONCLUSION

This chapter continued to explain what Wester Ross BR means in discourse and practice, introducing the challenge of a region that has not been developed sustainably. WRB actors see the (un)sustainability of the region as complex and contested, but most agree that action is needed to find balance between conservation and development. What this actually looks like in practice is more elusive and WRB remains cautious about working with larger industries, despite some directors arguing it would be beneficial to do so. So far, WRB has focused on creating a business supporter charter that celebrates the sustainability of smaller, local businesses whilst also seeking investment to support more sustainable livelihoods. The example of green jobs illustrates a desire to generate culturally specific and historically informed sustainability action in Wester Ross, which arises in the negotiation of more generic national narratives in the Scottish context.

The second half of the chapter explored how WRB actors approach natural and cultural heritage through the lens of moving beyond a nature–culture dichotomy. Despite having separate groups for natural and cultural heritage, WRB actors see these as interwoven and utilise a place-based and holistic approach to people and nature. Moreover, among the board, there is consistent emphasis on how WRB exists for both people and nature, as shown in the example of rewilding. The dissolution of thematic groups also means there are no longer any operational distinctions between natural and cultural heritage. WRB is therefore in an excellent position to advance a biocultural approach more explicitly. What this might look like in future could involve, for example, a cultural heritage approach to rewilding, or seeing the BR as a place for regenerative development encompassing the social, cultural economic and environmental.

Building on the discussions here, in the next chapter I continue to expand on how WRB actors negotiate nature–culture relations by focusing on their approach to managing change and conserving cultural heritage.

NOTES

1. Kurmo Konsa, 'Natural and Cultural Heritage: Framing Meanings and Practices,' *International Journal of Sustainability in Economic, Social, and Cultural Context* 12, no. 4 (2016): 9–18; Dennis Byrne, Sally Brockwell and Sue O'Connor, 'Introduction: Engaging Culture and Nature,' in *Transcending the Culture–Nature Divide in Cultural Heritage Views from the Asia-Pacific Region* (ANU E Press, 2013); Jeanne Bogert et al., 'Reviewing the Relationship between Neoliberal Societies and Nature: Implications of the Industrialized Dominant Social Paradigm for a Sustainable Future,' *Ecology and Society* 27, no. 2 (2022): 7; Bram Büscher and Robert Fletcher, *The Conservation Revolution: Ideas For Saving Nature Beyond the Anthropocene* (Verso, 2020).

2. Erik Aschenbrand and Thomas Michler, 'Why Do UNESCO Biosphere Reserves Get Less Recognition than National Parks? A Landscape Research Perspective on Protected Area Narratives in Germany,' *Sustainability* 13, no. 24 (2021): 13647.
3. Karl S. Zimmerer, 'The Reworking of Conservation Geographies: Nonequilibrium Landscapes and Nature–Society Hybrids,' *Annals of the Association of American Geographers* 90, no. 2 (2000): 2.
4. James Hunter, *On the Other Side of Sorrow: People and Nature in the Highlands* (Birlinn, 2014).
5. Hunter, *Other Side of Sorrow*.
6. 'Kickstarting Economic Transformation,' Scottish Government, https://www.gov.scot/news/kickstarting-economic-transformation/.
7. Zoe Russell, 'The Isle of Man Biosphere Reserve: An Entire Nation Approach to Sustainable Development,' *Environmental Policy and Planning* 25, no. 3 (2022): 273–86.
8. Zoe Malcolm et al., 'Towards a Circular Economy and Just Transition to Net-Zero in Rural Scotland: Resident Perspectives on Policy and Practice,' *Journal of Rural Studies* 108 (May 2024): 103300.
9. Johanna Wilkes, 'Reconnecting with Nature through Good Governance: Inclusive Policy across Scales,' *Agriculture* 12, no. 3 (2022): 3.
10. Rodney Harrison et al., 'For Ever, For Everyone,' in *Heritage Futures: Comparative Approaches to Natural and Cultural Heritage Practices*, ed. R. Harrison, C. DeSilvey, C. Holtorf, S. MacDonald, N. Bartolini, H. Fredheim, A. Lyons, S. May, J. Morgan and S. Penrose (UCL Press, 2020), 20–50; Rodney Harrison, 'Beyond "Natural" and "Cultural" Heritage: Toward an Ontological Politics of Heritage in the Age of Anthropocene,' *Heritage and Society* 8, no. 1 (2015): 24–42.
11. Maureen Reed, 'Conceptual Origins and First-Generation Biosphere Reserves,' in *UNESCO Biosphere Reserves: Supporting Biocultural Diversity, Sustainability and Society*, ed. M. Reed and M. Price (Routledge, 2020), 13–28.
12. Clio Kenterelidou and Fani Galatsopoulou, 'Sustainable Biocultural Heritage Management and Communication: The Case of Digital Narrative for UNESCO Marine World Heritage of Outstanding Universal Value,' *Sustainability* 13, no. 3 (2021): 1449.
13. Fraser Macdonald, 'Wild Beasts,' *London Review of Books* 43, no. 18 (2021): 44–5.
14. Alison Martin et al., 'Who Decides? The Governance of Rewilding in Scotland "between the Cracks": Community Participation, Public Engagement, and Partnerships,' *Journal of Rural Studies* 98 (February 2023): 80–91.
15. Tania Moreno-Ramos and Eduard Müller, 'Biosphere Reserves, Ideal Sites to Implement Holistic Approaches in Regenerative Development,' in *UNESCO Biosphere Reserves: Supporting Biocultural Diversity, Sustainability and Society*, ed. M. Reed and M. Price (Routledge, 2020), 254–69.

16. Roddy Maclean, 'Gaelic and Ecosystem Services: a Scoping Exercise' (NatureScot Report 1230, 2021), https://www.nature.scot/doc/naturescot-research-report-1230-ecosystem-services-and-gaelic-scoping-exercise.
17. Nadia Bartolini and Caitlin DeSilvey, 'Transforming Loss,' in *Heritage Futures: Comparative Approaches to Natural and Cultural Heritage Practices*, ed. R. Harrison, C. DeSilvey, C. Holtorf, S. MacDonald, N. Bartolini, H. Fredheim, A. Lyons, S. May, J. Morgan and S. Penrose (UCL Press, 2020), 347–56.
18. Nadia Bartolini, 'Fixing Naturecultures: Spatial and Temporal Strategies for Managing Heritage Transformation and Entanglement,' in *Heritage Futures: Comparative Approaches to Natural and Cultural Heritage Practices*, ed. R. Harrison, C. DeSilvey, C. Holtorf, S. MacDonald, N. Bartolini, H. Fredheim, A. Lyons, S. May, J. Morgan and S. Penrose (UCL Press, 2020), 375–95.

5

Conserving Cultural Heritage

UNDERSTANDING HERITAGE CONSERVATION OFTEN entails examining how actors engage in processes of 'caring for and attending to the past in the present'[1] within a wider 'endangerment sensibility' – referring to how specific heritages come to be defined as vulnerable and at risk of being lost.[2] Across natural and cultural heritage, diverse actors engage in attempts to 'arrest or reverse processes of loss and change', or may seek to 'work with change'.[3] Here I introduce WRB's focus on 'managing change' which embodies a biocultural approach to heritage conservation. This approach is rooted in a vision for more sustainable communities, landscapes and livelihoods – recognising the past has a role to play in the present and for the future. This approach, as I will show, helps to overcome the narrative tensions that appear in BRs elsewhere, where innovating for sustainable development and conserving cultural heritage have been challenging to reconcile.[4] Throughout the chapter I use examples of WRB projects and discussions related to traditional knowledge and skills, and people, places and stories to illustrate WRB's biocultural perspective on heritage-making practices. Additionally, I unpack how WRB actors perceive the role of local communities in heritage-making to offer insights into whose heritage is valued, at what scales and through what mechanisms.

MANAGING CHANGE

WRB's approach to conserving cultural heritage and landscapes reflects a view of heritage as being about the past, in the present, for the future and embedded in place-based nature–culture relations. This emerges in WRB's three pillars: living, learning and legacy. The legacy pillar states:

> People in the Highlands have been managing the landscape for centuries, and their current and historical knowledge are vital to the future of our

> environmental well-being. The Biosphere is inclusive by design – rather than keeping nature and people apart, it celebrates the way in which we interact with and take care of our natural and cultural heritage.

This challenges common-sense discourses of Highland landscapes as wild or people-less and highlights the value of place-based landscape knowledge. Ecological knowledge held by communities is often considered central to BR management[5] and recognised in biocultural heritage as a driver of more sustainable societies.[6] The legacy pillar celebrates nature–culture interactions, and building on Chapter 4, this shows that WRB transcend the nature–culture dichotomy. Although this would be even stronger were they to use the language of biocultural approaches. The argument that people have always managed Highland landscapes suggests that they will continue to do so, albeit not necessarily in the same ways as before. This is captured in the living pillar: 'New landscapes can develop that respect and learn from the past while meeting the changing needs of the future.' Additionally, WRB's learning pillar solidifies that communities should participate in the ongoing development and conservation of natural and cultural heritage. WRB embodies a notion that change is inevitable, and that neither community, heritage, nor landscapes are static, but rather living practices. As such, they are less concerned with preserving or returning to the past, and more with managing change. One key area in which WRB seeks to manage change is connected to an endangerment sensibility around the region's cultural heritage.

Traditional knowledge and skills

WRB actors have been particularly concerned about the region's declining cultural heritage practices; namely, traditional knowledge and skills. In Chapter 4, discussion about green jobs in Wester Ross highlighted the culturally specific skills and knowledges of the region, such as boat building. During such discussions, Norman argued that finding people in the area with traditional skills such as thatching, weaving, or working with lime mortar is a significant challenge. He argued:

> There are a huge number of traditional skills that people would have had in their local communities, that no longer exist, or which are very scarce. For us as an organisation, where we are supposed to be celebrating these sorts of cultural heritage features, retention of the skills to maintain them is a critical part of doing that.

Seumas agreed that only a few decades prior there was a much greater availability of trades and craftspeople in the area. Narratives of loss of traditional knowledge and skills seemed to reflect restorative nostalgia which is about rebuilding or the 'return of an object or experience lost'.[7] The Sustainable Development Group decided that it would be useful to discuss how to respond to loss with local communities. An online learning event was established to bring people together and share experience of traditional skills for sustainability. Shannon, a Wester Ross estate owner and crofter, was invited to speak at the event, related to renovating her nineteenth-century farm buildings. She outlined key challenges around: having the skills to maintain vernacular buildings, being able to work with lime, building drystone dykes, the availability of local materials, and potential to adapt and reuse older agricultural buildings for alternative uses. She explained how valuable it was to have had access to locally skilled labour and local materials, but was critical of the wider national context where there was little grant aid to support the conversion of rural vernacular buildings. She was also critical of the fact that most contractors had no skills in using traditional materials. Alongside Shannon, a representative of Historic Environment Scotland (HES) offered their perspective, focusing on managing historic buildings in the context of climate change. He explained first that HES see the historic environment as more than buildings encompassing the crafts and cultures of people and places. Like Shannon, he felt that over time, traditional skills have been devalued, going hand in hand with construction models based on unsustainable resource use, with long supply chains and copious plastic.

Following the presentations, discussion turned to reversing the decline of local skills and knowledge. It was noted that a good place to start is promoting greater awareness of locally specific practices and materials in Wester Ross. For example, how communities historically used shells to make lime mortar, and still could if they knew how. However, for those involved in rural skills training like Shannon, a key challenge is funding rural courses in small communities. Others pointed to ways to support living culture through in-situ practices within communities; for example, using community owned forests as sites for woodworking skills, or setting up a community mini-mill to process wool locally. Seumas described how his local community had been successful at supporting traditional boat building, but Covid-19 had stalled this: 'we are eighteen months into not building a boat'. The HES representative suggested boat building is exactly the kind of cultural heritage activity that they could fund, seeing it as an attractive way of 'making the culture living, as opposed to dead'. However, he framed the benefits around tourism, suggesting visitors 'want to see it [culture] alive; they don't want blue plaques everywhere; they want live humans. Hitting things and making things.' WRB could try to work with HES to fund activities that not only safeguard living culture, but contribute to sustainable tourism. Inspiration can be found in BRs in England and France, who have developed biocultural heritage tourism as a way to sustain and celebrate local skills and cultural practices like gin-making.[8] Importantly, this should recognise WRB's narrative that 'good places to visit, must first be good places to live' (see Chapter 3). Conserving cultural practices must be about sustaining common values among local people, rather than simply what visitors want. The boat building example in Seumas's community creates intergenerational skill transmission between senior school students, community members and retired traditional boat builders. These social connections allow for knowledges, memories and skills of the sea to be passed down and used in the present, for the future. This is akin to how biocultural heritage in Portugal's twelve BRs acted as a catalyst for conservation using the ecological knowledge and memory of communities for adaptation and innovation, alongside continuity.[9]

Returning to ideas to revive traditional crafts, knowledge and skills across the BR, Norman suggested developing a practical learning course focused on the range of things 'people would have done in this area' and shaped by the UNESCO link of 'people and place'. He argued that most learning in Scotland is geared towards certification and achievement and instead they could 'create Scotland's first folk school in Wester Ross Biosphere'. This would be different to the 'niche' skills training and formal institutional approaches that struggle in sparsely populated areas and which do not support people to make a living in Wester Ross. Whilst this idea has yet to manifest, it reinforces a recurring theme for WRB that cultural heritage can play a role in creating more sustainable rural livelihoods and economies. This became clearer when WRB developed a project proposal to establish a regional bioeconomy supporting rural livelihoods from innovative uses of cultural heritage. The idea built on WRB's collaboration with international partners in Norway and Iceland during the tourism project (see Chapter 3). During knowledge exchanges, WRB learned about a wool trail, a way of utilising cultural heritage to add value to wool supply chains and offer local producers and craftspeople new livelihood opportunities. In Wester Ross, wool is a resource associated with many traditional practices such as the 'age old skill' of dyeing with local plants and weaving (see Figure 5.1). Phoebe outlined the project to the board as a way to support crofters and crafters in Wester Ross who suffer from low wool prices, for whom shearing

Figure 5.1 Dyeing with plants, Applecross Heritage Centre.

sheep and processing wool generates 'negative income'. The project would create economies around the cultural heritage of wool locally, helping producers to mill locally and establish alternative, higher value uses. The proposal was submitted to a Scottish Government funding opportunity, but was rejected. Whilst WRB continues to seek opportunities to use the region's biocultural heritage to support local livelihoods, without funding the organisation is limited in what it can achieve. The UK becoming a signatory of the UNESCO intangible cultural heritage convention may open up future funding opportunities. If so, WRB could pilot biocultural heritage approaches to conservation that tackle two key gaps in Scotland, traditional craftsmanship and knowledges and practices of nature.[10]

LOST PEOPLE, PLACES AND STORIES

Largely, heritage-making in the BR has been on terms not of WRB's making. Rather than emerging from the priorities of local people or place-based knowledges, projects have been designed by external actors. Nonetheless, these carry forward a theme of responding to loss and decline, this time concerning people, places and their stories. In 2020, WRB joined a project designed to protect and share the rich natural and cultural heritage of Scotland's west coast, for visitors and locals alike. Led by UHI tourism researchers and two independent consultancies, it was supported by the natural and cultural heritage fund of NatureScot.

The project recruited thirty local 'story gatherers' to collect stories across Scotland's west coast on: histories, industries, migrations, environments, architecture and communities. Phoebe, with support from the board, proposed WRB agents cover the BR area and was successful in her bid. Phoebe, Coinneach and Mairi acted as story gatherers for sub areas of the BR and coordinated their activities through the Cultural Heritage Group. Another Wester Ross collector, Fionnlagh (introduced in Chapter 3), was also independently recruited to the project and covered part of the BR.

For WRB, the project brought immediate benefit in terms of income and allowed for a focus on conserving cultural heritage through gathering the stories of local people that were felt to be threatened and vulnerable. Coinneach, referring to the BR's older residents, argued the project would help to avoid 'losing another generation without capturing their stories that belong to the area and belong to them'. At a project workshop, Coinneach further explained how gathering stories of older residents can capture now lost experiences of everyday life in the BR. For example, times when Gaelic singing and cultural activities 'weren't separate or made special by any way, they were just part of the fabric of daily life'. Similarly, Mairi described her interest in story collecting as part of her experience of growing up locally in Applecross, in a home that was 'full of stories' from her grandpa who lived to be 100. Although involved in story collecting in the 1990s, she was saddened not to have been able to capture her grandpa's memories of Raasay before he died. Thus, both collectors conveyed a sense of capturing the BR's heritage from below,[11] and everyday heritage,[12] before it was lost forever.

Whilst responding to potential loss of everyday heritage, the project was also seen by both Coinneach and Mairi as a way to foster social connections in local communities. During the workshop, Mairi described how in the 1990s project, older people told their stories to children and her initial excitement for this project had been linked to getting out and talking to people. Coinneach argued that collecting stories from older people today shows them 'that they are valued while they are still alive' and helps to address contemporary social isolation. This is because often older residents 'no longer have a community around them' to share their stories. Unfortunately, Covid-19 limited the extent to which the project could foster social connection, and indeed, likely exacerbated social isolation among older residents. Nonetheless, the project brought some interesting themes to the fore, including the cultural heritage of the Clearances. Mairi spoke of local people in Applecross with stories about lost villages, stating sombrely, 'all that's left is stones now. The villages were cleared down to the shore, and the same in Torridon, up behind the village hall, there were villages up there that were cleared.' Another collector from the Highlands added, 'it's not only people that were cleared, but their songs and stories too'. Highlighting the loss of people, townships and stories captures the act of reflective nostalgia – the desire to remember.[13] I found other examples of this across Wester Ross too, such as 'Lost Inverlael', a project using community archaeology and research to capture stories of eviction. These stories were described as 'lost even within the local community' by the project coordinator and thus their recovery allows for new connections to present generations such as local familial connections to the lost township. Additionally, the material remnants of the Clearances – 'all that's left is stones' – are part of the biocultural heritage of BR landscapes. Across the region examples like Glenarigolach township (see Figure 5.2) convey landscape memories: tangible materialised human practice and ways of organising landscapes.[14] These sit alongside place-based memories which are the more intangible forms of knowledge and cultural practice that also represent 'ways of defining places and making sense out of them socially and culturally'.[15]

Figure 5.2 Glenarigolach township in the valley of Allt a Ghlinne. © Louise Pearson.

These memories are a vital part of challenging hegemonic interpretations of Highlands landscapes as empty and wild which can also exist locally in the BR. Coinneach, for example, told me of his frustration when landscapes 'seemingly empty' are interpreted in ways which fail to acknowledge the Clearances. For example, a local museum volunteer, writing in the local paper, had asked 'why didn't people in Wester Ross build anything?' Sounding dismayed, Coinneach explained 'of course the answer is that most buildings were destroyed', which he framed as part of a historical 'genocide'. Whilst some locals are less attuned to the Clearances, most I encountered felt 'they run deep in the feel of the place … it's a living landscape, the history is still there, you can see those abandoned houses' (estate owner). This is not only about how the Clearances are recognised as cultural heritage, but about how they act as a framework to interpret contemporary population struggles. Based on work in Easter Ross, the Clearances can be experienced as 'post memory' – 'a framework for interpretation and action in the present' set within narratives of historic loss and displacement.[16] Memory practices can shape place-based knowledge and reveal the dynamics of everyday life.[17] However, conflict can also arise when memories are (re)negotiated by local and external actors.[18] This emerged in the story gathering project when the question arose of whose stories are being collected, by whom, and for what purpose.

Whose stories, for what purpose?

Alan, although not directly involved in the stories project, had some awareness given updates from WRB board meetings. When the project first started, he joined a Cultural Heritage Group meeting seemingly to raise concern about external actors involved. He questioned the extent to which stories collected would be subject to the 'editorial control' of VisitScotland which he characterised as a 'top-down' organisation outside of the BR and felt WRB should not 'surrender our control' to communicate the region's cultural heritage. He was critical that the project was promoting wider west coast heritage tourism as an 'entertainment exercise', 'a North Coast 500 approach to things, which is let's cover 500 miles on the west coast and see as much as we can within the shortest period of time that we can see it in'. These concerns seem valid in the context if we agree with the assessment that Highlanders have historically not been 'authors of their own narrative'.[19] In Chapter 3 I introduced critiques of the North Coast 500 as an initiative seen to contribute to unsustainable tourism, and Norman has also described how 'the greatest threat to our heritage at the moment is too many visitors'. Given that sustainable tourism is about slowing down visitors to better engage them with local cultural heritage, to Alan, the coastal stories trail seemed to offer only a shallow engagement with place; a whistle-stop tour of the west coast. Alan's concern also reflects a wider trend in which local culture is commodified for tourist consumption which can negatively impact rural communities. Whilst biocultural heritage tourism can be about local livelihoods and sustainability in BRs,[20] it did not seem that local needs were a core focus of the project.

Responding to Alan's concerns, Coinneach explained that each story gatherer has 'discretion' about what content to put forward and community members sharing their stories will be 'representing themselves in their own words, and editorial control will not be surrendered'. Importantly for Coinneach, the project would give space for local voices to tell their stories and improve community relations. He noted that people moving into Wester Ross to live 'have never been told the stories, they know, but don't understand the names of the places they live so it is to bring them into the landscape'. He thus sought to articulate project benefits around social cohesion and sense of place.

However, Alan's concern was about the final curating of the stories and what purpose this would serve overall. In some respects, he was proven right, as I heard from a collector who was asked to summarise a story to make it digestible for online consumption – contradicting the idea that people had scope to tell their own stories. Ultimately, a project designed and driven by external actors operating at scales beyond the BR is likely to involve some loss of control over heritage-making. Although this project did directly involve local people, conservation of heritage was about wider consumption, an ex-situ approach, compared with 'in-situ' conservation that combines conservation with revitalisation of local communities and their heritage.[21] The latter seems more in line with WRB's own ethos of heritage-making.

HERITAGE-MAKING PRACTICES

Heritage-making can involve processes of collecting, curating, conserving and communicating heritage.[22] It is not only important to understand these processes, but to question who is carrying them out and for what purpose. For example, museum heritage-making often operates within a narrative of working 'on behalf of' the public, rather than seeking to build reciprocal relationships with specific people.[23] In contrast, WRB actors' ideal scenario seems to be that local people can define, manage and retain ownership over their own cultural heritage. Heritage-making processes are thus about building non-hierarchical relationships with local communities. An example of this emerged when WRB actors in the Cultural Heritage Group discussed ideas for a regional approach to BR community archives. It was felt that many existing resources are either localised, such as in Gairloch Museum, or too wide, such as *Am Baile* covering the Highlands. Thus, the idea of creating more community photographic archives with a BR focus was advocated by Anndra. Coinneach argued that WRB as a 'grassroots' organisation can play a role in helping to capture valuable materials in local communities. Phoebe, whilst agreeing in principle, argued that in practice any curating of materials must be based on asking people what they want to see preserved and following local communities priorities to define and interpret shared aspects of the region's history. She argued that we should 'share the narrative that everyone wants shared, rather than just ours', suggesting that they could upset people if they represent local heritage in the wrong way. Hence, on their own terms, as compared with their work with external actors and agendas, WRB are more process oriented, focusing on ensuring that people affected are directly involved in heritage definition and management. Whilst such a project has yet to come to fruition (largely an issue of funding and capacity), my final example of a 'co-created' project helps to elucidate the complexities of participatory methodologies for heritage-making.

WRB became a partner in an EU collaborative research project on co-creating cultural heritage narratives for sustainable development. The project was developed by UHI researchers and connected WRB with three other European BRs and universities in Czechia, Estonia and Norway. In early project development, WRB actors seemingly had little input into project design, although its title emphasised co-creation and some directors found it confusing. Mairi, at a Cultural Heritage Group meeting, said of the information shared with WRB, 'I had to read it about three times, I've got to confess, I kept thinking, what? It's a bit gobbledygook for me and I thought right, read it again'.

Alongside academic jargon, Elisabeth was critical about the lack of funding for WRB which made her reluctant to suggest Phoebe commit her limited time to getting involved. Phoebe agreed their role in the project would be 'peripheral', but that they should hopefully get something positive out it, even with minimal input. Coinneach was positive about the project's international dimension, enabling WRB to learn about strategies for 'sustainable cultural heritage engagement' in other BRs. These early conversations indicate some key barriers to co-creation.

A community BR like Wester Ross has limited capacity to be involved in unfunded work, and larger research projects tend to be designed without much direct input from those who later become the subjects/co-creators of the project, creating a disconnect about project aims.

Following some initial project meetings, Phoebe asked whether I (having volunteered for some time in the BR) could represent WRB in future. She explained the meetings were very 'academic', and that she felt her time was not well spent attending. After attending some online meetings on WRB's behalf, because of my existing knowledge, I was recruited to help UHI to deliver the project which was premised on using participatory methodologies to capture the region's 'heritage-in-the-making'.[24] Through workshops with WRB staff and directors, we co-produced a focus on a diverse range of individuals for interviews and participatory workshops. Rather than emphasise a specific element of cultural heritage (as other BRs had done) we were led by WRB actors' desire for an inclusive approach to working with multiple places and communities, and recognising the cultural heritage of all BR landscapes. This more open approach, whilst challenging initially, created space for WRB to use participatory workshops as part of regional place planning for Highland Council (see Chapter 3) whilst we focused on academic outcomes. Thus, co-creation in this context was about identifying pathways to future sustainability drawing on the BR's cultural heritage and landscapes, whilst pursuing different agendas in practice. However, despite valuable elements of co-creation and participation in project processes, some WRB actors still did not understand the aims or value of the project by its end. I would argue on this basis that future heritage-making in the BR must be co-created from the very beginning. This is the only way to address power relationships that result in more tokenistic involvement of local communities in larger research projects. With growing emphasis on the importance of participatory heritage-making, it is problematic that groups like WRB, whose heritage is directly involved, are not funded to participate. By funding community actors, this allows for time and capacity to build shared priorities around heritage. However, arguably in the absence of meaningful funding, it would also be helpful to shift away from predetermined outcomes and outputs towards a focus on process-driven heritage-making and relationship building. I argue similarly in Chapter 9 concerning approaches to nature conservation.

CONCLUSION

WRB actors perceive heritage in ways that overcome the nature–culture dichotomy, positioning Highland landscapes as a consequence of long-term human-environment interactions. Change and innovation are viewed positively, associated with learning from the past, in the present to respond to the needs of the future. When considered alongside Chapter 4, this illustrates there is no narrative tension for WRB between pursuing regional sustainability and conserving cultural heritage and landscapes. For WRB actors, there is an endangerment sensibility around threatened heritages, specifically local traditional knowledge and skills. Responding to this is about finding ways to work with and manage change, where the conservation of cultural skills and practices is part of innovating and adapting to support sustainable livelihoods. WRB's bioeconomy project for example, is indicative of how WRB embodies the biocultural heritage model, where resilient livelihoods are seen as the outcome of sustained, but also adaptive nature–culture relations.

However, as I explained in the second half of the chapter, WRB has struggled to engage in heritage-making on their own terms, predominantly involved in projects that are externally derived. However, such projects can respond to local priorities to capture and conserve the everyday heritages of the BR such as lost people, places and stories. For WRB heritage-making is not about conserving landscapes or knowledges for their own sake, but rather valuing social and intergenerational relationships and enabling place-based knowledge transmission within local communities. Additionally, marginalised cultural heritages can create opportunities to challenge hegemonic place myths such as notions of Wester Ross as predominantly natural and wild. Heritage-making is fundamentally contested with important questions about who defines heritage, through what means, and for what purpose. WRB actors seek opportunities for local people to define and manage their own heritage, but this has been difficult to implement. Whilst moves towards co-creation are positive, there is scope to better empower community actors like WRB to direct local and regional efforts. Importantly, this is about how in Wester Ross, and Scotland as a whole, communities can use traditional knowledge and craftsmanship, oral traditions and cultural heritage practices to create more sustainable futures. I will now discuss in depth crofting and Gaelic, which are two important, but threatened living heritage practices in the BR.

NOTES

1. Rodney Harrison, 'Beyond "Natural" and "Cultural" Heritage: Toward an Ontological Politics of Heritage in the Age of Anthropocene,' *Heritage and Society* 8, no. 1 (2015): 24–42.
2. Fernando Vidal and Nélia Dias, eds., *Endangerment, Biodiversity and Culture* (Routledge, 2014).
3. Caitlin DeSilvey and Rodney Harrison, 'Anticipating Loss: Rethinking Endangerment in Heritage Futures,' *International Journal of Heritage Studies* 26, no. 1 (2020): 4.
4. Erik Aschenbrand and Thomas Michler, 'Why Do UNESCO Biosphere Reserves Get Less Recognition than National Parks? A Landscape Research Perspective on Protected Area Narratives in Germany,' *Sustainability* 13, no. 24 (2021): 13647.
5. Hockings et al. 'Integrating Science,' 241–54.
6. Alexandria K. Poole, 'Where Is Goal 18? The Need for Biocultural Heritage in the Sustainable Development Goals,' *Environmental Values* 27, no. 1 (2018): 55–80; Rollo, 'Interconnected Nature and People.'
7. Raymond Orr, 'The Nostalgic Native? The Politics and Terms of Heritage and Remembrance in Two Communities,' *International Journal of Heritage Studies* 23, no. 7 (2017): 7.
8. Tim Wilkinson, 'Biocultural Heritage Tourism – a Review of Literature and Experiences,' 2019, https://www.bcht.eu/uploads/1/5/4/4/15448192/bcht_literature_review___appendixes.pdf.
9. Rollo, 'Interconnected Nature and People.'
10. Local Voices CIC, *Mapping Intangible Cultural Heritage Assets and Collections in Scotland* (Museums Galleries Scotland, Historic Environment Scotland, Traditional Arts and Culture Scotland and Creative Scotland, 2021), https://heritagecrafts.org.uk/wp-content/uploads/2021/08/Mapping-ICH-in-Scotland-Local-Voices-Aug-2021-w-Logos.pdf.
11. Iain J. M. Robertson, 'Afterword,' in *After Heritage: Critical Perspectives From Below*, ed. H. Muzzaini and C. Minca (Elgar, 2018): 169–80.
12. Tracey Ireland et al., 'Engaging the Everyday: The Concept and Practice of "Everyday Heritage",' *International Journal of Heritage Studies* 31, no. 2 (2025): 192–215.
13. Svetlana Boym, *The Future of Nostalgia* (Basic Books, 2001).
14. Karl-Johan Lindholm and Anneli Ekblom, 'A Framework for Exploring and Managing Biocultural Heritage,' *Anthropocene* 25 (March 2019): 1–11.
15. Lindholm and Ekblom, 'A Framework for Biocultural Heritage.'
16. Siân Jones, '"Thrown Like Chaff in the Wind": Excavation, Memory and the Negotiation of Loss in the Scottish Highlands,' *International Journal of Historical Archaeology* 16, no. 2 (2012): 346.
17. Rollo, 'Interconnected Nature and People.'

18. Anneli Ekblom et al., 'Conservation Through Biocultural Heritage – Examples from Sub-Saharan Africa,' *Land* 8, no. 1 (2019): 1–15; Lindholm and Ekblom, 'A Framework for Biocultural Heritage.'
19. Michael Newton, *Warriors of the Word* (Birlinn, 2009).
20. Tim Wilkinson, 'Biocultural Heritage Tourism – a Review of Literature and Experiences,' 2019, https://www.bcht.eu/uploads/1/5/4/4/15448192/bcht_literature_review___appendixes.pdf.
21. Álvaro Fernández-Llamazares and Mar Cabeza, 'Rediscovering the Potential of Indigenous Storytelling for Conservation Practice,' *Conservation Letters* 11, no. 3 (2018): 3.
22. Rodney Harrison et al., 'For Ever, For Everyone,' in *Heritage Futures: Comparative Approaches to Natural and Cultural Heritage Practices*, ed. R. Harrison, C. DeSilvey, C. Holtorf, S. MacDonald, N. Bartolini, H. Fredheim, A. Lyons, S. May, J. Morgan and S. Penrose (UCL Press, 2020), 20–50.
23. Helen Graham, 'Publics and Commons: The Problem of Inclusion for Participation,' *ARKEN Bulletin* 7 (2017): 150–68; Helen Graham, 'Horizontality: Tactical Politics for Participation and Museums,' in *Engaging Heritage: Engaging Communities. Heritage Matters*, ed. B. Onciul, M. L Stefano and S. Hawke (Boydell and Brewer, 2017), 73–90.
24. Iris C. Bohnet et al., 'Co-Creating Cultural Narratives for Sustainable Rural Development: A Transdisciplinary Learning Framework for Guiding Place-Based Social-Ecological Research,' *Current Opinion in Environmental Sustainability* 73 (2025): 101506.

6

The Past, Present and Futures of Crofting

Crofting is an agricultural land tenure created out of the Highland Clearances (see Chapter 1). It involves tenancy or ownership of small plots of land ('crofts') and shared use of common grazings – the most widespread form of common land remaining in Scotland.[1] Information on crofts in Wester Ross BR is not readily available, but Crofting Commission data suggest that across Applecross, Gairloch, Glenelg, Glensheil, Kintail, Lochalsh, Lochbroom and Lochcarron there are approximately 2200 crofts. Half of these are tenanted, whilst a quarter are owner occupied and the remainder are part tenanted/part owned. The crofting system in Scotland is thought to be in a bad way, given challenging legal, policy and democratic conditions.[2] The benefits and viability of crofting locally are also contested, although it remains valued as a cultural connection to land in the Highlands and Islands, and is associated with population retention in rural communities.[3] Drawing on critical theory and heritage studies, crofting can be conceptualised as counter-hegemonic to dominant ideologies of sporting, conservation and tourism[4] and common-sense discourses of 'wildness'.[5] It is an embodied heritage from below[6] that constitutes a form of sustainable small-scale agriculture for alternative post-neoliberal societies.[7] For example, on the Isle of Harris, crofting communities 'trouble the norms of private property' through land commoning embodied in the notion of *dùthchas*.[8] However, crofting varies in practice across the Highlands and Islands. In some places, including Wester Ross, the effects of socioeconomic and agrarian change in the last seventy-five years have created a significant shift from traditional to more intensive land practices[9] and from collective to more individualised practices.[10]

I focus in this chapter on outlining the pasts, presents and futures of crofting in Wester Ross, unpacking the nuances surrounding heritage, community and sustainability. I begin by explaining how crofting and crofters are invoked as cultural heritage, before discussing their position in contemporary communities, and as a sustainable land use and livelihood. I avoid essentialising a Wester Ross crofting 'community' as counter-hegemonic, or as a collective – whether class-based[11] and/or relating to ethnic identity.[12] Instead, I draw out the complexities of crofting as fragmented and unsustainable in the BR based on the diverse perceptions and experiences of WRB actors, communities, crofters and national crofting/government bodies. Given the challenges facing crofting, I conclude the chapter by thinking towards how the BR might help to create new crofting futures.

CROFTING AS HERITAGE

WRB recognise crofting as 'a historically important land use' that has declined significantly over time but 'remains relevant to local communities today'. Their website explains that crofting is a land use practice that can 'enhance' and 'reduce' biodiversity – the latter connected with 'extensive sheep grazing' across Wester Ross. In this simple description, crofting emerges as valued heritage, community practice, and a contested sustainability issue. The narrative of decline surrounding crofting in Wester Ross was also central to many actors interpretations, conveying land abandonment and changing communities. Historically, many more people were living and crofting in Wester Ross than today. A local resident of Gairloch, citing the museum's crofting township maps from the 1840s, told me there were 'so many more houses' and the population was much larger, evidenced in the many ruins and abandoned crofts across the area. Alongside material remnants of the Clearances, remnants of past crofting are part of the region's landscape memories. Such remnants, like ruined blackhouses and disused croft buildings, are seen as part of the 'special character' of landscapes, such as the Wester Ross National Scenic Area and NTS's Kintail estate. Adverts for croft houses, describe ruined croft buildings as 'adding character' (and development potential) to properties across Wester Ross. Whilst some actors like NTS and NatureScot characterise landscapes of abandonment within positive narratives of 'wildness' – this is often resisted by locals. Shannon, an estate owner and crofter felt that although the landscapes where people lived 150 years ago are 'more abandoned than ever' they are still not wild. Moreover, Seumas characterised abandoned crofting townships as 'graveyards of unsustainable practice'.

Narratives about crofting are prominent in the BR's three museums of Applecross, Gairloch and Ullapool. Generally, exhibits tell local and regional stories of crofting with displays describing historic practices and technologies (see Figure 6.1). A key focus is often the manual labour and hardship associated with life on the croft, how crofters engaged in a variety of activities to survive and the collective nature of crofting. For example, peat cutting and harvesting were once 'social occasions' within the community (Ullapool Museum). Decline over time is captured in Applecross Heritage Centre: 'crofting, as a way of life, is a thing of the past', 'until the 1950s, Applecross was very much a crofting and fishing community'. More optimistically are statements like 'crofting has changed, but hopefully, not vanished'. An Ullapool Museum booklet on crofting suggests that it was 'the preoccupations of modern life' that 'threatened' crofting, which has 'struggled during the last century' due to an ageing population, loss of skills passed through generations, speculation around land and housing, neglect of crofts and absenteeism, and policymakers subsidising industrial agriculture.

Figure 6.1 Crofting tools, Gairloch Heritage Museum.

The Balmacara estate (owned by NTS since 1946) is an example of where heritage interpretation brings historic and contemporary crofting together. In place of narratives of decline is a 'thriving' crofting landscape connecting land, people and nature. The estate is 75 per cent croft land with eighty-two crofts over eight townships, a 'true Highland crofting estate'. An NTS booklet explains estate management involves 'careful consideration of heritage' and support for 'modern crofting'. In Plockton visitor centre a display presents local perspectives on contemporary crofting, including how it contributes to landscape aesthetics, 'supports' the cultural landscape and biodiversity, but also 'you cannot live off crofting'. Norman, representing NTS, said he has always recognised the value of the estate's crofting landscape – but this has not always been shared by superiors. He has thus had to advocate for telling the crofting story. This may be down to the crofting estate being seen as a burden given the complexities of acting as a landlord for multiple crofting townships. There have been tensions in Plockton, for instance, between crofters and the community about the right to use the village as commons. Whilst conflict rarely appears in heritage interpretations of crofting, local actors told me crofting has always created tensions over land. An Applecross crofter challenged romantic notions of crofting as harmonious citing historic and ongoing conflicts about the creation croft boundaries. Indeed, Norman once described how crofters often fight over very little; they 'end up in court over a small piece of land'. Both conflict and change have always been present as Norman aptly summarises: 'crofting is not a museum piece, it's cultural heritage, but it's not something from the past, it's still going and it has evolved since day one'. However, change has not necessarily been for the better.

THE DEATH OF CROFTING COMMUNITIES

In 2019, a *Crofter* article was published titled, 'The Death of a Crofting Community?'[13] It states that historically as place-based communities, the strength of crofting townships lay in people living and working there. Today, a very different community has taken shape, one in which the proliferation of 'the non-resident outsider' adds 'nothing except to the apparent emptiness of the place'.[14] In Wester Ross the idea of an absent community emerged when Seumas said: 'with crofting, you can see plenty of sheep on the hill and deer and so on, but you don't see the crofters because there are few and far between'. In Applecross I was shown by a local crofter the many neglected crofts that were supposedly owned by absentees. He claimed most were living in England and had no intention of working the land or allowing for someone locally to do so in their absence. Crofting regulations stipulate crofters should be resident within thirty-two kilometres of their croft and put their croft to purposeful use, but across Wester Ross, this seemed contrary to reality. Whilst the Crofting Commission can permit absences for periods of time, in one case a crofter cited an owner had been absent since the 1970s. In Kinlochewe, a crofter who was selling a croft told me an English couple came to view it and admitted they had no intention to work the land and would build a holiday home. He said he refused to sell to them because he felt the land must remain in crofting for someone to live and work locally.

Many crofting townships in Wester Ross are in a dire state, some having only one or two active crofters. The issue is not only absenteeism, but whether those living on their crofts can engage in crofting as they age. A local in Applecross explained, 'the pool of traditional crofters is getting smaller and the people older ... too old to put their sheep out on the hill as they used to'. Moreover, fewer people overall are crofting, and in some townships 'no one uses the common grazings anymore'. This explains aspects of the death of crofting communities in Wester Ross. In response many argue for improving access to crofts among new entrants. However, WRB director Michael suggests that even in townships where there only a 'few people keeping going', young people struggle to access crofts because crofting communities are not very 'inclusive' and it is hard to get into the 'power structure'. Crofts are often passed down through family inheritance and a former employee of the Crofting Commission, living in Wester Ross, explained that individuals often refuse to be the one to break the line of inheritance, even if they have no interest in living on and working the croft themselves.

How to deal with a lack of available crofts and croft tenancies can be contentious. At a Scottish Crofting Federation (SCF) meeting, access to crofts was raised with some arguing for stronger enforcement of crofter's duties to reside on their crofts via the Crofting Commission or the transfer of unused crofts to new tenants or owners via landlords. This was emotive, with the idea of landlords or the Commission proactively evicting people seen as a continuation of historic land dispossession and going against the cultural heritage of crofting. Another point against enforcing the 'purposeful use' of crofts was given to me by a former SCF employee, who said the rule is unjust because its 'forcing people to use ten acres of unproductive land when others with land are not obligated in the same way'. Why should a crofter need to make sustainable use of a marginal piece of boggy land, when non-crofting land users and owners are not held to any standards of use? This conveys a paradox for crofting. On the one hand, crofting must be contextualised within Scotland's wider, inequitable system of land ownership, and historic land injustice to protect the hard-won rights of crofters. On the other hand, protecting the rights of individual crofters to use (or not) their crofts seems to contribute to the death of crofting as a community-based, collective system of land use. As one of my interviewees put it, even the 'strongest advocates' of crofting can contribute to its decline through their individual actions.

On individualisation across Wester Ross, crofting was often perceived as a hobby, and croft amalgamation or 'croft collecting' was occurring – where individuals gained multiple crofts in a township. The latter was argued to be evidence that crofting is no longer a communal system but a mechanism for land grabbing at a local level by 'selfish' individuals. Indeed, as crofts become part of larger units, this counters the idea that crofting can maintain a rural population and exist as a form of community.[15] Alternatively, one might consider taking on additional crofts as an effort to make a living from the land in a context where it is increasingly challenging to do so. Nonetheless, a key issue across Wester Ross seems to be that communal structures of crofting are failing. Crofting common grazings committees are supposed to 'help sustain communal working' and management of community assets.[16] However, many are not functioning well in Wester Ross; they rely on one or two individuals, and some refuse to join or run a common grazing committee because of personal financial liability and local conflict. Absentees also do not participate in the committees; as an Applecross crofter said, 'they do not want to know'. In Wester Ross, crofting seems to represent an 'underuse context', and in a similar context in a German BR, actors beyond the fragile common pasture organisations were needed to help promote sustainable development and conserve common grazing practices.[17]

'The right to buy was a folly'

Individualisation in crofting has been tied to legislative change, for example, how the right to buy crofts incentivised turning leased crofts into privately owned properties. According to a former Commission employee and crofter in Wester Ross, whilst the logic was about empowerment through land ownership, 'introducing the right to buy was a folly, because it undermined that basic principle of crofting'. Crofter and estate owner Shannon similarly felt once crofts became a 'free market asset' it enabled them to be sold off here and there, leading to houses being developed 'which are just dead, no one lives there'. In Gairloch and Applecross, I heard complaints about croft land being used for housing development, which although supported when it can provide affordable housing for a young person, is seen as problematic when done to resell for personal financial gain. For critics, this is ultimately about a desire to value land for its social, cultural and environmental values and community benefits, which contrasts with a feeling that some individual crofters are 'property developers'. A non-crofting resident described that: 'all crofting land is community land, and it shouldn't be possible for one individual to be able to sell it for profit or individual gain'. For Norman there is 'nothing sustainable' about a system based on buying and selling crofts to the highest bidder. He finds it troubling that despite a history of struggle, many crofters today are treating land 'in exactly the same way as the private landowners were doing' to make profit from it. It certainly seems that across Wester Ross, crofting is reproducing 'dominant norms of property that rely on practices of privatisation and enclosure', treating land only as 'a commodity with exchange value'.[18]

However, this problem is also Scotland-wide, as evident from an SCF meeting about improving access to crofts where attendees voted that the top three barriers were: unused/neglected crofts not made available; market price and competition; crofts being bought for house sites. Crofting is shaped by capitalist relations and private property logics and some argue for market intervention to make crofts affordable for young people, whilst others see crofters as a marginalised group with a legitimate right to sell land for financial gain. On the Isle of Harris, the idea of moving beyond more individualised forms of crofting is found in the notion of crofting tied to *dùthchas* and narratives that 'the land does not belong to you, but you belong to the land'.[19] However, this did not seem common in Wester Ross. In fact, in some local communities the idea of encouraging collective ownership of land was highly sensitive. A local crofter told me that crofting commons and common grazing committees could easily translate into a collective community buyout from the estate owner. However, they felt there would be 'uproar' if this was openly discussed in their area. The former Commission employee perceived that differences between communities in Wester Ross and Harris seem to reflect how in the former, crofters do not want to share responsibility for land with the wider community, and prefer remaining under the tenancy of a private landlord than a community arrangement. As explained by Coinneach, 'sometimes, benign neglect from an absentee landlord is better than massive in-fighting within a community'. For him, there are few local communities in Wester Ross that have a shared sense of purpose. Instead, there are multiple agendas, within crofting, and between crofters and communities, where people want to see different uses of croft land that are challenging to reconcile.

A SUSTAINABLE LAND USE AND LIVELIHOOD

As noted at the beginning of this chapter by WRB, crofting as a 'sustainable' land use is contested. SCF's Facebook page describes how crofting is good for biodiversity and is 'a sustainable way to produce food, grow communities and protect the planet'. Commenting on the post, a well-known crofter argued this is only true where small-scale food production methods are embraced, which often they are not. Indeed, different forms of crofting can either enhance or reduce biodiversity. A crofter in Kinlochewe argued that crofting practices today are a product of the 1950s, tied to government subsidies that have resulted in extensive sheep grazing in Wester Ross (see Figure 6.2). Again, this is true for the Highlands more widely, that sheep-farming, although largely unprofitable, is 'kept going by public subsidy'.[20] The Kinlochewe crofter, was a strong advocate that 'crofting has to change' and he felt the Crofting Commission and SCF were 'failing crofting' by not realising the future can be about more than raising sheep. For him, among other crofters I encountered, it would be better to subsidise alternative, sustainable practices.

At the heart of contestations about the future of crofting as sustainable land use is a tension that exists in Wester Ross and nationally between so-called 'traditional' and 'modern' crofting. The foreword

Figure 6.2 Sheep grazing in Wester Ross.

to the Scottish Government's Crofting National Development Plan states:

> Traditional crofting has a role to play in our ambition to re-people the Highlands and Islands, but it is also important to encourage modern approaches to crofting and diversification into such things as renewable energy projects, tourism, woodlands and beekeeping.[21]

The idea of a dichotomy between traditional and modern crofting in Wester Ross was conveyed by an Aultbea crofter, who explained, 'I am frowned upon because I've got ponies on the croft here, which obviously aren't the traditional thing'. They also reported that a neighbouring crofter was trying to rewild their croft which was 'not going down well' with other crofters. Similarly, Coinneach wished to see peatland restoration on the common grazings in his township, but felt other crofters would be resistant. He noted that since taking on the croft, they have 'flat out rejected the notion that I've got any interest in the common grazing, because I don't have any animals there'. Peatland restoration is important nationally, seen by NatureScot and the Scottish Government as part of how crofting can address the climate crisis. However, environmentally focused initiatives can be perceived by crofters as a threat to 'the actual productive use of land, which is what crofting is ultimately for' (crofter, SCF meeting) – implying livestock grazing. It is common across Europe to find the mentality that landscapes should be frozen in time in their current state, without recognising what has come before or what could come after.[22] Hence, it may be useful to dissolve the dichotomy between traditional and modern crofting by recognising, as Norman does, that crofting has already changed and will continue to change. What this change looks like in practice needs to include past traditional land use practices and more recent innovations. Some landscapes in the BR are at risk from under-grazing from a conservation perspective, reflecting how European landscapes have nature value because of traditional livelihoods and land practices.[23] Others are at risk from overgrazing, and so what practices are needed depends on the specific conditions of a landscape. Examples of sustainable crofting are often based on mixed use, rather than a single purpose. For example, woodland crofts benefit ecological systems and can still allow for livestock grazing. Examples such as conservation grazing and transhumance are also culturally relevant practices that could lead to more sustainable crofting landscapes.

Crofting as a sustainable land use practice must also be about creating more self-sufficient crofting livelihoods. Crofting was never designed to allow for self-sufficiency, but to provide wage labourers for capitalist industries. Coinneach hoped to one day make a living from his croft full-time and was saddened that most in Wester Ross cannot 'create a livelihood ... where they place their feet on the ground and where they place their head at night'. For him crofting is much more than a hobby, it is a cultural connection to land, rooted in an environmental ethic – central to his identity. However, in the current context he is forced to make a living beyond the croft. WRB, as described in Chapter 5, have already been attempting to support croft livelihoods, such as through their bio-economy project which was about adding value to crofting products like wool. Norman has also mentioned on several occasions an idea to develop a scheme to pay crofters a premium for 'heritage' products, produced in sustainable or traditional methods. Crofting livelihoods could be strengthened if crofts are valued and funded as a sustainable method of food production, emphasising the need for agroecological principles. Examples, such as Cosaig Growers in Glenelg, have been highlighted at WRB events as cases of good practice, where crofters run a market garden selling produce locally that is grown using no-dig methods and without plastic or chemicals. Other examples for supporting crofting livelihoods, include social crofting which sees crofters utilise their land in partnership with the health and social care sector.[24] Therein crofts are no longer a small parcel of land entirely surrounded by legislation, but rather 'spaces of wellbeing' for rural communities. Ultimately a sustainable future for crofting and crofters must be about heritage, sustainability and community.

TOWARDS NEW CROFTING FUTURES

WRB actors recognise that crofting in Wester Ross has a long way to go before it is sustainable. But the question of how change in crofting might be achieved, and by whom, is unsettled. Whilst there is appetite among WRB actors to create a more sustainable system of crofting in the BR, there has been little progress on this in practice. Crofting is seen as a complex and contentious issue especially for Phoebe, who admits, 'I'm not an expert, I don't know that much about it'. Norman, who is more knowledgeable, has tended to imply that it is national political actors who can improve the situation of crofting. Discussing how to bring 'vast' areas of unused croft land in Wester Ross into more productive use, he stressed that 'big questions' must be asked of Scottish Government and the Crofting Commission for their lack of action. He feels that 'nothing is being done' about the lack of access to crofts because crofting is 'a big political hot potato'. Similarly, a crofter felt that 'everyone's terrified of crofting, all politicians are terrified of crofting, they don't know how to deal with it, what to do about it, it's such an emotive topic'.

During my observations of the Scottish Parliament Cross-Party Group on Crofting (CPGC) I gained some insight into how SCF, the Crofting Commission, members of the Scottish Parliament, and Scottish Government envision action on crofting. A recurring theme was crofters calling for the Commission to tackle enforcement problems and government to prioritise crofting and enact legislative reform. Both were at times criticised for being disconnected from the realities of crofting communities. In response, the Commission cited their insufficient resources or capacity meaning they were forced to focus on 'low hanging fruit', such as self-report breaches of crofting duties, and said there was little they could do about absenteeism unless it was officially reported. Scottish Government representatives were unable to answer questions on when crofting law reform might take place, but assured the group that crofting was valued, citing financial support through various grants. Commitments to ensure 'crofting can reach its full potential' were reiterated and a national development plan for crofting was produced. When the plan was published in 2021, SCF were disappointed by its content and the failure to address legislative reform. Years later, in 2025, the Scottish Government under John Swinney included crofting law reform in the Programme for Government. The Commission has also been given a role for crofting development, which may help to make changes happen in local communities. Whilst national action is positive, relying on it arguably limits the possibility for prefiguring more sustainable futures for crofting in the BR.

Elsewhere, following an anarchist heritage sensibility, I have suggested that prefigurative practices could help to address crofting challenges beyond hegemonic institutions.[25] WRB as a community-led regional actor has a significant role to play in creating collaborative action among crofters, communities and national actors like SCF to create more sustainable futures for crofting in practice. Ultimately this is about enacting a form of crofting where the means creates the end, starting by treating crofting as a collective biocultural heritage practice. I advocate thinking about what Wester Ross crofting could look like if actors took inspiration from Biocultural Heritage Territories – which are models of bottom-up food systems governance (see Chapter 1). Moving beyond private property models, a focus on collective heritage in Wester Ross could draw on *dùthchas* as a more ethical relationship with land. I return to this in the following chapter. It is also about balancing conservation and development through in-situ models that create resilient livelihoods,[26] which is already an aim of WRB. Wester Ross is no different to Peru's Parque De La Papa, in the sense of a need to adapt agricultural systems to climate change[27] and resist threats to such systems from neoliberal policies and place myths that devalue small-scale agriculture. I return to the question of regional food futures in Chapter 8; however, it is clear on the basis of previous chapters, that WRB creates new potential to foster a more collective approach to crofting in the BR.

CONCLUSION

Crofting in Wester Ross is complex. It is a valued aspect of the region's heritage, it remains part of, but is declining among communities, and its sustainability as a land use and livelihood is contested. Narratives about past crofting bring to the fore how this once more prevalent collective experience in Wester Ross was rooted in forms of hardship that ought not to be romanticised. Crofting was and still is a difficult living from the land, but nonetheless remains valued by people as a part of cultural heritage and connection to place. Heritage actors narrate the decline of crofting in Wester Ross tied to wider societal and economic change. However, crofting estates like Balmacara and actors like WRB reinforce crofting is important to communities today. Focusing on perceptions of crofting in Wester Ross, the most prominent narrative is that of unsustainability. From absenteeism, to unaffordable prices, individualism and extensive sheep grazing, it is difficult to see how crofting on the whole in Wester Ross is a model of sustainable nature–culture relations. Whilst there are examples of good practice, WRB actors are among those that focus on a need for change, arguing that crofting has a long way to go to be sustainable.

Thus far, change has been elusive, tied to the emotive and political nature of crofting and tensions between individual rights and safeguarding a collective system. WRB has had little resource and capacity to work towards more sustainable crofting, and most lobby for national actors to address the problems. However, thinking about alternatives and the future of crofting in Wester Ross, it would be fruitful, I suggest, to shift focus towards changing practices and relations in the here and now. WRB could advocate for crofting as a collective biocultural heritage and work towards collaborative regional scale action to improve the governance, practices and values of contemporary crofting. This is about moving beyond individualism and marketisation and overcoming conflict associated with the traditional–modern dichotomy. Whilst there are no easy solutions, change will be required to ensure sustainable futures for crofting in the BR. I turn now to Gaelic, which like crofting, is a valued, yet contested and threatened heritage in Wester Ross.

NOTES

1. Katrina Myrvang Brown, 'New Challenges for Old Commons: The Role of Historical Common Land in Contemporary Rural Spaces,' *Scottish Geographical Journal* 122, no. 2 (2006): 2; Katrina Myrvang Brown, 'Understanding the Materialities and Moralities of Property: Reworking Collective Claims to Land,' *Transactions of the Institute of British Geographers* 32, no. 4 (2007): 4.
2. Iain MacKinnon, 'Crofting Policy and Legislation: An Undemocratic and Illegitimate Structure of Domination?,' in *Land Reform in Scotland: History, Law and Policy*, ed. Jayne Glass et al. (Edinburgh University Press, 2020).
3. Bryan Hains et al., '21st Century Crofting: Strengths and Opportunities for Community Development,' *Journal of Agriculture, Food Systems, and Community Development*, 8 May 2013, 47–60.
4. Fraser MacDonald, 'Viewing Highland Scotland: Ideology, Representation and the "Natural Heritage",' *Area* 30, no. 3 (1998): 3.
5. Rick Rohde, 'Written on the Surface of the Soil: West Highland Crofting Landscapes During the 20th Century,' in *Repeat Photography: Methods and Applications in the Geological and Ecological Sciences*, ed. R. H. Webb, D. E. Boyer and R. Turner (Island Press, 2010), 248–64; Zoe Russell, 'Common Sense Discourses of Nature: A Gramscian Analysis of Conservation Designations in the Scottish Highlands,' in *Heritage and Environment* (ICC, 2021), 47–66.
6. Iain J. M Robertson, 'Hardscrabble Heritage: The Ruined Blackhouse and Crofting Landscape as Heritage from Below,' *Landscape Research* 40, no. 8 (2015): 8.
7. Mark Shucksmith and Katrina Rønningen, 'The Uplands after Neoliberalism? – The Role of the Small Farm in Rural Sustainability,' *Journal of Rural Studies* 27, no. 3 (2011): 3.
8. Fiona Mackenzie, *Places of Possibility: Property, Nature And Community Land Ownership* (John Wiley Sons, 2013).
9. Rohde, 'Written on the Surface.'
10. Brown, 'New Challenges for Old Commons'; Brown, 'Materialities and Moralities of Property.'
11. James Hunter, *The Making of the Crofting Community* (Birlinn, 2000).
12. Iain MacKinnon, 'The Invention of the Crofting Community: Scottish History's Elision of Indigenous Identity, Ideology and Agency in Accounts

of Land Struggle in the Modern Gàidhealtachd,' *Scottish Historical Review* 98, no. 1 (2019): 1.
13. John Bannister, 'Death of a Crofting Community?,' *The Crofter* 117: 7, https://www.crofting.org/wp-content/uploads/2020/03/crofter117.pdf.
14. Bannister, 'Death of a Crofting Community?'
15. Matthew Hoffman, 'Private Property in the Context of Community: Property and Community,' *American Journal of Economics and Sociology* 77, no. 1 (2018): 1.
16. Appointment of Common Grazings Committees. Crofting Commission, https://www.crofting.scotland.gov.uk/common-grazings/appointment-of-grazings-committees/ (accessed 11 June 2025).
17. Florian Brossette et al., 'Adapting Common Resource Management to Under-Use Contexts: The Case of Common Pasture Organizations in the Black Forest Biosphere Reserve,' *International Journal of the Commons* 16, no. 1 (2022): 1.
18. Mackenzie, *Places of Possibility*, 24.
19. Mackenzie, *Places of Possibility*.
20. James Hunter, *On the Other Side of Sorrow: People and Nature in the Highlands* (Birlinn, 2014).
21. Crofting: National Development Plan. Scottish Government, 2021. https://www.gov.scot/publications/national-development-plan-crofting/.
22. Eugene Costello, 'Hill Farmers, Habitats and Time: The Potential of Historical Ecology in Upland Management and Conservation,' *Landscape Research* 45, no. 8 (2020): 8.
23. Costello, 'Hill Farmers, Habitats And Time.'
24. Zoe Russell et al., "Spaces of Well-Being: Social Crofting in Rural Scotland," *Journal of Rural Studies* 86 (August 2021): 145–54.
25. Zoe Russell, 'An Anarchist Imagination for Critical Heritage Studies: Prefiguring Equitable and Sustainable Futures in Crofting and Beyond,' in *The Routledge International Handbook of Heritage and Politics*, ed. Gönül Bozoğlu, Gary Campbell, Laurajane Smith and Christopher Whitehead (Routledge, 2024).
26. Krystyna Swiderska et al., 'Indigenous Peoples' Food Systems and Biocultural Heritage: Addressing Indigenous Priorities Using Decolonial and Interdisciplinary Research Approaches,' *Sustainability* 14, no. 18 (2022): 11311.
27. Matthew Sayre et al., 'You Can't Grow Potatoes in the Sky: Building Resilience in the Face of Climate Change in the Potato Park of Cuzco, Peru,' *Culture, Agriculture, Food and Environment* 39, no. 2 (2017): 103.

7

Gaelic Language and Culture: Loss and Revival

SCOTTISH GAELIC IS PART of the Celtic languages family related to Manx and Irish. It has a complex history in Scotland but was once the dominant language.[1] From the later sixteenth century, Gaelic was stigmatised and repressed, followed by periods of both romanticism and persecution in the eighteenth and nineteenth centuries. For example, the 1872 Education Act made education synonymous with English, fostering a colonised mentality and deficit ideology among Gaels.[2] Only more recently, since 1985, has Gaelic Medium Education (GME) become available in Scotland. From the twentieth century, more positive attitudes towards Gaelic seen it valued in discussions about development in the Highlands and Islands and its relationship to land and crofting.[3] Nationally, revitalisation efforts have helped to grow speaker numbers, particularly in urban centres like Glasgow, but have failed to prevent the current 'crisis' in vernacular communities.[4] Gaelic 'as a community vernacular is now weaker than ever before'[5] and the Scottish Languages Act 2025 has only just recognised Gaelic as an official language.

This chapter outlines local actors' perspectives on the past, present and future of Gaelic loss and revival in Wester Ross. I begin by discussing Gaelic as heritage and introducing narratives of decline experienced locally over time, unpacking a complex politics of language, identity and place in BR communities. I then offer perspectives around Gaelic revival in local communities which draws out the notion of Gaelic as difficult heritage tied to colonial legacies and the devaluing of the language and culture. I turn next to discuss Gaelic as a lens for sustainability action, focusing on WRB's work around Gaelic in the landscape. WRB position Gaelic as a vital part of the BR's cultural heritage and relevant to contemporary communities. I connect local and regional understandings to wider literature on Gaelic as a model for articulating 'the relationship between nature and society to the mutual benefit of each'.[6] This leads on to a critique of Scottish conservation policy where Gaelic approaches to nature are marginalised in mainstream scientific frameworks. I conclude by suggesting how WRB could help create a 'third cultural space' for more sustainable nature–cultures in future.

GAELIC AS DIFFICULT HERITAGE

WRB's strategic plan states Gaelic language and culture are 'a vital thread that runs through the rich fabric of life in Wester Ross'. However, Gaelic has declined significantly over time, especially during the twentieth and twenty-first centuries. Elisabeth told me, 'there are no pockets of Gaelic speaking in Wester Ross'. In 1891, 75–100 per cent of the population of Wester Ross could speak Gaelic,[7] whereas today the figure is around 10 per cent (BR nomination form). Wester Ross faces challenges that are widely shared, namely, the dispersed nature of the speaking community and the weakness of intergenerational transmission.[8] In smaller local communities I encountered one or two Gaelic speakers, such as a Kinlochewe crofter whose wife was trying to learn so that he would have someone to speak to locally. WRB's website described the loss of Gaelic as 'rapid and devasting' with 'huge amounts of knowledge of the local landscape dying with it'. It highlights the important work of Gairloch Museum, home to a significant collection of Gaelic resources. Interpretation within the museum tells the story of Gaelic in Gairloch, including the history of the language and a rich cultural heritage including music, place names, literature and oral traditions, some of which are preserved in the museum. In Gairloch, Gaelic was the first language for locals, few of whom spoke English 'until the 1880s and as late as the 1950s'. However, Gaelic had declined significantly by the end of the twentieth century, meaning 'the language is never likely to be heard as freely as it once was'. At the time of my visits the museum was playing a film of local post-war stories, in which an older woman solemnly said, 'living here and growing up was so much connected with Gaelic, you were aware of it disappearing in a way. There are places I know by name, but I'll never hear them mentioned again.' Other locals in the film described how Gaelic was seen as 'old-fashioned' and older speakers perceived as 'stupid'. Many who could speak Gaelic chose not to 'because that's the way the world was going'. In the BR there is a clear intergenerational transmission gap where many, despite having grown up in Gaelic-speaking families, were not taught the language. For Coinneach this was experienced as 'a feeling of loss', leading him to learn as an adult and become an active proponent of Gaelic revival in Wester Ross. Local voices in the film suggested that the decline of

Gaelic went hand and hand with the decline of crofting (see Chapter 6). Discussing this with Coinneach, he felt that 'the death of Gaelic and the death of crofting' were interconnected, and that he had come to see them as in a relationship of 'mutual aid' – they 'need each other'. I asked WRB's Gaelic Development Officer (GDO) Adaira about these connections and she explained:

> There will be crofters who maybe don't feel any connection to Gaelic whatsoever. But does that mean that there is no connection? I think there probably is quite a big connection, but I think it's less strong than it was because people's understanding of Gaelic is less, but then people's understanding of crofting is less as well. At one point, a lot more people used to speak Gaelic and a lot more people used to do crofting. I think those ties are generally fragmenting. I personally do think there's a huge connection. It's just, I don't think everybody sees that anymore.

A biocultural lens would explain this fragmentation in relation to how hegemonic cultural, political and economic forces have led to the loss of distinct cultural practices, languages, knowledges, values and governance systems (see Chapter 1). Challenging this requires drawing attention to peoples, cultures and relationships with nature that have been 'othered' in the master narrative of capitalism and the Anthropocene.[9] In the Scottish context this must, however, be understood in the context of debates about Gaelic cultural identities and place.

Gaelic revival in Wester Ross invokes relationships between language, identity and place. These are set within arguments about Gaelic as 'Scotland's language',[10] which can invoke tensions between those that consider *Gàidheal* an ethnic, indigenous identity[11] and those that find this view essentialist.[12] It has been argued that someone speaking Gaelic who is born in Scotland is as likely to be accepted as a Gael as someone who has the blood and lives in the *Gàidhealtachd*, but without the language – because Gaelic identity is open and fluid, not fixed and given.[13] In Wester Ross, Gaelic cultural identity tended to be defined in relation to place-based relationships:

> I'm not a Gaelic speaker, I was brought up in a Gaelic culture at a time when Gaelic was very much discouraged by Gaels. When I first moved here, I was four, and when I played with the neighbouring kids, they only spoke Gaelic and I only spoke English. Now they don't speak any Gaelic, no one speaks any Gaelic here. I'm not claiming my affinity with the Gaelic culture is really through the language, it's more through ... the people I grew up with, were the last of the old timers. It was a completely different world ... it was a fishing and peat cutting way of life. (Local resident, Applecross, 40–50, male)

Hence there is a sense of place-based Gaelic culture even for those without the language, although tied to relations with those that did have it. For Elisabeth, however, who moved to Wester Ross as a Gaelic learner from another part of Scotland, her sense of identity in relation to Gaelic also brought out boundaries between 'natives' and 'learners'. She told me, 'native speakers wouldn't speak to me ... they would speak back in English'. Whilst she felt things have changed a bit since then, for her it was hard to maintain her Gaelic: 'I'm getting worse because I'm not using it'. Unwillingness to speak Gaelic across the native–learner divide could be about local–incomer dynamics (see Chapter 3) in certain cases, but it is also evidence of the devaluation of the language among the native speaking community.

In Wester Ross, I heard about the indifference and hostility towards Gaelic from within Gaelic speaking families, tied to beliefs that Gaelic is not worth passing on to the next generation – a 'waste of time'. Fionnlagh explained how Gaelic has been deemed detrimental to 'progress', arguing that 'if you get told as we did ... that your language and culture is pointless then you start to believe it'. Adaira described how anti-Gaelic attitudes often come from a place of insecurity, linked to a complicated history: 'we're not maybe as proud of who we are as we could be'. These attitudes help to explain why generally it is incoming families to Wester Ross, rather than locals, that have children in GME: 'we've got four Gaelic schools, but most of the kids are coming from English households' (Elisabeth). Phoebe as a parent herself told me:

> It's nothing against Gaelic, but the fact was, all the local families, you know, that grew up here, and have their own kids here, they put their kids in the English programme. It's the more affluent incomers, English and Scottish, who put their kids into Gaelic.

This situation has created a disconnect in Wester Ross between the younger GME population and the older speaking population with Gaelic as a family heritage.

Part of the difficulty around sustaining Gaelic through families is that it embodies elements of a 'difficult heritage', which although meaningful, invokes an 'unsettling and awkward' past.[14] For Coinneach, Gaelic heritage can lead to the intergenerational transmission of 'trauma'. He told me how his father had a 'brutal experience' with Gaelic and so 'he didn't feel that it was safe to teach it to us', nor did he identify himself as a speaker in any national census. I also had heard previously from a local resident of Applecross about how she was beaten in school for speaking Gaelic, or speaking English using Gaelic grammar patterns.

Another element of Gaelic heritage is narratives of loss and displacement in music and poetry, which Coinneach felt made it easy to associate the language with a sense of grief and despair. Additionally, he described that in Wester Ross community councils would have been places to go to hear local voices full of energy and good intention but historically these spaces have been 'colonised' because 'all of a sudden, the local voices are displaced'.

Finally, the difficulty of Gaelic heritage also lies in how it is valued (or not) depending on context and usage. Whilst few oppose Gaelic in heritage contexts, recognising its role in the past, it can be deemed irrelevant to modern society and visions for the future. The Gaelic Champion of Gairloch Museum told me how whilst valued as local heritage, most on the museum board did not want to actively use or promote Gaelic in the community. Some locally perceive Gaelic as inherently tied to party politics and arguments for Scottish independence, but as Fionnlagh explained to me, it was actually a conservative politician that advocated for Gaelic at a time when the Highlands and Islands Development Board saw 'no role for Gaelic in what they were trying to do'. Historically, Gaelic has not been part of visions for the future development of the Highlands and Islands.[15] Some also seem to imply Gaelic is irrelevant in present times because 'hardly anyone speaks it' (estate owner) and it is pointless to learn when everyone has English. Hence, there are many narratives at play in Wester Ross about Gaelic, and the combination of difficult heritage and a devaluation of Gaelic locally help to explain why in an era of Gaelic revitalisation traditional Gaelic communities are not thriving.[16]

TOWARDS REVIVAL

On Gaelic revival, Coinneach challenged the narrative of Gaelic as irrelevant to the present by arguing that billions of people already use it given that Scottish placenames make one a de facto Gaelic user. He amongst others also spoke positively about progress made through GME provision, Gaelic film and media and online learning resources like the app Duolingo. Such examples reflect a wider Scottish context in which revitalisation and institutionalisation have led to more official support for the language.[17] Contradicting the above narratives, Wester Ross residents are also positive about how Gaelic has been increasingly valued and supported:

> I'm in the generation where Gaelic was being dropped like a hot potato, it was, you know, frowned upon. Now it's the other way round, if you have

> it, you hang onto it. When I first went to work in the Crofting Commission, we were in a building with Scottish Natural Heritage and they had Gaelic tutors, teaching everybody that wanted to learn, it was great. (Local resident, 60–70, male)

However, despite a wider sense of progress, Coinneach felt that there have been many 'missed opportunities for acculturation in Wester Ross, welcoming outsiders in and making outsiders insiders' through the sharing of Gaelic. It is in this context that WRB approach their work.

WRB actors already recognise that among local communities, different groups have had different experiences with Gaelic requiring bespoke approaches to Gaelic development. This is essential to creating opportunities for processes of acculturation where: 'it's not about who speaks Gaelic and how Gaelic you are. Anyone has the right to speak it' (Adaira, WRB GDO). Among WRB's board, there are speakers of different levels of fluency, who came to the language in different ways, through family upbringing or as adult learners. Importantly, most see Gaelic revival not only as a linguistic issue, but part of wider cultural revitalisation in the BR:

> We're fairly conscious of the importance of keeping Gaelic alive … but it's not just Gaelic … I'm deeply involved in Shinty, and music, these are the traditional aspects of the culture, the community, it's too easy to say that everything's alright, it isn't alright. (Seumas)

As discussed in Chapter 5, WRB actors are concerned about the loss of traditional knowledge, skills and practices in the region, of which Gaelic is a part. Gaelic development is intricately related to the future of economy, place, culture and sustainability in ways that differ from the lowlands.[18] Initially, WRB actors have prioritised language revival within communities trying to make new spaces for Gaelic to be shared and valued. This has taken precedence over making WRB materials bilingual, because as Elisabeth argued, 'it is quite nice to see it in Gaelic, but it's a little bit of lip service'. For her, advancing projects supporting the oral culture and history are more important such as through the story collecting project (see Chapter 5).

Indeed, some of the stories Coinneach had collected were from his father's generation where 'Gaelic was unwelcome' and 'would hold you back'. He described how in such a context Kay Matheson made significant contributions to revival in the community including 'a renewed sense of cultural confidence', bringing people together in ceilidh and song.

Recordings made by her are part of the Gaelic resources of Gairloch Museum and a valuable resource for 'future generations'. Coinneach also had stories related to Roy Wentworth, another key figure in revival who carried out Gaelic work in the Gairloch area. However, Coinneach noted the work 'died with him', and thus he felt Gaelic revival cannot rest on individuals and must be a collective effort to shape living culture and everyday life in Wester Ross. One of Coinneach's ideas for how to do this was to 'reclaim the ceilidh, in the sense of visiting, rather than dancing' as an aspect of community. During interview, he explained 'the ceilidh is just a visit and a cup of tea, like this' and was 'the most natural part of Gaelic culture'. However, admittedly he struggled to think about how this would work in practice when most efforts for Gaelic revival are tied to formalised funded projects. He felt perhaps one route would be to fund young Gaelic speakers as story collectors and house visitors, to meet with older people to record their Gaelic songs and stories, reducing isolation and potentially creating meaningful intergenerational social relationships.

Gaelic development

Coinneach has been a key figure driving WRB's Gaelic development work forward. This started with a recognition that WRB ought to have a Gaelic strategy based on community priorities. Cautious about how to proceed in light of local politics, a meeting was held to learn from Gairloch Museum who had knowledge and experience of Gaelic development in practice. Jane, former WRB director based at the museum, agreed a Gaelic strategy would be a good step for the BR but also noted working with local communities had been challenging. She explained the difficulties engaging people locally who have most knowledge of the language and its cultural heritage. She said those most able to help were 'very seldom positive' about the museum's Gaelic work. They have also struggled with recruiting people for paid Gaelic work and once had to return unspent project funding to *Bòrd Na Gàidhlig*. Nonetheless, the meeting was pivotal in leading WRB to apply for a funded GDO.

Discussing the rationale for their application, Coinneach argued they should aim to connect the two disparate Gaelic speaking groups in Wester Ross: school leavers who have few opportunities to use the language and the 'dying population of native speakers' whose 'community has died around them.' These groups were seen as a priority because of the need to reach older people 'before the living historical memory dies' and to encourage younger generations to use and value the language in everyday life. The latter was linked to a comment from Carla (NatureScot advisor to WRB) that her child had come out of GME feeling that Gaelic was not relevant beyond school. For Elisabeth, a GDO could also help break down barriers between 'native speakers and learners'. She felt no other languages have such a strong distinction between these categories and '*Is fheàrr Gàidhlig bhriste na Gàidhlig sa chiste*' – it is better to have broken Gaelic than dead Gaelic.

The proposal for a GDO also had a strong theme of Gaelic in the landscape building on WRB's unique position as a UNESCO BR connecting people and nature. It referenced biocultural heritage which Coinneach had taken an interest in following our conversations and a report I had published on it. He was especially interested in how Gaelic language decline goes hand in hand with decline in biodiversity and knowledge of the landscape. Indeed, Gaelic speakers are usually seen as part of an older generation of local residents 'who were most intimately acquainted with the landscape' and 'have passed away taking their knowledge with them' (Applecross Historical Society). Following recruitment of the GDO a central work stream has been to conserve this knowledge through Gaelic placename collection. Work had already begun in Applecross and Torridon and WRB were keen to see this extended across the whole BR. WRB's first GDO conducted desk-based research on placenames funded by NatureScot and Historic Environment Scotland. These feature on a digital story map, including names that reflect historic land uses and practices such as *Càrn a' Bhreabadair* (the Weaver's Cairn) and *Àirigh an t-Saoir* (the Carpenter's Shieling). WRB's GDO was later replaced by Adaira, whose work also began with placenames. Specifically, she conducted oral histories with local people around Balmacara estate funded by NTS:

> I've gathered over sixty new names, particularly from one lady who really knew her community and was over ninety years old. She was so inspiring. I heard placenames that have not been recorded and if I hadn't interviewed her, they might get lost.

For her, Gaelic place names unlock the history of places in the BR. She felt it was important to raise awareness of these names so they are not forgotten or lying dormant. Such names, which are abundant across the BR, have relevance to land use histories and practices, local mythologies and interpretations of the landscape.[19] Whilst desk-based research on these is valuable, the oral histories method in particular has been attributed to successful conservation and community participatory governance in Portuguese BRs.[20] Community participation is at the heart of WRB's work, based on bringing more people into Gaelic, speakers and non-speakers. Seumas bemoaned how Gaelic placenames were ignored on a daily basis by visitors and hillwalkers, such as the local *Taigh Mhic an Toisich*, a ceilidh place to tell spooky tales about the nearby standing stone *Clach nan Con-fionn*.

Gaelic placenames, for Seumas, reflect a deeper cultural heritage of Wester Ross: 'it is great to record the names – but it's the meaning behind them that gives us a clue to the fragments of nearly lost heritage – the bones of *dùthchas* if you like … man's relationship with his landscape.' His view aligns well with biocultural heritage where language conservation is not only tied to biodiversity conservation but sustaining 'the values particular to a language and culture'.[21] *Dùthchas* is one such value, a recognised nature–culture relationship in the BR. In Chapter 6, I suggested that *dùthchas* might be drawn upon as a culturally specific approach to crofting, partly because WRB actors already value and draw on *dùthchas* in their thinking. Coinneach for example, connects it to a relational and dialogical way of engaging with landscape with Gaelic being 'a mode of communication', 'a medium for the landscape speaking back to us, and us listening'. For Adaira, *dùthchas* is a feeling that 'exists in everything', it is more than just a word which makes it 'impossible to explain' and yet 'so incredibly meaningful'. She explained to me that 'it goes back through generations of my family, and your family. And how we're all connected and how we want to move forward as a community, as a world.' This captures the bidirectionality between humans and the natural world in Gaelic culture[22] and *dùthchas* as a kin-centric concept.[23] Moreover, WRB now cite *dùthchas* as a central principle of the BR:

> The word *dùthchas* is used to describe a sense of belonging between the people and the land in which they live. There is no English translation for the word but it has a special meaning in Gaelic-speaking communities. This special word is rooted in the work that we do. Wester Ross Biosphere works towards encouraging a strong connection between people and the land around them to create a sustainable future.

Dùthchas is arguably used here as an inclusive way into Gaelic because whilst it holds special meaning to speakers of the language it can represent a more widely applicable sense of local people's cultural connection to land and each other. It goes hand in hand with how Adaira, through a new Gaelic blog, is trying to 'get different people, different perspectives and different levels of Gaelic' represented. The blog highlights the multiple ways that people locally use and value Gaelic in everyday lives, livelihoods and relationships with place. Ultimately, WRB's Gaelic development work is making the language and culture increasingly visible and valued as part of creating sustainable futures in the BR and the GDO post funded by *Bord Na Gaidhlig* has been vital in making this happen. However, in the Scottish context more could be done to value Gaelic in relation to sustainability.

A THIRD CULTURAL SPACE

Place-based ways of knowing through Gaelic ontologies such as *dùthchas* are not currently part of mainstream Scottish conservation policy and practice.[24] Instead, the dominant approaches are rooted in capitalist and scientific frameworks that marginalise cultural heritage and communities. Part of the problem is evident in the example of how NatureScot commissioned a report on Gaelic and Ecosystem Services.[25] Whilst drawing attention to Gaelic and proposing useful ideas for research the report maps Gaelic according to the hegemonic discourse of nature as service provider. It does not articulate what a Gaelic worldview on its own terms would mean for conservation policy and practice in Scotland. Traditional knowledges of indigenous peoples are often grafted onto non-indigenous frameworks in ways that seem like inclusion, but which reproduce patterns of 'epistemological dominance'.[26] Such approaches simply recognise there are diverse nature–culture relations but do not take them seriously as a framework for conservation policy or practice. NatureScot cited the Gaelic and Ecosystem Services report as evidence of meeting Aichi target 18 of the Convention for Biological Diversity, 'traditional knowledge is respected and integrated'. In contrast to citing a report, in Bolivia, the target was met through 'integrated community-based management by indigenous peoples, campesino communities and small-scale producers'.[27] A similar approach in Scotland would mean support for community conservation initiatives like WRB which centre Gaelic ontologies and place-based knowledges. BRs are also themselves models to integrate traditional ecological knowledge and scientific knowledges.[28] True integration means 'not subsuming or incorporating one knowledge within an otherwise dominant paradigm' but rather creating a 'third cultural space' for listening, learning and developing innovative approaches.[29] WRB could help create a third cultural space – especially through collaborations with mainstream conversation actors like NatureScot and the National Trust for Scotland (see Chapter 9). Ultimately, this would mean valuing communities, cultures and local knowledges in Scotland's policies for nature and landscape.

CONCLUSION

Gaelic language and culture are an important aspect of heritage in Wester Ross BR. They are also relevant to contemporary communities and how WRB understand nature–culture relations. I began by demonstrating how Gaelic as heritage is shaped by narratives of loss. Whilst the reasons for the decline and devaluing of Gaelic in the BR are similar to those across Scotland, I offered insight into lived experiences of people in Wester Ross around the intergenerational transmission gap and Gaelic as difficult heritage. Gaelic has been seen as irrelevant to the present and future due to experiences of internal colonisation that in part help to explain the wider crisis in vernacular communities in the Highlands.

WRB actors support Gaelic revival, and position Gaelic as central to the present and futures of communities and landscapes in the BR. A core focus is on developing an inclusive approach to regional language and culture. WRB's Gaelic development work also illustrates that Gaelic is valued locally, especially as part of place-based knowledges and for connecting people and nature through *dùthchas*. Whilst this is having an impact regionally, nationally, there is a need for a third cultural space to create better dialogue regarding the relationship between scientific and local cultural knowledges of nature and landscape. A third cultural space could help to centre *dùthchas* and move beyond common-sense neoliberal approaches to nature such as ecosystem services and natural capital which serve the interests and agendas of elites rather than local communities. I return to the issue of regional–national conservation politics in Chapter 9, but first, I explore how a community Biosphere negotiates local–global relations in discourse and practice.

NOTES

1. Wilson McLeod, *Gaelic in Scotland: Policies, Movements, Ideologies* (Edinburgh University Press, 2022).
2. Paul Meighan, 'Languages Do Not "Die", They Are Persecuted: A Scottish Gael's Perspective on Language "Loss",' *Bella Caledonia*, 19 July 2023, https://bellacaledonia.org.uk/2023/07/19/languages-do-not-die-they-are-persecuted-a-scottish-gaels-perspective-on-language-loss/.

3. McLeod, *Gaelic in Scotland.*
4. Conchúr Ó Giollagáin, Gòrdan Camshron, Pàdruig Moireach et al., *Gaelic Crisis in the Vernacular Community: A Comprehensive Sociolinguistic Survey of Scottish Gaelic (GCVC)* (Aberdeen University Press, 2020).
5. McLeod, *Gaelic in Scotland*, 6.
6. Meg Bateman, 'The Landscape of the Gaelic Imagination,' *International Journal of Heritage Studies* 15, nos. 2–3 (2009): 2–3.
7. McLeod, *Gaelic in Scotland.*
8. McLeod, *Gaelic in Scotland.*
9. Stefania Barca, *Forces of Reproduction: Notes for a Counter-Hegemonic Anthropocene* (Cambridge University Press, 2020).
10. Sharon Macdonald, 'The Gaelic Renaissance and Scotland's Identities,' *Scottish Affairs* 26 (First Series), no. 1 (1999): 100–18.
11. Iain MacKinnon, 'Recognising and Reconstituting Gàidheil Ethnicity,' *Scottish Affairs* 30, no. 2 (2021): 2.
12. Timothy Armstrong et al., 'Gaelic and Identity: A Response to Iain MacKinnon,' *Scottish Affairs* 31, no. 1 (2022): 1.
13. Frank Bechhofer and David McCrone, 'What Makes a Gael? Identity, Language and Ancestry in the Scottish Gàidhealtachd,' *Identities* 21, no. 2 (2014): 2.
14. Sharon Macdonald, *Difficult Heritage: Negotiating the Nazi Past in Nuremberg and Beyond* (Routledge, 2009).
15. McLeod, *Gaelic in Scotland.*
16. Camshron, 'Resisting Dismissal in the *Gàidhealtachd*.'
17. See McLeod, *Gaelic in Scotland*, 174–274.
18. Gòrdan Camshron, 'Resisting Dismissal in the *Gàidhealtachd*,' *Scottish Affairs* 30, no. 2 (2021): 240–50.
19. John Murray, *Reading the Gaelic Landscape: Leughadh Aghaidh na Tire* (Whittles Publishing, 2014).
20. Maria F. Rollo, 'Interconnected Nature and People: Biosphere Reserves and the Power of Memory and Oral Histories as Biocultural Heritage for a Sustainable Future,' *Sustainability* 17, no. 9 (2025): 1–33.
21. Alexandria K. Poole, 'Where Is Goal 18? The Need for Biocultural Heritage in the Sustainable Development Goals,' *Environmental Values* 27, no. 1 (2018): 57.
22. Bateman, 'Gaelic Imagination'; Newton, *Warriors of the Word.*
23. Paul J. Meighan, 'Dùthchas, a Scottish Gaelic Methodology to Guide Self-Decolonization and Conceptualize a Kincentric and Relational Approach to Community-Led Research,' *International Journal of Qualitative Methods* 21 (2022): 16094069221142451.
24. Déirdre Ní Mhathúna, 'Traditional Ecological Knowledge and the Relevance of *Dùthchas* in *Gàidhealtachd* Environmental Futures,' *Scottish Affairs* 30, no. 2 (2021): 2.

25. Roddy Maclean, 'Gaelic and Ecosystem Services: A Scoping Exercise,' (NatureScot Report 1230, 2021), https://www.nature.scot/doc/naturescot-research-report-1230-ecosystem-services-and-gaelic-scoping-exercise.
26. Cash Ahenakew, 'Grafting Indigenous Ways of Knowing onto Non-Indigenous Ways of Being: The (Underestimated) Challenges of a Decolonial Imagination,' *International Review of Qualitative Research* 9, no. 3 (2016): 3.
27. 'Aichi Target Pages. Aichi Target 18.' Convention on Biological Diversity (accessed 12 June 2025), https://www.cbd.int/aichi-targets/target/18.
28. Marc Hockings, Ian Lilley, Diane Matar et al., 'Integrating Science and Local Knowledge to Strengthen Biosphere Reserve Management,' in *UNESCO Biosphere Reserves: Supporting Biocultural Diversity, Sustainability and Society*, ed. M. Reed and M. F. Price (Routledge, 2020), 241–54.
29. Hockings, 'Integrating Science.'

8

Wester Ross in the World: The Local–Global Nexus

BRs and the MAB programme operate at the local–global nexus promoting local solutions to global problems. As pathways for reconnecting people and nature, BRs can bridge the local and global by seeking to implement the Global Sustainable Development Goals (SDGs)[1] or more radically new forms of planetary citizenship.[2] As multi-scalar sustainability initiatives, BRs take regional action shaped by global discourses and adapting to distinct local and national contexts. Herein, I unpack what this means for WRB actors in practice. I draw attention to how scalar relations are key to meaning-making, recognising that scale is not neutral or static.[3] I start by introducing how WRB actors 'think global and act local', explaining perspectives on the community Biosphere as part of a global sustainability agenda and WRB's work on the SDGs. Next, I discuss interactions between WRB actors and other BRs in the World Network, highlighting relations of solidarity and inequality and arguing there is a lack of regional spatial justice for Wester Ross. Finally, I discuss regional sustainability as scalar politics focusing on WRB's aim to re-localise food in light of leaving the European Union and the Covid-19 pandemic.

THINK GLOBAL, ACT LOCAL

The UNESCO MAB programme is underpinned by the idea of BRs as constituting a kind of 'planetary concern'.[4] For example, embodied in their vision is 'a world where people are conscious of their common future and interaction with our planet, and act collectively and responsibly to build thriving societies in harmony within the Biosphere'.[5] In Chapter 2 I introduced that planetary logics can be problematic in zoning;[6] however, here I am concerned with the global in WRB's organisational practice. As organisations, it is argued that BRs should translate global agendas and agreements into local practice,[7] with action guided by MAB strategies such as the LIMA Action Plan (2016–25) and the Roadmap for Biospheres (2015–25).[8] I asked Phoebe about managing global, national and local priorities and she explained that lack of time and capacity meant it was only possible to focus on 'local stuff'. Whilst occasionally considering the national UK MAB strategy she would rarely consult international documents. It is not uncommon for local agendas to be prioritised in BRs, which are themselves shaped by global logics and policies.[9]

In Wester Ross this is clear around WRB's work with the SDGs. Phoebe, when representing WRB and explaining the BR to external audiences, cites the SDGs and Scotland's support for them. Explaining what this means for the BR she has said, 'the old adage, think global, act local remains as pertinent as ever'. Moreover, she has talked of how the integration of social, economic and environmental alongside community development offers, 'great potential to challenge the direction of global forces and return to a more equal, social and sustainable world'.

One of WRB's projects has been the creation of a BR SDG trail as a way to 'show real-life examples of the SDGs in practice'. There are currently twenty-five sites on the trail although not all SDGs are represented as some are repeated. Each has a physical post and is part of a digital map, for example: Goal 4 Quality Education is posted in relation to a Gairloch school climate change project; Goal 7 Affordable and Clean Energy is based at BroomPower community-owned hydro scheme; Goal 15 Life on Land is based at community-owned Kirkton woodlands managed for reforestation, food growing and education; and Goal 8 Decent Work and Economic Growth is based at Gairloch and Loch Ewe Action Forum, a community enterprise providing year-round employment (see Figure 8.1). This has been a simple way for WRB to marry a global sustainability agenda with local life and raise awareness of sustainable development regionally.

However, the SDGs do not necessarily enable new kinds of 'collective planetary rethinking' beyond neoliberalism.[10] First, they fail to recognise biocultural heritage as a sustainability pathway which marginalises local ecological knowledge and cultural heritage.[11] These are important areas for WRB as explained in previous chapters. Second, the SDGs reproduce a narrative that economic growth can be reconciled within sustainability – as embodied in SDG 8. However, never-ending growth is a pathway towards more environmental harm.[12] Aligning with the SDGs might therefore limit the radical potential of WRB and BRs to promote transformation that, in Phoebe's words, challenges 'the direction of global forces'. An alternative mentality for a global sustainability

Figure 8.1 Sustainable Development Goal post.

agenda could be for WRB to demonstrate 'marginalized, alternative and experimental ways of inhabiting the Earth' in practice.[13] This requires moving beyond mainstream sustainable development which is part of capitalist hegemony.

What it means to think global and act local in Wester Ross has also emerged in discussions among WRB actors concerning their identity as a BR. As discussed in Chapter 2, WRB had some early challenges with social media communications. Concerned about this, Phoebe had asked the board to consider developing a Wester Ross specific strapline similar to UNESCO's 'connecting people and nature today to inspire a positive future'. The idea of a clear message would help to share things 'directly linked to Wester Ross Biosphere'. Whilst this was not about distancing from UNESCO, Alan interpreted her comments as such. He argued, 'we are representatives of the international ... why wouldn't we try to broaden our perspective so that we think globally while we're acting locally?' Similarly, Coinneach had also previously argued that WRB has been 'forced to be very inward looking and very community-based' due to the Covid-19 pandemic and felt the BR would benefit from being more 'international in our outlook ... to share and support across national boundaries'. Further commentary by Alan also drew out the positionality of WRB as community-led and a UNESCO BR in a global network. He argued that Wester Ross is just one area in Scotland and the world that can 'offer a local perspective' but which should be aligned with 'a broader perspective on environmental responsibility' beyond the BR. Similarly, Robert then added, 'we've got a responsibility' to the wider world because 'it's our mess ... that we're trying to clear up'. He felt WRB must not isolate in a 'green bubble' and only focus on 'clearing our own place up' but acknowledge global environmental problems. Citing India as an example, he explained how the Global North has a responsibility, having exported its unsustainable industries to the Global South. Thus, WRB has a 'bigger thing to think about'. Such sentiments also came to fore through Coinneach's vision of Scotland as an independent country:

> if we acknowledge our collective contribution to the global wellbeing whilst acknowledging our contribution to global suffering, we are stepping onto a path to independence with a view to creating a true state of interdependence. We can path find, we can demonstrate by living our truth another way of being and not winding back the clock but moving forward leaving no one behind.

Situating Wester Ross BR and Scotland in the wider world, these perspectives evidence the 'active production of local, regional and international relations' as an inherent part of building solidarities for alternative approaches to sustainable development.[14] The community Biosphere is about cultivating regionally specific sustainability and Robert's comments indicate awareness that colonial modernity shapes Global North–South relations through historic and contemporary exploitation, extraction and dependency on cheap labour and resources.[15] In practice, WRB actors negotiate relations of solidarity and inequality as one UNESCO BR among many in a global network.

SOLIDARITY AND INEQUALITY

The World Network of BRs (WNBR) is a 'vibrant network' for global learning about locally applied practices.[16] Whilst solidarities can be built within BRs,[17] they can also be built between them. Solidarity embodies feelings of 'mutual identification' and relations of reciprocity that involve non-hierarchical forms of power and resource sharing.[18] This aptly describes relations between WRB and Galloway and Southern Ayrshire (GSA) BR in relation to the business supporter charter (see Chapter 5). For Phoebe, sharing resources and learning with other BRs is 'invaluable' because of the limited time and resources available to her. Additionally, WRB have cultivated reciprocal relations and learning with other BRs globally through thematic and regional networks such as NORDMAB, EUROMAB and UKMAB. For Phoebe and Elisabeth, relationships with other BRs are often most meaningful where there is a sense of mutual identification, which has tended to mean regions and organisations facing similar sustainability challenges like rural depopulation or unsustainable tourism. WRB's most valuable relationship was with MU BR in Canada (see Chapter 4), where regular knowledge exchanges have taken place in both countries over several years. This has focused particularly on how BRs can follow a social enterprise model, with WRB learning from MU to adapt this for Wester Ross. Phoebe has cultivated a close friendship with Pierre, MU's manager, who has offered her moral support and MU's time and resources on a basis of reciprocity. Pierre has also supported WRB's board to think more about how the BR can fulfil the UNESCO mandate through an entrepreneurial mindset. Directors learned of MU's success with this model, moving from reliance on grant funding towards financial autonomy and organisational sustainability. MU generates income by working within and beyond the boundaries of their rural BR, accessing urban wealth through sustainability consulting which is used to subsidise charitable activities. Although I showed above that WRB actors think beyond their boundaries, in practice some find it difficult to think of WRB operating outside of Wester Ross. Pierre encouraged the board to think about the BR not as 'governing a territory', but as a 'regional development office' and facilitated a bespoke session for staff and directors to generate ideas to take this forward.

Reflecting on the session at a board meeting shortly after, directors agreed the learning had been 'invaluable' and it was agreed that the next reciprocal exchange would be WRB staff visiting MU to share their expertise around sustainable tourism management. Regarding how to pursue the social enterprise work, board discussions recognised that WRB and MU had different governance models. Alan felt WRB was 'bottom-up' and must listen to and act as a voice for the community, compared with MU which is more 'top-down'. Norman agreed that WRB is unique as a fully community-led BR but suggested MU's resources could be adapted to suit their context. For example, MU's use of UNESCO BR principles as 'checkpoints' for consulting work was an approach that could be tailored for WRB's purposes. Relations of solidarity with MU have led WRB to become more entrepreneurial. Recently they have acted as consultants for sustainability work within and beyond their boundaries and delivered a workshop with MU on the entrepreneurial model at the World Congress of BRs in China.

Concerning WRB's relations with other BRs, alongside solidarity, I observed 'unity-in-diversity', part of the planetary consciousness of anarchist geographer Elisée Reclus. Therein, difference is valued as part of a shared global community[19] and a similar ethos is found among WRB actors who recognise difference and diverse cultural experiences as a valuable learning opportunity. However, time and capacity are limitations to the scope of this in practice. WRB has tended to form relations with actors that whilst different in some ways are very similar in others as BRs in the Global North. There is thus potential to expand unity-in-diversity by working more globally and building solidarity with BRs in the Global South. This is a vital step towards taking global responsibility as described by Robert, and for decolonising sustainability (see Chapter 11).

Whilst relations of reciprocity and solidarity have been positive for WRB, interactions in the WNBR have also magnified inequalities. Early into my research, Phoebe told me:

> It can be depressing sometimes going to national and international UNESCO meetings because it feels like we haven't done anything. And everyone looks at us cross-eyed when we say we operate on a budget of like £15,000 a year. So that's hard, it's a hard feeling. I've learned to not have that mindset anymore and say, but look at what we've done, this is really little to you guys, but you might have a national government behind you, you might have a whole department behind you.

BRs are generally under-resourced but for Phoebe WRB felt like 'the little hick brother'. Whilst UNESCO MAB emphasise that states should support and integrate BRs at a national level this varies significantly. Funding is dependent on modes of governance and usually tied to government involvement.[20] Interacting with other UK BRs and internationally can emphasise vast differences in resource, staffing and funding. As Phoebe explained, her mindset has changed over time partly because although underfunded, as a community Biosphere outside of government 'we can do whatever we want'. Indeed, WRB actors can more easily transcend the nature–culture dichotomy (Chapter 4) as compared with the Isle of Man's government-led model requiring departmental working and stakeholder collaboration across policy siloes.[21] Nonetheless, BRs that are more detached from state administrations must balance freedom against the uncertainty of funding.[22]

A key source of frustration for Phoebe and WRB directors has been disparity of funding between Scotland's two BRs. GSA BR were awarded £1.9 million investment by the Scottish Government's non-departmental public body South of Scotland Enterprise (SSE). The funds were unrestricted and could be used for core costs and to employ more BR staff. Whilst very supportive of the success of GSA, there was a feeling of injustice. Elisabeth asked the board, 'if Galloway and South Ayrshire are getting this much money, what's so different down there that's not up here?' She answered her own question when she followed with, 'it's all political'. She felt the Scottish Government had needed for some time to invest in the south of Scotland and 'this is one way of doing it'. Lack of Scottish Government support for WRB was seen as a 'major stumbling block' (Elisabeth) and Elisabeth and Norman speculated if GSA BR was more successful due to engagement with national politicians. Additionally, they noted GSA's governance involves three local authorities and thus already has government buy-in. Nonetheless, Norman challenged the disparity between the two regional development agencies for south Scotland and the Highlands especially in financial terms. To make clear the extent of this, I estimated based on figures provided by Phoebe that WRB has received approximately 1 per cent of the value of core funding that GSA has received from SSE. Hence, why Norman and others are disgruntled and confused about how their situation differs. They rightly feel that their own regional development agency, Highlands and Islands Enterprise (HIE), should invest in WRB as SSE has done with GSA. I would frame this as a problem of regional spatial justice, a concept used in Wales to describe a region's capacity to create new futures specific to their needs and conditions, and to move beyond a national one-size-fits-all approach to development.[23] The current lack of regional spatial justice in Wester Ross must be understood by examining the wider scalar politics of development in Scotland alongside WRB's relationship with HIE.

REGIONAL SPATIAL JUSTICE

From the Victorian period through industrialisation and modernisation, the Highlands and Islands were constructed as a 'problem' region based on 'the assumption that there was something inherently wrong with the people and the area'.[24] The 'problem' persisted until the 1960s, with political debates focused on 'modernisation' and how to 'integrate the region, economically and socially, into the rest of Scottish society'.[25] The Highlands and Islands Development Board was set up to improve social and economic conditions and enable the region to contribute to the national economy. It later became HIE. On the whole, development in the Highlands has been about population retention, employment opportunities and more recently, sustaining the region's cultural practices such as Gaelic and crofting. Whilst many agendas align with WRB priorities, there are wider scalar politics at play that have limited the BR's capacity to enact regional sustainable development.

For WRB, HIE is an obvious potential funder given their remit for regional economic and social development but support from them has varied. Phoebe told me they were 'on board' in the beginning but then 'fell off the face of the earth and didn't want to talk to us, didn't want to know'. Elisabeth felt that within HIE perceptions of the BR were not always favourable. When Norman spoke of an upcoming meeting with a HIE representative, Elisabeth forewarned that, 'he has not been a fan of Wester Ross. He doesn't really see it as an entity ... he's not against the Biosphere, but didn't see Wester Ross a significant area to him.' HIE subdivide the Highlands and Islands into specific territories with Wester Ross part of a larger area with Skye and Lochaber. WRB are thus operating at a regional scale misaligned with HIE territories. Norman, at a Sustainable Development Group meeting, argued that:

> for our area, one of the problems we have is that we don't actually have a development plan, whether it be sustainable or otherwise. HIE don't have an intention of creating one for Wester Ross, they're looking at it on a bigger area basis and as usual Wester Ross will probably end up being the poor cousin to places like Skye.

Wester Ross as the 'poor cousin' and WRB as the 'little hick brother' are indicative of regional spatial injustice for sparsely populated rural areas like Wester Ross. Robert expressed that HIE 'have not done that much for Wester Ross', often focusing on larger industries and populated areas like Fort William. Returning to the BR as place-making, as discussed in Chapter 3, the designation and organisation in such contexts can represent a mechanism through which to establish regional autonomy in rural regions that have been excluded in mainstream development and planning. For Norman a sustainable development plan for the BR is less about having an institutional mechanism in the planning system but rather a strategic plan for 'how you develop the area sustainably'.

Importantly, he thought it could foster cross-sectoral working and help resolve tensions across conflicting regional interests. Presenting the idea to the board he described, 'you've got the environmental people as well as the development-focused people, industrial people. We need to bring them together and try to develop some sort of consensus.' As discussed in Chapter 4, the BR region has not been developed sustainably and here Norman saw a path forward to addressing this. He suggested WRB could play a role by faciliating similar participatory processes as were used in the context of community-led sustainable tourism. Given that HIE had recognised the benefits of collaborative regional working in that context and funded their work, he felt they could do so again for development. Norman's approach arguably reflects how rural development in diffuse power contexts requires developing 'strategic agendas' and using emergent processes that embody multiplicity and non-linearity.[26]

However, one of the anticipated challenges to funding such work through HIE was the BR not being an appropriate scale of action. Norman noted that development is often either 'very localised to individual communities to take responsibility and develop ideas themselves or it's done strategically at a much higher level'. The regional, collaborative approach of WRB is 'not the way most things are being done these days unfortunately'. Seumas was also critical about how HIE funding was increasingly about community development as income generating activity; a shift away from a narrative that 'HIE get money from central government, let's have our chunk of it'. This gets at how 'community self-help' has been seen as a way of reducing subsidy dependence; a central narrative of rural development in the Highlands.[27] Such trends are shaped by a neoliberal agenda in Scotland which is transmitted by local and regional enterprise organisations like HIE.[28]

Economic growth is at the heart of such agendas, with the Scottish Government pursuing the paradoxical 'sustainable' economic growth,[29] whilst HIE state: 'strong, capable and resourceful communities are vital for the social and economic growth of the Highlands and Islands'. Challenging the common sense of economic growth,[30] the idea of spatial justice encourages a shift away from viewing regions as places to pursue one-size-fits-all development for the sake of growing the national economy. Instead, regions should have agency and capacity to pursue alternative visions of regional wellbeing.[31] Such thinking aligns with arguments that BRs should 'imagine and enact alternative visions to "development" rather than a "greener" version of the same'.[32] Alternatives to western models of development include degrowth, *Buen*

Vivir, Ecological Swaraj,[33] which emphasise principles of sufficiency, participation and ecological and human wellbeing.

In WRB's discussions about development economic growth was never explicitly mentioned as a goal or as problematic. One exception was WRB's former youth ambassador who challenged the normalisation of economic growth in business speakers' narratives at the sustainable tourism conference (see Chapter 3). Whilst individual WRB actors likely differ in their views about economic growth, I would argue that the BR is a model for regional spatial justice and a mechanism to foster alternatives to capitalist development. Although not explicitly anti-capitalist, one case that evidences this potential, is how WRB have sought to remake food systems to better serve local communities. Additionally, working towards more sustainable food in Wester Ross also illustrates one final example of how WRB negotiate scalar power relations at the local–global nexus.

Sustainable food futures

A key source of investment in Wester Ross has been European Union (EU) funding and locals often suggested the region's local economies were dependent on Europe: 'communities like Applecross cannot survive without people coming from Europe to work in local businesses'. An Applecross business owner told me that there are no working-age people in the area to take jobs and younger people often leave for university. Farmers and crofters such as Shannon also described dependence on export of products like lamb to Europe. For many the prospect of leaving the EU threatened local economies and communities. However, once Brexit (Britain's Exit from the EU) became a reality some started to discuss opportunities for new regional food futures. The chairperson of the Scottish Crofting Federation, for example, had told me that the Scottish Government had channelled EU funding for 'less favoured areas' (associated with crofting) into larger more 'productive' farms on the east. Thus, Brexit created possibilities for a new agricultural funding model that would better support crofting.

WRB's Sustainable Development Group also discussed the implications of Brexit whist developing a funding proposal for a local food hub. Brian suggested that Brexit could be to 'the advantage of local fisherman to sell more product locally'. He felt it was folly that the amazing seafood of Wester Ross is rarely eaten as a staple food in the BR. He among others had some optimism that new local food production and consumption relationships could be created in the BR and reduce overall dependency on European and global markets. The Covid-19 pandemic further strengthened WRB actors' sense that alternatives to a globalised food system were necessary. The pandemic had highlighted the 'enormous vulnerabilities' of a global food system based on industrial production, complex supply chains and concentrated markets.[34] WRB actors conveyed the unsustainability of a situation where all of the food consumed in Wester Ross is imported whilst food produced is exported:

> We don't grow our own or grow very little ... what we do produce here goes east (Seumas).

> So much of our product is produced in crofting and fisheries ... but it all disappears off elsewhere instead of being used locally (Norman).

Tackling this was part of the rationale for a BR local food hub that would improve sustainability by reducing food miles and the dependency of communities on complex global supply chains. Existing community responses to the pandemic were cited in discussions as evidence that it was possible to produce and consume more locally. For example, in Glenelg, Anndra spoke of local people 'ramping up efforts to provide local food'. Norman said for the first time in a long time, fresh local seafood was available direct from fishers at Plockton pier. To ensure a new local food hub would be supported by communities and serve their needs, an online event was held to take the idea forward and gain input from the perspective of consumers, producers and the Open Food Network – a digital platform. Norman explained to attendees that if local producers can provide food for local people in the pandemic, then why not do it all the time: 'why should we be giving all of our best things away to Spain and Italy and France and wherever, when we need them here?'

The practical challenges of establishing a regional, localised food system were identified as lack of critical mass and competition with supermarkets that have a monopoly on cheap food, making locally produced, ethical products relatively less affordable. For Norman a key element of local production–consumption relations must be fair prices to producers as a means to support viable agricultural livelihoods for crofters and fishers. However, he felt the cost need not always be fully borne by consumers, as organisations like the National Trust for Scotland could offer premiums for produce grown sustainably using cultural heritage practices. Unfortunately, despite a great deal of work including community engagement, WRB's funding application for the local food hub was unsuccessful. One of the reasons given was a lack of engagement with business.

Although unsuccessful in this particular case, WRB's approach to sustainable food has not only been reactive to wider scalar changes like adapting to Brexit and Covid-19 but part of a longer-term focus on regional sustainability requiring a localised food system and strengthening rural livelihoods. In line with my arguments above about connecting with BRs and communities beyond the Global North, WRB could further develop their approach to regional food futures through knowledge exchange with communities in Biocultural Heritage Territories such as the Parque de la Papa. As I mentioned in Chapter 6, these are bottom-up food systems that produce wellbeing and sustainability through small-scale, culturally appropriate agriculture.[35] They are one of many global alternatives to unsustainable industrial agricultural models and monocultural commodity production.

CONCLUSION

BRs are multi-scalar initiatives and because scale is never neutral or fixed, scalar relations must be unpacked. Starting with the local–global nexus I explained how WRB actors 'think global and act local'. Although community focused, WRB as a community Biosphere is also positioned within a global sustainability agenda. This has meant translating the SDGs into local practice and debating the BR's position as an actor in the Global North potentially reproducing exploitative relations with the rest of the world. To a certain extent WRB actors challenge colonial modernity, but have yet to create decolonial practices. They have built relationships of solidarity and reciprocity with BRs in the Global North who face similar regional problems and with whom they share valuable resources. As such, WRB has been embodying the principle of unity-in-diversity – an ethos that recognises regionally specific sustainability solutions can be part of wider planetary consciousness. If applied to working with BRs in the Global South this could contribute towards decolonising sustainability.

I also discussed the inequalities within the World Network of BRs, with WRB particularly under-resourced in the Scottish context. Disparity between the community Biosphere and GSA BR in the south of Scotland is arguably a case of regional spatial injustice – Wester Ross lacks agency and capacity to develop according to its own regional needs and priorities. This is compounded by a challenging relationship with HIE, scalar misalignment in development and mainstream agendas shaped by neoliberal common sense. As an alternative to the status quo, WRB actors envision a more collaborative approach to sustainably develop the area across sectors and from the bottom up. WRB actors are also pursuing alternatives for a local food system, challenging the status quo of scalar relations to prioritise sustainable rural communities and livelihoods. Building on my conclusions from earlier chapters, a more radical approach could manifest in WRB and BRs generally with a move away from mainstream sustainable development in the pursuit of alternatives, including regenerative development and biocultural heritage.

Having focused this chapter around issues of development, the next chapter turns to nature conservation in the Scottish context, unpacking WRB's relationship with NatureScot and possibilities for multi-scalar, biocultural conservation.

NOTES

1. Miren Onaindia, Cristina Herrero, Alberto Hernandez et al., 'Co-creation of Sustainable Development Knowledge in Biosphere Reserves,' in *UNESCO Biosphere Reserves: Supporting Biocultural Diversity, Sustainability and Society*, ed. M. Reed and M. F. Price (Routledge, 2020), 269–81.
2. Tania Moreno-Ramos and Eduard Müller, 'Biosphere Reserves, Ideal Sites to Implement Holistic Approaches in Regenerative Development,' in *UNESCO Biosphere Reserves: Supporting Biocultural Diversity, Sustainability and Society*, ed. M. Reed and M. F. Price (Routledge, 2020), 254–69.
3. David C. Harvey, 'Heritage and Scale: Settings, Boundaries and Relations,' *International Journal of Heritage Studies* 21, no. 6 (2015): 577–93.
4. Silvia Posocco, 'Zoning: Environmental Cosmopolitics in and Around the Maya Biosphere Reserve, Petén, Guatemala,' *Nature and Culture* 3, no. 2 (2008): 213.
5. UNESCO, 'A New Roadmap for the Man and the Biosphere (MAB) Programme and its World Network of Biosphere Reserves.' United Nations Educational, Scientific and Cultural Organization, 2017, https://unesdoc.unesco.org/ark:/48223/pf0000247418.
6. Posocco, 'Zoning: Environmental Cosmopolitics,' 213.
7. Maureen Reed and Martin F. Price, 'Introducing UNESCO Biosphere Reserves,' in *UNESCO Biosphere Reserves: Supporting Biocultural Diversity, Sustainability and Society*, ed. M. Reed and M. Price (Routledge, 2020), 1–10.
8. Diane Matar and Brandon Anthony, 'Sense and Sustainability: The Story of Biosphere Reserves in Lebanon,' in *UNESCO Biosphere Reserves: Supporting Biocultural Diversity, Sustainability and Society*, ed. M. Reed and M. F. Price (Routledge, 2020), 135–48.
9. Matar and Anthony, 'Sense and Sustainability.'
10. Colin Sterling and Rodney Harrison, 'Introduction: of Territories and Temporalities,' in *Deterritorializing the Future: Heritage in, of and after the*

Anthropocene, ed. R. Harrison and C. Sterling (Open Humanities Press, 2020), 24.

11. Alexandria K. Poole, 'Where Is Goal 18? The Need for Biocultural Heritage in the Sustainable Development Goals,' *Environmental Values* 27, no. 1 (2018): 57.
12. Sterling and Harrison, 'Territories and Temporalities,' 4.
13. Sterling and Harrison, 'Territories and Temporalities,' 25.
14. Manuel Peters, 'Culture, Heritage and Solidarity in the Context of Sustainable Development,' in *Perceptions of Sustainability in Heritage Studies*, ed. M. T. Albert (DeGruyter, 2015), 143.
15. Saurabh Arora and Andy Stirling, 'Colonial Modernity and Sustainability Transitions: A Conceptualisation in Six Dimensions,' *Environmental Innovation and Societal Transitions* 48 (2023): 100733.
16. Maureen Reed and Martin F. Price, 'Unfinished Business: The Present and Future Contributions of Biosphere Reserves To Sustainability Science,' in *UNESCO Biosphere Reserves: Supporting Biocultural Diversity, Sustainability and Society*, ed. M. Reed and M. F. Price (Routledge, 2020), 323; Alicia D. Barraclough et al., 'Global Knowledge–Action Networks at the Frontlines of Sustainability: Insights from Five Decades of Science for Action in UNESCO's World Network of Biosphere Reserves,' *People and Nature* 5, no. 5 (2023): 1430–44.
17. Raphaël Mathevet and Catherine Cibien, 'The French Biosphere Reserves: Looking For Ecological Solidarity and Stewardship,' in *UNESCO Biosphere Reserves: Supporting Biocultural Diversity, Sustainability and Society*, ed. M. Reed and M. F. Price (Routledge, 2020), 114–24.
18. Uri Gordon, 'Power and Anarchy: In/equality + In/visibility in Autonomous Politics,' in *New Perspectives on Anarchism*, ed. N. Jun and S. Wahl (Lexington Books, 2010), 64.
19. John Clark, ed., *Anarchy, Geography, Modernity: Selected Writings of Elisée Reclus* (PM Press, 2016).
20. Martin F. Price, 'The Evolution of the Biosphere Reserve Network in the United Kingdom,' in *UNESCO Biosphere Reserves: Supporting Biocultural Diversity, Sustainability and Society*, ed. M. Reed and M. F. Price (Routledge, 2020), 89–101.
21. Zoe Russell, 'The Isle of Man Biosphere Reserve: An Entire Nation Approach to Sustainable Development,' *Journal of Environmental Policy and Planning* 25, no. 3 (2022): 273–86.
22. Jan Těšitel and Drahomíra Kušová, 'The More Institutional Models, the More Challenges: Biosphere Reserves in the Czech Republic,' in *UNESCO Biosphere Reserves: Supporting Biocultural Diversity, Sustainability and Society*, ed. M. Reed and M. F. Price (Routledge, 2020), 125–34.
23. Rhys Jones, 'Governing the Future and the Search for Spatial Justice: Wales' Wellbeing of Future Generations Act,' *Fennia* 197, no. 1 (2019): 8–24.

24. Katie Louise McCullough, 'Resolving the "Highland Problem": The Highlands and Islands of Scotland and the European Union,' *Local Economy* 33, no. 4 (2018): 433; see also Malcolm Gray, 'Crofting and Fishing in the North-West Highlands, 1890–1914,' *Northern Scotland* 1, no. 1 (1972): 89–114.
25. John Burnett, *The Making of the Modern Scottish Highlands* (Four Courts Press, 2011), 104.
26. Mark Shucksmith, 'Disintegrated Rural Development? Neo-Endogenous Rural Development, Planning and Place-Shaping in Diffused Power Contexts,' *Sociologia Ruralis* 50, no. 1 (2010): 12.
27. James Hunter, *The Claim Of Crofting: The Scottish Highlands and Islands 1930–1990* (Mainstream, 1991).
28. Danny MacKinnon, 'Regulating Regional Spaces: State Agencies and the Production of Governance in the Scottish Highlands,' *Environment and Planning A: Economy and Space* 33, no. 5 (2001): 5.
29. Andrea Ross, 'The Future Scotland Wants – Is It Really All about Sustainable Economic Growth?,' *Edinburgh Law Review* 19, no. 1 (2015): 66–100.
30. Giorgos Kallis, *Degrowth* (Agenda Publishing, 2018), 73.
31. Rhys Jones et al., 'From Territorial Cohesion to Regional Spatial Justice: The Well-Being of Future Generations Act in Wales,' *International Journal of Urban and Regional Research* 44, no. 5 (2020): 895.
32. Susanne Stoll-Kleemann and Tim O'Riordan, 'The Challenges of the Anthropocene for Biosphere Reserves,' *Parks* 23 (March 2017): 93.
33. Ashish Kothari et al., 'Buen Vivir, Degrowth and Ecological Swaraj: Alternatives to Sustainable Development and the Green Economy,' *Development* 57, nos. 3–4 (2014): 3–4; Kallis, *Degrowth*.
34. Jennifer Clapp and William G. Moseley, 'This Food Crisis Is Different: COVID-19 and the Fragility of the Neoliberal Food Security Order,' *Journal of Peasant Studies* 47, no. 7 (2020): 1411.
35. See Matthew Sayre et al., 'You Can't Grow Potatoes in the Sky: Building Resilience in the Face of Climate Change in the Potato Park of Cuzco, Peru,' *Culture, Agriculture, Food and Environment* 39, no. 2 (2017): 100–8; Krystyna Swiderska et al., 'Indigenous Peoples' Food Systems and Biocultural Heritage: Addressing Indigenous Priorities Using Decolonial and Interdisciplinary Research Approaches,' *Sustainability* 14, no. 18 (2022): 18; Thierry Winkel et al., 'Mobilising Common Biocultural Heritage for the Socioeconomic Inclusion of Small Farmers: Panarchy of Two Case Studies on Quinoa in Chile and Bolivia,' *Agriculture and Human Values* 37, no. 2 (2020): 2.

9

Towards Biocultural and Convivial Conservation

BRs are a participatory governance model shaped by local–global relations, and embedded in specific national contexts. This chapter focuses on the politics of scale in Scotland, teasing out local–national tensions that shape debates about who has responsibility for conserving and managing nature. The national scale and statist logics are treated as hegemonic in conservation practices where natural and cultural heritage are protected 'for the nation'.[1] However, it is important to consider the narratives and practices within national actors to move beyond binary representations of power[2] and stereotypes of conservation stakeholders.[3] In the first half of the chapter, I outline WRB's relationship with NatureScot, Scotland's national public body for nature conservation, and discuss local views on the role of state and third sector actors in conserving nature. This brings to the fore contestations regarding the extent to which communities like WRB should hold responsibility for nature, discussed amidst wider contexts of austerity and state retreat.

The second half of the chapter focuses on alternatives to mainstream conservation such as convivial conservation, which aims to transcend capitalism and nature/culture dichotomies.[4] Convivial conservation emphasises the need for better dialogue and a process-driven approach to living better with each other and with nature. I discuss the multi-scalar, biocultural approach of WRB, comparing this to the rigidity of national actors like the National Trust for Scotland and NatureScot where scales and values seem more fixed. Finally, I outline how WRB actors compare the BR to national parks as a way to position themselves as an alternative and garner more support for the community Biosphere.

NATURE CONSERVATION IN SCOTLAND

NatureScot is Scotland's public body for nature conservation. As introduced in Chapter 2, NatureScot did not push for BR designation in Wester Ross, but agreed to support it if communities wanted it. NatureScot has since then remained at arm's length from WRB, providing minimal financial support and a board advisor. Each year, WRB and the advisor request funding from NatureScot. Around £10,000 was offered in the first few years which funded Phoebe as a part-time coordinator. This funding has never been guaranteed and advisors often asked for more with little success. Funding was later halved to £5,000, channelled through implementation of a sustainable tourism project (see Chapter 3) and then withdrawn. NatureScot has also given small sums left over from annual underspends, which although beneficial for short-term projects and events, was not useful for longer term core work.

Alison was WRB's first advisor, who on retirement was replaced by Carla, another local resident of the BR. When Carla left, the role was briefly re-allocated but weakening ties between WRB and NatureScot led to the loss of a board advisor. Phoebe once spoke positively to the board about feeling 'valued' by the public sector whilst working with NatureScot, but this was largely due to interpersonal relationships and support from the likes of Alison and Carla. More recently it is felt that NatureScot have not supported WRB. Phoebe, for example, asked for help to deliver the BR's ten-year periodic review due in 2026. This is an important milestone with UNESCO which results in continuation or withdrawal of the BR designation. Phoebe's email to request help was forwarded on as WRB's contact had left the organisation and the person who then received it replied bluntly that NatureScot had no capacity or funding to support them.

Lack of support from NatureScot for WRB was once attributed by Alison to the community-led governance. She told me during interview that whilst the BR had originally piqued some interest among NatureScot directors, when they learned about its powers and governance (no powers and community-led) she said it became 'difficult to make the case for it'. NatureScot do support community empowerment, stating online, for example, that this is a 'top priority' for themselves and Scottish Government.[5] This has not, however, translated into support for WRB as a biocultural model for community-based conservation. Alison offered some context about NatureScot's way of working, which she felt was changing due to austerity. The organisation was forced to work more closely to its legislative remit (which does not involve BRs) and there had been many staff reductions, centralisation and a focus on populated areas deemed higher value for money. Research has showed how austerity impacted collaborative governance in North Devon BR, with national agencies withdrawing from BR partnership activities that do not directly serve their legislative remit.[6] However, Alison was positive that NatureScot was increasingly people-centred rather than about conservation for its own sake. In Wester Ross many locals held negative views of NatureScot and conservation in general (see Chapter 2). Understanding these conservation conflicts (and possibilities for cooperation) requires consideration of 'local political, cultural, and individual histories, as well as the development of conservation relations over time'.[7]

Whose responsibility, at what scale?

Describing the disconnect between national conservation and local communities in Wester Ross, a former employee of NatureScot, told me that most decisions are made by 'pen pushers' in the central belt who have often never set foot in the Highlands. Estate owner Shannon also shared that when NatureScot opened offices in Inverness, people locally said, 'they're just moving Edinburgh people up there'. Although a national body, NatureScot is associated with the lowlands and centralised political governance. Such sentiments also apply more widely in the Highlands, for example in Easter Ross local people said, 'Edinburgh is coming' to refer to visits by Historic Scotland, the national heritage conservation body.[8] Social and physical distance between conservationists and local communities in the BR is a challenge for advancing more convivial conservation because it is in the everyday and informal spaces where commonalities across difference can be built over time.[9] Where there are interactions, these can fuel tensions, such as when conservationists 'come from out of the area and sometimes they don't know some of the very localised flora and fauna'. One example I heard was from a gamekeeper who was frustrated that a red squirrel conservation project was advised by a NatureScot conservationist who had only ever worked with grey squirrels. Some involved in conservation thus had the impression that NatureScot lack ecological knowledge relevant to Wester Ross. However, Carla, who lives in Wester Ross and works for NatureScot, told me that the residual 'wariness of government agencies of any kind' in Wester Ross has a longer history, beginning with the Nature Conservancy Council and Scottish Natural Heritage. Indeed, Seumas told me, 'SNH have not always been able to work well with local communities and have got themselves into trouble quite often'. As has been discussed in previous chapters, local actors can be critical of how conservation agendas (such as rewilding, or the designation of protected areas) exclude local culture, communities and livelihoods and are implemented top-down (see Chapters 2 and 4). Alongside the state, local communities have been wary of conservation carried out by landowners and charitable organisations. Seumas perceived some progress in recent relationships:

> I am also a member of the John Muir Trust, and I know some of the problems that they've experienced working with local communities, although actually I think they're doing quite a good job … I'm not trying to sell John Muir Trust, but they and the Scottish Wild Life Trust I think have learnt that it's very important to work with communities and to get them on your side. And if you don't get them on your side, then you are lost.

Whilst advocating for greater community inclusion in conservation decision-making, there were also some conflicting narratives locally about the responsibility of communities versus national bodies to manage nature in Scotland. Michael, for example, questioned whether communities would be empowered and deliver conservation outcomes if responsible for managing large estates in Wester Ross. Reflecting on his local area, he felt it would be positive if a smaller piece of land was taken over from a private landowner whereas 'taking land off a conservation charity to put into the community, I'm not quite sure where the benefit lies'. He argued that compared to public bodies or charities, a community 'will be unable to match the level of expertise available in the existing organisation'. Similarly, Shannon felt that national government not local communities should hold responsibility for Scotland's natural resources. For example, the Forestry Commission must manage forests 'for the people' and public ownership must remain a government priority to care for 'national assets'. Thinking of her local area where there is community-owned forestry, she similarly cited lack of expertise and the fluctuation of community capacity as potential issues. In contrast, Callum, an employee of Forestry and Land Scotland, said that 'communities buy forests because the state isn't doing what they want it to do'. He argued communities do 'amazing things' without the money and resources of a public body, and taking on responsibility for managing and conserving assets like forests drives forward local priorities. For example, the community-owned woodland in Lochcarron is being managed by local people to deliver multiple local priorities: diversifying to improve conservation values, showcasing cultural heritage values of the woodland, providing leisure, employment and education opportunities and building affordable housing. Hence, conservation agendas are usually situated by local communities amidst wider aims for local planning and development (see Chapter 2).

WRB actors have debated whether conservation is the responsibility of the state, communities and/or the third sector. At a meeting of the Natural Heritage Group, participants were reviewing and producing WRB's response to the draft Highland Biodiversity Plan. Brian argued that countryside rangers would be a 'core method of delivering' and asked the group, 'do we actually think NatureScot should be leading it? Should it be their responsibility?' Michael, a former Cairngorms National Park ranger, felt 'there should be a national service, similar to the coastguard, the police'. An NTS volunteer agreed, arguing the current approach is 'disjointed, what there is left of it'. Brian seemed to agree that a national approach would be the most 'economic' mode of delivery and partnership working with NatureScot could 'actually make it work properly' and shift from reliance on volunteers. He felt that conservation in Scotland needs greater investment and that whilst communities should participate, 'it shouldn't be up to lots of small groups, disparate organisations doing a bit here and there, because it needs a strategic approach'. Elisabeth cautioned the group that there would be no budget attached to implementing the plan and she felt WRB ought to create their own regional plan to progress some of the priorities for biodiversity in the BR. However, without funds, Brian suggested the BR could also play role by raising awareness and holding knowledge exchange events to create dialogue among conservationists, landowners and communities.

The subject of rangers re-emerged in WRB's discussion of green jobs (see Chapter 4). Here, the idea of WRB employing rangers for conservation in the BR became more palatable to Brian following discussion with Norman. Brian was initially reluctant, arguing that the government should not expect the third sector to run public sector green jobs, especially when it was government who cut funding for green jobs in the first place. With funding now available, 'we should be making a strong case that the government's agencies should be doing these things'. Norman, however, said given NatureScot, Highland Council and conservation charities are cutting ranger services, the BR has a role in delivery. He described the wider policy context as one in which the Scottish Government and its agencies are focusing on central populations, with funding for areas like Wester Ross receding. Despite having previously felt WRB should not be employing rangers to avoid being seen as an 'authority' or a 'national park on the cheap', Brian came round to WRB taking responsibility. These discussions reflect how BRs under austerity negotiate a 'vacuum' as state actors retreat and non-state actors become service deliverers.[10] WRB is, however, only a small organisation run by volunteer community members which makes employing rangers difficult. Phoebe shared that Galloway and Southern Ayrshire (GSA) BR have part time rangers, but speculated these were employed by local government given the BR's partnership model. Ultimately, both WRB and Highland Council separately applied to NatureScot requesting funding for rangers. Thus, a partnership was set up where three rangers, employed by the council would work in the BR area and raise awareness of WRB. These seasonal roles were geared towards managing the environmental impacts of unsustainable tourism, public access rights and visitor capacity issues. Whilst important, they were not necessarily focused on resolving conflict and moving towards convivial, biocultural conservation.

CONVIVIAL AND BIOCULTURAL PERSPECTIVES

Resolving tensions between conservationists, communities and land managers is at the heart of calls for convivial conservation in Scotland. What this means in practice is as simple as 'having a blether and getting people on board', recognising that conflict is overcome through communication, cooperation and respect.[11] This idea emerged in the perspective of Matthew, CEO of a national conservation charity with personal and professional experience in Wester Ross. Matthew felt that 'animosity' between conservationists and communities is often 'overplayed' by those not working 'on the ground'. Speaking of NatureScot and Forestry Land Scotland he said, 'they think they can hear the local voice, but they don't because they are not going out on the hill with people, or spending time with them to get beneath the knee jerk reaction'. From his perspective, although local communities or specific groups can coalesce against conservation agendas, usually this was due to a perceived threat to their livelihood, not a sign they do not value nature. For him, conservation must account for historical contexts where livelihoods on estates and within crofting have become dependent on the wealth of the landowning community and government subsidies. Conflict emerges when public debates on conservation translate into a feeling that 'somebody's attacking them' and their way of life. To move forward, he described the need to build trust through meaningful private conversations and create mechanisms that build collective confidence in change and through which those affected can 'assert what they want their future to be'.

WRB is well placed to facilitate both of these in the BR. As a community Biosphere there is time and scope to build everyday informal relationships and the organisation has already created new spaces for collective future-making in some contexts. Generally, too, WRB have been advancing convivial conservation by creating spaces to 'have a blether and get people on board' through in-person and online knowledge exchange events. These have often overcome binaries of 'professional-subaltern'[12] and nature–culture in subjects like managing wildfires, tackling invasive species and community climate action where communities, land managers, estate owners and conservation agencies collaborate. Managing Change in our Land and Seas was an online event funded by NatureScot underspend which focused on climate change and community participation in diverse BR habitats from woodlands and forests to blue spaces and uplands. It enabled sharing of existing good practice and identification of priority action for the future, and discussions often implied a biocultural approach. Discussions made reference to the folklore and cultural traditions of woodlands, such as foraging, alongside traditional uses of timber and woodland pasture as a means to support conservation of nature, cultural heritage practices and livelihoods in communities. On the biodiversity of the BR's marine protected area, whilst national policy change was advocated, it was also suggested that unsustainable dredging practices could be replaced with community cultural practices linked to seaweed cultivation, which can be used as fertiliser by crofters, as a food or fuel source, and for local products. Raising awareness about species decline and threats to the seabed was also seen as key to involving communities in marine conservation given that valuable habitats and species are usually 'out of sight out of mind'. In the uplands discussion, rewilding was argued as a way to restore peatlands not only for biodiversity benefits, but for local community benefit, through improved water quality and flood management. The cultural heritage significance of peat was also seen as a central reason for communities to be more involved in decision-making around these landscapes for the future. Such conversations have been well attended and are facilitated by independent chairpersons in inclusive ways. They are designed with WRB's process-oriented approach in mind, which is rarely about a fixed outcome and how to get there, but about building trust and relationships across sectors and actors in the BR. The process of creating such spaces involves WRB actors negotiating scalar politics, given that different actors have different priorities associated with specific values at specific scales.

Communities often focus on local scales and issues and landowners on estate boundaries, whilst NatureScot are nationally focused. With a regional focus, WRB exists in the critical messy middle, a multi-scalar, participatory organisation working to accommodate diverging interests.

For example, the Sustainable Development Group deliberated on what topics to choose for several knowledge exchange webinars; some were seen as regionally or nationally important, others more localised but important to communities. For Norman, deer management was central to the 'mismanaging of the vast majority of the BR' and something which 'nobody talks about'. However, it was seen as more of a national or regional issue, with Phoebe unsure what role communities might play compared with other topics like local food or where collaborative action might be easier. However, the Managing Change event raised community stalking and community deer larders as ways in which local people could contribute to and benefit from action on deer management in Scotland.

More recently, a WRB funding proposal for a collaborative conservation project also illustrated elements of multi-scalar, biocultural conservation. It was about 'growing biodiversity together', aiming to engage local people in ecosystem restoration, drawing on cultural heritage knowledge among crofters and gardeners, 'addressing local concerns' whilst contributing to 'restoring Scotland's rainforest, heathlands, coastal wildflower grasslands, wetlands, soils, ecosystem links and native wildlife'. The project conveyed a sense of moving towards a 'third cultural space' by integrating local ecological knowledge and scientific conservation agendas (see Chapter 7). It was also indicative of biocultural heritage where cultural heritage and biodiversity are interwoven. Sadly, the proposal was not funded; a missed opportunity to overcome the nature–culture dichotomy and advance convivial conservation in practice.

WRB's rejected projects over the years also led me to question whether this occurs due to confusion about the multi-scalar, multi-actor approach which focuses on processes rather than outcomes. The idea of working flexibly across scales, with different actors is often about accommodating multiple values and nature–culture relationships. This may appear ambiguous compared with set outcomes from working in a specific local area, and may be perceived as less achievable at the scale of regional collaboration. WRB projects convey that BRs are spaces where 'different modes of living ... engender different natures' going beyond multiple perspectives on a singular nature.[13] This is challenging to communicate as a complex view of nature–culture relations and WRB tends to reject the mainstream 'deliverology' mentality which is about predetermined outcomes rather than processes.[14]

WRB resists what is known in heritage conservation as 'practising perspectivalism', a model for identifying multiple values among stakeholders but using overarching expertise to offer 'a perspective on all perspectives'.[15] This is part of scalar power relations, reflecting a sense that conservation values must be 'either/or' and never 'both/and'. Values are either at a national or a local scale and conservation decisions require that these are traded off according to an organisation's predetermined agenda. This can be illustrated using the example of the National Trust for Scotland (NTS), who invited me to deliver a workshop on the BR and WRB for their staff based centrally and in Wester Ross. I argued that WRB work across the nature–culture divide and focus on the process of building relationships with multiple communities and stakeholders across scales without a predetermined outcome in mind. During discussion, an NTS staff member said on reflection, 'for us, scale is an issue ... it's at what level do we make decisions. Is it the local property scale? Is it more regional? Or is it that national scale?' Here we see the either/or dilemma, where choosing a scale becomes associated with choosing one set of values over another. However, for multi-scalar conservation, it is important to 'cut free from assumptions about the stability and essential characteristics of scale'.[16] Another NTS staff member argued that whilst certain arguments are acceptable at local level they are not acceptable at a national one, which is a problem because, 'we are guided by higher-level decision making in the Trust'. Relying on higher level decision-making does seem to have limited the space available for local values and cultural heritage to play a role in conservation management, as the Trust falls back on the sense of retaining some overarching authority tied to a hegemonic model of conservation policy and practice.

Norman argued that NTS must move away from top-down decision-making because it has operated 'feudally' at times. He felt things were getting worse and rather than collaborating with 'staff, volunteers, communities of interest or resident communities' those at the top are 'assuming that they know better in their ivory tower'. In contrast, he told his colleagues how WRB as an organisation is 'about bringing people together, it's about facilitating those discussions rather than necessarily delivering hard and fast projects its more about facilitating the process'. He felt NTS, in its position as one of the largest landowners in Wester Ross and an actor conserving both biological and cultural heritage, should play a role in such processes, for example as part of a plan for sustainably developing the BR (see Chapter 8). WRB's process-driven approach, for Norman, is about moving beyond predetermined ideas of 'what heritage is and what is right and what's wrong', recognising that 'you won't get a consensus on every last thing, but you will begin to have those conversations' with a flexible approach allowing for 'some progress and change'. These ideas demonstrate the ethos of convivial conservation and alternatives to the 'deliverology mentality' that move from outputs towards valuing relationships over time.[17]

Convivial and biocultural approaches also transcend the nature–culture divide, which is not the norm in mainstream nature conservation in Scotland or indeed globally. This came to light when I interviewed Carla after she replaced Alison as NatureScot advisor to WRB. She recalled:

> I'm still getting up to speed, I have to say that last meeting it was kind of slightly bamboozling, the amount of stuff they were covering and you know – it's like a spider web isn't it, lots of these little kind of, everyone getting involved in every other bit. I think that's great, that's not a criticism, it's just, you know some of it is not anything that I can help with, you know the cultural heritage stuff, even though I'm interested in that, that's not our role.

The meeting, as was the norm for WRB, covered a wide range of issues across nature–culture boundaries. Although not what she was used to in her work at NatureScot, Carla saw value in the Biosphere as a practical mechanism for making the most of the region's diverse nature–culture relations where 'it's about it all fitting together'. However, for Phoebe it has been challenging to pursue such an approach in practice, when key actors do not value this biocultural approach. She explained WRB's two main funders NatureScot and HIE have 'completely different remits and mandates [and] ne'er the twain shall meet'. She felt both were stuck in rigid professional/sectoral binaries – 'I'm in conservation' or 'I'm in development'. It has been hard to foster collaborative action and to convince funders to invest in WRB's process-driven approach, where sustainability is a holistic mentality. Nonetheless, they continue to advocate for a multi-scalar, multi-actor model across the nature–culture binary, and thus offer a regional alternative to mainstream conservation models in Scotland.

'Why vote for a national park when you've got a Biosphere?'

Since the 1940s, Wester Ross has been considered by campaigners as a possible site for a national park. More recently, the prospect re-emerged when the Scottish National Party (SNP) and Scottish Green Party coalition government agreed to introduce a new park in Scotland. This prompted debate among WRB as to whether it may be beneficial to have both designations. Indeed, globally there are crossovers with national parks and BRs which can operate similarly.[18] In Scotland, national park objectives have historically been interpreted hierarchically, with conservation taking priority if ever there is a conflict with other objectives such as economic development.[19] In contrast, no such prioritisation exists for WRB, and this ambiguity is what makes BRs harder to understand than national parks, which are more obviously spaces for nature.[20] I would argue WRB are closer to a Biocultural Heritage Territory (BCHT) than a national park, centring community governance and positioning conservation amidst wider aims for resilient livelihoods, local food systems and cultural heritage. Alongside examples from previous chapters, priorities for biodiversity conservation include removal of rhododendron, which for WRB actors is not only about invasive species management, but a way to support local economies and communities through the creation and sale of rhododendron biochar.

WRB actors' deliberations about a new park highlighted their own interpretations of the similarities and differences between the BR and Scotland's national parks. Whilst most agreed the two have overlapping remits as place-based approaches to conservation and development, there were diverging perceptions about the benefit of national park status. Alan emphasised how WRB have achieved a lot on a 'shoestring budget' under the UNESCO remit and said, 'we are already doing it and whether you call us a national park and give us money to run it as a national park'. He spoke positively about John Muir and American national parks as inspiration for 'protecting' and 'preserving' the Biosphere. However, Coinneach was highly critical of this; he argued that US national parks removed indigenous people from land and erased their culture, an injustice that was part of the 'turning wheel of colonisation'. Seumas also held the view that national parks have 'very little to do with human interaction with their environment' and are more focused on 'preventing development'. The board also discussed governance structures and power, with parks noted as having greater authority and autonomy and a legal role in planning. As state-driven models, national parks have built-in competencies to control development for conservation whilst BRs may not.[21] Whilst WRB actors had a desire for more autonomy and resource, most resisted that this should come through national park status, as a kind of top-down state authority. They maintained that the difference and value of the BR lies in being community-led and working from the bottom-up through participatory processes. It was also speculated (and later proven to be accurate) that communities in Wester Ross would not support a bid for a national park.

It was agreed at the time that any decision would need to be led by communities, and in the meantime, WRB might consider how to achieve greater recognition and funding for the BR by taking advantage of a new national park being on the political agenda. This was tied to funding of GSA BR (Chapter 8), as Norman argued they had perhaps been so successful because funding the BR was an easy way for an SNP government (less keen for more parks) to invest in already existing alternatives. He suggested that WRB might be treated the same and felt it was a good time to reach out to HIE to have a conversation about funding them as an alternative to a national park. Alongside contacting HIE, the board felt WRB must make a stronger case for itself to the Scottish Government and political representatives. Norman argued that when considering sustainability, conservation and cultural heritage: 'we are in a strong position to argue, why vote for national park when you've got a Biosphere? Just fund it properly.' He said national parks cost around £5 million a year and WRB could run well on even just one tenth of that amount. Phoebe agreed that WRB could deliver a similar remit to a park with only 'a few crumbs off the table'.

In their advocacy it would make sense for WRB to position themselves not only as a UNESCO site, but as part of a wider global move towards biocultural approaches.[22] This should be about advocating for themselves as a community Biosphere and acting in solidarity with the campaign for BCHTs as a community model that, like WRB, offer a 'fairer, effective and lower-cost alternative to protected areas'.[23] Such advocacy could help advance convivial conservation, shifting from protected areas, to promoted areas. The UNESCO status is a way to do this but the emphasis should be on WRB's unique capacity to offer in-situ community-based conservation. Additionally, WRB could consider how best to hold NatureScot and the Scottish Government to account on the idea that community empowerment is a 'top priority' – drawing attention to the specific needs of rural communities and the lack of support for the Highlands' only community-led BR in Wester Ross.

CONCLUSION

In Scotland, as elsewhere globally, there is a need for alternative conservation models that overcome the nature–culture dichotomy. WRB is a model for this in the Scottish Highlands, where action is needed to overcome regional conflict and enact ecological, economic and social restoration. However, at present WRB as a community Biosphere is undervalued and has received insufficient support. WRB's relationship with NatureScot is fraught and there have been missed opportunities over the last decade to empower communities through the BR as a convivial, biocultural model of conservation. I have outlined how the scalar politics of conservation are playing out in contestations about who is responsible for conserving what natures, at what scales; and that WRB are actively negotiating the spaces between community, state and third sector in conditions of austerity. I also articulated how WRB differ from mainstream conservation approaches, particularly in terms of their process-driven approach which is about facilitating conversations and allowing for multiple values and relations with nature. Importantly, such relations are not subsumed under one dominant logic or authority, nor are they shaped by a nature–culture dichotomy. This is quite different from the 'either/or' approach of mainstream conservation actors, who have tended to separate natural and cultural heritage values and see the local and national as fixed scales in tension. Finally, I showed how through comparison with the national park model, WRB actors perceive themselves as an alternative rooted in community-led governance and bottom-up working. To better value this model, WRB could advocate for itself as part of the wider global agenda for biocultural conservation within which conservation is balanced alongside the wider social and economic realities facing local communities.[24] However, part of the challenge in advancing change is the complex politics of land ownership and management in the BR, which is the subject of the next chapter.

NOTES

1. Lisa Breglia, *Monumental Ambivalence: the Politics of Heritage* (University of Texas Press, 2006), 179.
2. Siân Jones and Tom Yarrow, *The Object of Conservation: An Ethnography of Conservation Practice* (Routledge, 2022).
3. Sam Staddon, 'Conservation's All about Having a Blether and Getting People on Board: Exploring Cooperation for Conservation in Scotland,' *Conservation and Society* (2021), https://doi.org/10.4103/cs.cs_20_58.
4. Bram Büscher and Robert Fletcher, *The Conservation Revolution: Ideas For Saving Nature Beyond the Anthropocene* (Verso, 2020).
5. 'Our Approach to Community Empowerment,' Nature Scot, 2025, https://www.nature.scot/about-naturescot/our-work/community-empowerment-and-scotlands-environment/our-approach-community-empowerment.
6. Nick Kirsop-Taylor, Duncan Russel and Michael Winter, 'The Contours of State Retreat From Collaborative Environmental Governance Under Austerity,' *Sustainability* 12, no. 7 (2020): 1–16.

7. Staddon, 'Having a Blether.'
8. Siân Jones, 'Making Place, Resisting Displacement: Conflicting National and Local Identities in Scotland,' in *The Politics of Heritage: The Legacies of Race*, ed. J. Littler and R. Naidoo (Routledge, 2005), 94–114.
9. Staddon, 'Having a Blether.'
10. Kirsop-Taylor et al., 'State Retreat.'
11. Staddon, 'Having a Blether.'
12. Jones and Yarrow, *Object of Conservation.*
13. Uta Berghoefer, Ricardo Rozzi and Kurt Jax, 'Many Eyes on Nature: Diverse Perspectives in the Cape Horn Biosphere Reserve and their Relevance for Conservation,' *Ecology and Society* 15, no. 1 (2010), 18.
14. Staddon, 'Having a Blether.'
15. Jones and Yarrow, *Object of Conservation*, 208.
16. David C. Harvey, 'Heritage and Scale: Settings, Boundaries and Relations,' *International Journal of Heritage Studies* 21, no. 6 (2015): 589.
17. Staddon, 'Having a Blether.'
18. Maureen Reed, 'Conceptual Origins and First-Generation Biosphere Reserves,' in *UNESCO Biosphere Reserves: Supporting Biocultural Diversity, Sustainability and Society*, ed. M. Reed and M. F. Price (Routledge, 2020), 13–28.
19. Adam Barker and Aileen Stockdale, 'Out of the Wilderness? Achieving Sustainable Development Within Scottish National Parks,' *Journal of Environmental Management* 88, no. 1 (2008): 181–93.
20. Erik Aschenbrand and Thomas Michler, 'Why Do UNESCO Biosphere Reserves Get Less Recognition than National Parks? A Landscape Research Perspective on Protected Area Narratives in Germany,' *Sustainability* 13, no. 24 (2021): 13647.
21. Aschenbrand and Michler, 'UNESCO Biosphere Reserves Get Less.'
22. See Peter Bridgewater and Ian Rotherham, 'A Critical Perspective on the Concept of Biocultural Diversity and its Emerging Role in Nature and Heritage Conservation,' *People and Nature* 1, no. 3 (2019): 291–304; Jarrod Cusens, Alicia Barraclough and Inger Måren, 'Participatory Mapping Reveals Biocultural and Nature Values in the Shared Landscape of a Nordic UNESCO Biosphere Reserve,' *People and Nature* 4, no. 2 (2022): 365–81; Maureen Reed and Martin F. Price, eds., *UNESCO Biosphere Reserves: Supporting Biocultural Diversity, Sustainability and Society* (Routledge, 2020), 321–32; Maria F. Rollo, 'Interconnected Nature and People: Biosphere Reserves and the Power of Memory and Oral Histories as Biocultural Heritage for a Sustainable Future,' *Sustainability*, 17, no. 9 (2025): 1–33; Elke Schüttler, Roy Mackenzie and Lucas Muñoz-Petersen, 'Biocultural Conservation in Biosphere Reserves in Temperate Regions of Chile, Estonia, Germany, and Sweden,' in *Field Environmental Philosophy* (Springer, 2023), 483–502.

23. Krystyna Swiderska, Alejamdro Argumedo and Michael Pimbert, 'Biocultural Heritage Territories: Key to Halting Biodiversity Loss,' *International Institute for Environment and Development*, 2020, https://www.jstor.org/stable/resrep29050.
24. Rollo, 'Interconnected Nature and People,' 1–33.

10

The Politics of Land Use and Ownership

How societies use and manage land is central to sustainability challenges.[1] Land is embedded in power relations, evident in historic and ongoing enclosures of land and sea for capital accumulation.[2] Land power must be put in the service of wider societies[3] in order to create more sustainable futures. For many critical thinkers and activists, this involves defending and reinventing alternatives such as commons.[4] There is a long history of struggle over land in Scotland, culminating in policy and legislative agendas for land reform and community empowerment. This includes new community right-to-buy regimes which are underpinned by sustainable development.[5] Currently, 2.9 per cent of land in Scotland is under community ownership[6] with the Highlands and Islands having the highest concentration of community owned assets.[7] Community land purchase and land reform processes are arguably normalising communal models of property,[8] yet the 'vast private estates' of Wester Ross are evidence that land reform in Scotland has a long way to go.[9]

According to the BR's nomination to UNESCO, large privately owned estates are 'the most significant form of land holding' in Wester Ross. There are approximately seventy-nine estates covering just over one million acres of land, the largest being Letterewe, Heights of Kinlochewe and Tournaig, which owners describe as 'The Last Wilderness of Scotland'. Land ownership in the BR is also linked to beneficiaries of Britain's system of plantation and enslavement in the Caribbean colonies.[10] In Wester Ross, >206,481 acres were purchased between 1726 and 1939 by families with financial connections to British slavery[11] – just one example of the many ways in which land embodies colonial relations.

In this chapter I outline perspectives of WRB actors, landowners and local residents on land use and ownership in the BR. Unpacking the complexities and politics of land, I consider the role of the UNESCO

BR in advancing sustainable land management and compare it to other models in Scotland, such as national parks and regional land use partnerships. The second half of the chapter focuses on changing local relations between communities and landowners using an in-depth case study of Applecross. This case helps to articulate the ways that local people problematise or reproduce the status quo and how collective land and asset ownership are seen as a pathway to more sustainable, thriving communities.

THE GOOD, THE BAD AND THE UGLY

For many WRB actors the topic of land brings out historic and contemporary injustices and power relations. Phoebe, although more neutral publicly, expressed how: 'land management always comes back down to land ownership and that makes me angry'. Molly, former staff member and director, described land as a complex issue because in the BR there are 'so many different land owners and potential uses'. Especially regarding land for housing and security for people to live in the BR, the issue 'is visceral, it's very emotional for people'. Anndra outlined how land shapes the fate of local communities:

> We've still got this legacy of old, aristocratic people that are keeping people out of their land, just so they can run it as a deer forest, or a place where they can have their own sport. The biggest offender here just outside of Glenelg is Sheik Mohammed [bin] Rashid Al Maktoum, who owns everything that you can see when you come over the hill from here. The Highland Clearances continue with him. The few people that were here 25 years ago when I first came here, are no longer on that land, they've been pressured to move away, houses demolished, so that it's just an empty place where nothing happens.

The Sheik mentioned is a billionaire, the ruler of Dubai who bought his estate in Wester Ross for £2 million. Land is regularly sold at market prices unaffordable to the majority, such as Ledgowan estate (£4.5 million) or Inverbroom Estate which was recently bought for £17.5 million by the Scottish Wildlife Trust. Whether private or charitable, large land owners are seen as holding power over communities and their relationships with land, and rarely working with or for local people. Speaking of Anders Polvsen, owner of a large rewilding estate, Coinneach argued:

> He seems to have a notion of conservation that's not connected to the wellbeing of the communities that live in the area. And has a notion of the landscape being devoid of people, or at the expense of the rule of people.

Both green lairds and traditionally managed estates are seen to play a part in upholding power relations that exclude communities. For Norman the problem is that 'there is no system of making landowners, whether they are large scale or small-scale landowners, accountable for their sustainability or lack of it'.

However, WRB actors are cautious about how the BR might advocate for more sustainable land management practice. Anndra, for example, in discussions with the board felt that action around land management practices relates to land ownership, which 'becomes very political, and I don't think that's our role'. In contrast, Robert, a Highland Councillor held stronger views on land reform and told me: 'I have no problem with the Biosphere taking on landowners'. This meant encouraging those with the largest areas of land to use it sustainably, not just for 'running some deer and pheasants for shooting'. However, often the focus is on the need for stronger legislation in Scotland as a whole, such as when Michael suggested landowners that manage land unsustainably should have their estates forfeited.

Although Scotland's landownership system does need reform, there is also a role for BRs to encourage regional collaboration among landowners for sustainable landscape stewardship. Coinneach recognised this when he argued of landowners: 'we need these people to come to the table and not feel castigated or judged'. So far, however, Norman told me, WRB has 'failed' to engage with landowners and especially larger private estates. He felt alongside WRB's lack of resource that most owners are not interested in seeing any change to current land management, which makes it challenging to engage with them. Landowner engagement has also emerged in discussions about BR funding. Alan argued that WRB should be proactive with rich benefactors such as the Sheik, who have at times contributed funds for community projects. This particular suggestion was resisted, with Seumas citing the fourteenth-century proverbial saying, 'if you want to sup with the devil, you need a lang spoon'. However, not all landowners in Wester Ross are cut from the same cloth and there may be scope for WRB to work with landowners that align with the BR ethos. During my fieldwork I interviewed some landowners and three family-owned estates seemed to be engaging with local communities and advocating sustainability.

In one case, the estate owner, an older woman, had visited the area often as a child and inherited the estate from her father. She has since lived there full-time and is involved with the local paper and hosting the Highland Games. A close relationship with the community is something she inherited from her father, who was seemingly always available to talk to local people informally. For her, the estate has always tried to support the community and she felt people locally viewed them positively as a result, whereas the idea of 'wicked landowners' removing people from land came from outside the area. She suggested that maintaining good relations with the community meant keeping out of local politics and only supporting positive things. Indeed, the estate became a WRB business supporter, and she said of the Biosphere, 'I'm 100 per cent behind it'. When the Scottish Land Commission (SLC) visited her area promoting good practice protocols for community engagement with land, she felt this overly formal – 'they want you to have meetings or something' – but nonetheless said land reform is 'a power for good'. The extent to which local communities are involved in estate decision-making was unclear, with most benefit linked to public access. However, the perceived 'sense of familiarity' is an important aspect of creating positive relationships between landowners and communities.[12]

Another example is Shannon, a younger woman, who also inherited an estate from her father – the same crofter I introduced in Chapter 6. She described how landowner ownership is 'very transparent' in her area because people know her and that she lives and works on this land. It 'hasn't passed from hand to hand' having been in her family since the 1950s. She has lived there since she was two weeks old and has run the estate full time for the last twenty years. She also supported the BR because it is 'about the interaction between man and the environment' which is 'a good way to describe ourselves and a model for sustainability'. The estate is also a WRB business supporter and Shannon is an active supporter of land reform with public-facing roles that evidence this claim. Lastly, I spoke with a younger male whose family has owned a Wester Ross estate since the late 1990s. He took part in BR consultations and although not particularly engaged with WRB, seemed to mirror their priorities. He argued, 'in any Biosphere it is very important to maintain the human culture' and tourism must first work for local people (see Chapter 3). The estate was also engaged in native woodlands conservation and a red squirrel reintroduction project. Akin to the previous two cases, he believed local communities around the estate, 'know where to find us, we're not difficult to get a hold of'. He felt there was a 'good relationship with the local community' and that if anything was wrong, they would reach out. He also participated in local community events, and argued that estates 'have a big part to play' in local culture. His view was that landowners not interested in this should not own a Highland estate, because it is the spirit and culture of local communities that make an estate special.

Although land ownership is contentious in the BR, there are opportunities to move towards sustainable regional land management by building relationships with landowners. In Germany, BR administrations have initiated a process of landscape-scale stewardship, within which stakeholders are brought together and encouraged to adopt shared responsibility for sustainable futures.[13] Whilst such a process is unlikely to involve absentee landowners, it could begin without them and engage not only private estate owners, but the wider range of community and charitable owners in the BR, such as the National Trust for Scotland (see Chapter 9), as part of a collaborative approach. Taking steps towards a regional partnership in the BR also aligns with wider Scottish policy.

Towards collaborative regional land management

The 2020–1 Programme for Government stated an intention to introduce Regional Land Use Partnerships (RLUPs) in Scotland. Scotland's Third Land Use Strategy explained:

> RLUPs will help national and local government, communities, land owners and stakeholders work together to find ways to optimise sustainable land use in a fair and inclusive way – meeting local and national objectives and helping achieve Scotland's climate change targets through land use change and good land management that supports a sustainable future.[14]

Several pilot sites have been established to test governance options and approaches to partnership working across Scotland, on the basis that RLUPs should integrate with existing structures rather than add a new layers of bureaucracy. When first announced WRB were uncertain about RLUPs but interested in how this would overlap with the BR. They were invited by the SLC to early stakeholder discussions, but had no capacity to attend a meeting held in person in Edinburgh. It was suggested I might represent WRB, but this was refused by organisers. SLC later produced recommendations for RLUPs which were brought for discussion by Norman to the board and the Sustainable Development Group. He argued that the recommendations 'didn't really provide any answers'. He explained how BRs are briefly mentioned in the report as a part of justifying the regional approach, and that Galloway and Southern Ayrshire BR had been involved in consultations. Norman felt the model for RLUPs suited Galloway's governance more so than WRB, 'because that's what they are already, they are a mixture of statutory bodies'. It was agreed that WRB could engage more moving forward and an SLC representative was invited to present about RLUPs at a learning event on partnerships for land management. There, Norman expressed his concern to the representative that it was being assumed bodies such as Highland Council and WRB have existing resources to take on the responsibilities of an RLUP. He stated, 'for us, that's not an option, because we are not resourced at all'. The Commission representative said their recommendations do not specify who should be the 'accountable body' and that financing is for Scottish Government to determine, if and when RLUPs are rolled out across Scotland. Some attendees saw potential in RLUPs as 'game changers' for achieving regional priorities and targeting funding, and of WRB, it was agreed, 'the Biosphere is a great model for that, if people actually understood how it worked'.

Following on from ideas about sustainably developing Wester Ross through collaborative action (Chapter 8) and arguments about the BR as an alternative to a national park (Chapter 9), there is an opportunity for WRB to lead on an RLUP, or to seek greater investment in the BR as an already existing alternative. RLUPs are currently being conceived through the lens of hegemonic approaches to land – embodying common-sense discourses of natural capital and ecosystem services.[15] As I suggested in Chapter 9, we might also look to alternatives like Biocultural Heritage Territories, which as models for land use and ownership focus on the land rights of communities and indigenous peoples. This is about how land underpins self-determination, with stewardship following culturally specific worldviews for holistic wellbeing of people and nature. We should not be limited to thinking about Scotland's land futures through the lens of mainstream, hegemonic policies. Whilst RLUPs might be better than no action at all, I would argue the community Biosphere offers greater scope for regional spatial justice and ethical relations between people and land. Additionally, there must be more support for communities locally to take on collective ownership of land as a way of destabilising hegemonic land power.

COMMUNITIES, LAND AND SUSTAINABILITY

When it comes to land ownership, many local residents were critical about the lack of transparency in Wester Ross. Locals were often unsure who owned large estates in their area: 'I don't think I could pick her out in a crowd. Everything is dealt with through the factor who lives on the east coast and is very hands off' (Aultbea crofter, 40–50). Communities tend to have little influence over land management, although this is not usually contentious, but rather, accepted as the norm. In contrast, advocating for community land ownership can be sensitive, as I noted in Chapter 6 related to competing crofting and community visions for land. Nonetheless, there are examples of community ownership in Achmore, Applecross, Aultbea, Coigach, Gairloch, Isle Martin and Kyle of Lochalsh. Some ownership originates in the 1990s; the chairperson of Fernaig Community Trust told me their buy-out in Achmore is 'very small by national standards' but still able to provide immediate benefits to people locally in terms of access to land for agricultural activities, and recreational benefits. Additionally, Isle Martin is a community-owned island which was gifted to the community from the Royal Society for the Protection of Birds in 1999, and is managed today for natural and cultural heritage, education and recreation and sustainable economic activity. More recently, Coigach Community Development Company purchased Badentarbet estate with help from the hedge fund millionaire Ian Wace. I conclude the chapter with the case of Applecross, to illustrate tensions around land governance in the BR and the role of land in supporting sustainable rural communities.

Applecross: A' Chomraich/*The Sanctuary*

Applecross, located in the southern part of Wester Ross BR, is a peninsula with a collection of villages that are home to around 200 residents. The population has declined over time, and an *Economist* article in May 2025 discusses the threat of further depopulation linked to a lack of land for housing. The Applecross Trust currently owns 95 per cent of the peninsula (see Figure 10.1).[16] The history of the Applecross Estate is detailed in Applecross Heritage Centre. The estate was owned by the Mackenzies for 300 years until 1855 when it was sold to the Duke of Leeds and upon his death, sold in 1861 to Lord Middleton. From 1929 it was owned by the Wills family who had it for three generations starting with Captain Arnold Stancomb Wills, who was succeeded by his son and grandson. The Wills family are beneficiaries of slavery-produced tobacco.[17] The estate was put into a charitable trust in 1975 and is managed today for conservation of archaeological heritage and environment, sporting and woodland restoration. The Trust own holiday cottages and residential properties and are the landlord for twenty crofting townships.

Estate governance has been a key source of tension, linked to a lack of community representation on the Trust's board. The trustees are a small group of individuals, none of whom live in Applecross.

Figure 10.1 Map of Applecross Estate. © OS Base Map, estate boundary data Andy Wightman.

The chairperson Keith, based in Edinburgh, has been involved in the estate for over forty-five years, acting previously as the Wills's solicitor. He helped to set up the Trust to take over ownership from the family. In 2012 a land reform campaign led by Andy Wightman targeted the Trust, branding it as a 'nepotistic clique' and calling for democratisation. Keith felt this was based on the 'misconception' that someone was owning 68,000 acres of land and 'not engaging'. He explained that the Wills family have completely moved out, the Trust is 'trying to modernise', and that trustees do not 'take anything out of the Trust' financially. Rather, they are on the board because 'we think that the preservation of the traditional way of life is worthwhile'. According to most locals the land action campaign had not helped relations with the estate, and may even have set them back, and there was frustration that it was directed from outside of the area. However, describing the Trust one local resident told me it was 'very much a fiefdom … owned by King Richard as we called him'. Local sentiment was often thus in line with the land action campaign, challenging the lack of local representation in Trust governance. Another local resident argued, 'there needs to be more transparency and local control'. They felt the Trust was out of step with Scottish Government and SLC advice on the importance of communities having influence over land in their local area. Whilst locals are sometimes invited to listen in on board meetings, this feels like 'lip service' with 'local governance missing'. Some felt that community representatives would help to build 'local knowledge' and 'awareness of community issues' into Trust governance. One resident who had attended a Trust board meeting described it as 'embarrassing' how little trustees 'understand or know about anything in Applecross'. They explained, 'their local knowledge is shocking, because it seems one of the only prerequisites of being a trustee is that you don't live here'.

A resident born and raised in Applecross also reported how Trust representatives had been explicit in the view that living locally makes one unsuitable to be a trustee, because of being too 'emotionally' attached to the place. They felt this akin to a colonial mindset: 'the natives cannot be trusted'. Some locally perceived the reluctance to allow communities more control over land as tied to a fear that it will encourage changes which threaten the 'character' of the area. When locals have asked the Trust to define this character, answers have been vague. I asked Keith about the special character of Applecross and he said:

> You'll know it when you see it. It brings people in time and time again, because there are just sort of intangibles there. It's the, well the old family used to call it the wilderness and the wilderness is not dead, it's an ecosystem which is unique.

These conceptualisations are also part of the Trust's website description of Applecross as a 'haven' away from the 'bustle and noise that many people experience on a day-to-day basis'. Drawing on the Gaelic name,

A' Chomraich (the Sanctuary), the Trust seems to define the character of Applecross through the tourist gaze as a wilderness rather than as a living, working community. This is also in line with the presence of an Applecross Wild Land Area that covers most of the estate. Locals not only resist these narratives but see them as a threat to much needed local development, without which 'the community will not survive'. According to Keith, the estate is managed for the benefit of the public:

> The Trust is quite different from private ownership, in that we're a mini sort of national trust. We are there for the public benefit, rather than for the benefit of the community. We take actually nothing out of it ourselves. It's all, for the benefit of the wider public, otherwise known as tourists. [laughs]

This approach was seen as problematic for some local residents. As one explained, the Trust seeing itself as a 'quasi-national park' serving the public rather than residents, 'is the worst of all worlds, because under a benevolent laird, you at least get some of the scraps, you know, the benefits of hanging onto someone's coattails whose got shitloads of money'. The idea of the Trust as a charity preserving wildness and supporting tourism can make residents involved in community development nervous given the implications for fragile local infrastructures.

Despite ongoing tensions, both Keith and local residents have described relations as improving over time. Part of the process of relationship building recently has been facilitated discussion through a new Applecross forum. The forum created space for dialogue where there was none before and for Keith, relations have been 'transformed completely'. However, for him, the main catalyst was:

> the removal of the family with their sort of traditional landowner aura about them. I mean they were actually quite benevolent, but the locals didn't perceive that and I'm not certain that they [the family] actually understood what the locals' life was like.

Some agreed the removal of the Wills family did help disrupt local deference to landowner authority. For example, with 'King Richard' gone a 'window of opportunity' has opened for people whose families were tenant crofters under the Wills. These people who are 'indigenous' to Applecross will not feel deference towards the new laird, because 'no one's even met him'. However, some challenged the sense in which a 'traditional landowner aura' has been removed, with attitudes in the Trust branded by some as sexist, classist and feudal. Such attitudes are a barrier to meaningful partnership working between lairds and communities.[18]

Local residents involved in development for the benefit of communities have found the Trust's discourse of supporting a 'sustainable community' as only occurring on 'their own terms'. I was told the Trust want to retain 'their current power over the community'. This power seemed both material and immaterial not only around ownership of land and housing, but through normalisation of inequalities. A local resident explained that different segments of the community either challenge or support the status quo and the Trust, based on their economic situation. There is argued to be a 'clear split' in the community between the haves and the have nots. A community of older residents, largely retired who own their crofts and houses, have little issue with the Trust, who they associate with acts of 'estate benevolence'.[19] For instance, free firewood is a sign that the Trust is 'good to us'. In contrast, some are struggling with housing, or unable to access land, which means 'the landowner can seem very overpowering, and non-engaging'. This often refers to younger people with little security of tenure or employment who seek change, but are simultaneously too precarious to challenge the Trust directly. Finally, there is a large portion of people 'in the middle' who are against change, either because they support the status quo, or are simply uninterested, or dislike the people that want change.

A key actor aiming to reconfigure relations around land for more just futures is Applecross Community Company (ACC), which works for all in the community, but emphasises local development. Their Action Plan for 2020–5 states a vision for the 'small (but amazing) community of Applecross to be sustainable, resilient and prosperous'. ACC staff and trustees often felt frustrated by the lack of opportunities for development to support community viability and self-sufficiency. This includes difficulties in working with the Trust, acquiring Trust land, and lack of public infrastructures. Despite many challenges, the company has managed to purchase land through the support of the Scottish Land Fund to deliver their strategic priorities and community land use plan. Some of ACC's work has been contingent on whether the Trust will engage and sell land for development. The Trust were often reluctant, with buyouts on their terms and certain sites off limits. It has been easier for ACC to take on public assets from Highland Council and land from NHS Highland. ACC currently owns land and manages assets including local broadband, a fuel station, public toilets, an affordable housing development, a site for housing and business units, a community woodland, allotments and a community garden and a community hydro scheme. As mentioned in Chapter 2, the community has taken on the responsibility to meet local needs, and collective ownership of assets is seen as vital for the community 'to develop and become stronger and viable in the future' (Development Officer). Community land ownership is seen as holding potential for 'tackling the climate emergency' and becoming 'self-sufficient', such as how local food growing can address overreliance on external food sources (see also Chapter 8). Regarding woodlands, community ownership was seen as giving locals and future generations 'permanent control of decision making about the woodland and the benefits derived from it' (Development Officer).

Compared to other parts of Wester Ross, Applecross can seem like an extremely active community and ACC staff described feeling 'very lucky' to have paid development officers to advance their work and navigate the complexity of land and asset purchases. For local communities in Wester Ross, land reform and community empowerment processes can feel bureaucratic and complex to navigate. Significant time and resources are required and the onus is on community organisations to initiate and sustain community assets over the long term. Whilst on the one hand community land ownership is an alternative to neoliberal property norms, there is also a sense in which communities taking on such responsibility is part of the wider turn in neoliberal governance through community. Neoliberal capitalism has created uneven development and left some local places lacking in public services and resources to meet their needs; meanwhile large private landowners have a monopoly on land.

CONCLUSION

The politics of land use and ownership in Wester Ross BR are complex given the diversity of uses and owners alongside the emotive and visceral nature of issues facing local communities. Much of the BR is managed by absentee land owners and decisions are made without community involvement. Moreover, there is no system for making landowners accountable for their sustainability or lack of it. WRB actors convey the need for change, but what this looks like in practice is yet to be determined. As a UNESCO BR, some actors see the need for caution given the political nature of land, but WRB can and should play a role in advancing sustainable land management. Elsewhere in Europe this has involved the process of facilitating a network of landowners for sustainable landscape stewardship. Were similar approaches taken in Wester Ross, this would demonstrate the value of the BR as an alternative to hegemonic models for regional land management. It would help to bring together landowners for whom community, heritage and sustainability are already of importance and build momentum around existing good practice.

Globally many community actors are defending and reinventing the commons, and this is relevant to some communities across the BR, especially in places like Applecross. WRB could also strengthen their role by supporting such local communities to take on land ownership and assets where there is a desire to do so, facilitating dialogue between landowners and local actors. However, the case of Applecross shows the challenges of engaging with private owners who often hold different views about who land is managed for. A focus on wildness and tourism, for example, is at odds with the needs of local communities to sustain a viable population. Wester Ross on the whole faces these challenging conditions and large scale private land ownership is limiting the possibilities for more sustainable communities in the BR.

NOTES

1. Patrick Meyfroidt et al., 'Ten Facts about Land Systems for Sustainability,' *Proceedings of the National Academy of Sciences* 119, no. 7 (2022): e2109217118.
2. Wendy W. Wolford et al., 'Global Land Deals: What Has Been Done, What Has Changed, and What's Next?,' *Journal of Peasant Studies* 0, no. 0 (2024): 1–38.
3. Michael Albertus, *Land Power: Who Has It, Who Doesn't and How That Determines the Fate of Societies* (Basic Books, 2025).
4. Silvia Federici, *Re-enchanting the World: Feminism and the Politics of the Commons* (PM Press, 2018).
5. Andrea Ross, 'The Evolution of Sustainable Development in Scotland – A Case Study of Community Right-to-Buy Law and Policy 2003–2018,' *Sustainability* 11, no. 1 (2019): 1–18.
6. 'Community Ownership,' Scottish Land Commission (2022), https://www.landcommission.gov.scot/our-work/ownership/community-ownership.
7. 'Community Ownership in Scotland 2022,' Scottish Government (2023), https://www.gov.scot/publications/community-ownership-in-scotland-2022/.
8. Carey Doyle, 'Rethinking Communities, Land and Governance: Land Reform in Scotland and the Community Ownership Model,' *Planning Theory and Practice* 24, no. 3 (2023): 429–41; Fiona Mackenzie, *Places of Possibility: Property, Nature and Community Land Ownership* (John Wiley Sons, 2013).
9. Mackenzie, *Places of Possibility*.
10. Iain MacKinnon and Andrew Mackillop, 'Plantation Slavery and Landownership in the West Highlands and Islands: Legacies and Lessons,' *Community Land Scotland* (2020), https://www.communitylandscotland.

org.uk/wp-content/uploads/2020/11/Plantation-slavery-and-landownership-in-the-west-Highlands-and-Islands-legacies-and-lessons.pdf.

11. MacKinnon and Mackillop, 'Plantation Slavery and Landownership.'
12. Annie J. McKee, 'Legitimising the Laird? Communicative Action and the Role of Private Landowner and Community Engagement in Rural Sustainability,' *Journal of Rural Studies* 41 (October 2015): 27.
13. Klara J. Winkler and Jennifer Hauck, 'Landscape Stewardship for a German UNESCO Biosphere Reserve: A Network Approach to Establishing Stewardship Governance,' *Ecology and Society* 24, no. 3 (2019): 3.
14. 'Scotland's Third Land Use Strategy 2021–2026. Getting the Best from our Land,' Scottish Government, 2021, https://www.gov.scot/publications/scotlands-third-land-use-strategy-2021-2026-getting-best-land/pages/4/.
15. Mark Reed et al., 'Land Use Partnerships Using a National Capital Approach: Lessons for Scotland,' 2022, http://dx.doi.org/10.7488/era/2229.
16. Economist, 'Scotland's outdated land laws threaten the future of rural towns,' *The Economist*, May 2025 (last accessed 4 September 2025), https://www.economist.com/britain/2025/05/01/scotlands-outdated-land-laws-threaten-the-future-of-rural-towns.
17. MacKinnon and Mackillop, 'Plantation Slavery and Landownership.'
18. McKee, 'Legitimising the Laird?'
19. McKee, 'Legitimising the Laird?'

11

Alternatives for Just and Sustainable Futures

I argued in Chapter 1 that more just and sustainable futures require us to move beyond common-sense hegemonic discourses and practices rooted in neoliberal capitalism, colonialism and a nature–culture dichotomy. One way of doing this is to recognise that 'there are many alternatives'[1] for development and diverse nature–culture relations. This chapter synthesises ideas from previous chapters to theorise WRB as an alternative through the lens of hegemonic and non-hegemonic politics, following my 'both/and' perspective.[2] I start by treating WRB as an example of community governance and collective action. Community governance involves transformations from the bottom up, addressing structural and systemic sustainability challenges through 'horizontal relations in place' that are bound up in global relations.[3] Community initiatives can invoke 'additional, substitute or oppositional' alternatives and I map WRB against this typology.[4] This helps to explain how a community Biosphere can reproduce, work alongside or challenge the status quo of hegemonic relations. Thereafter I shift to a non-hegemonic lens, using assemblage thinking and anarchism to theorise WRB's horizontal relations and prefigurative politics. I then consolidate my arguments around biocultural heritage which I have referenced throughout the book as an inspiration for alternative nature–culture relations. Finally, I theorise WRB in relation to planetary thinking as an alternative to the hegemony of the Anthropocene. The chapter shows the complexity, relationality and multiplicity of WRB and situates the unique case of a community Biosphere in the Scottish Highlands in wider global agendas for more just and sustainable futures.

THE MANY ALTERNATIVES OF A COMMUNITY BIOSPHERE

BRs can adopt approaches that are top-down, multi-stakeholder or community-led.[5] As an entirely community-led BR, WRB is fairly unique in the World Network and certainly in the UK. What community participation means for BRs led by government (such as the Isle of Man) is quite different from that of a community Biosphere like WRB. Indeed, some BR managers do not always see the direct relationship between community participation and sustainable development,[6] whereas for WRB these are inseparable. Globally, community participation is also more highly valued in Latin American BRs compared to North America and Europe and in more populated regions.[7] WRB contradicts this wider trend from a sparsely populated rural region of Scotland. Given the centrality of community to WRB it makes sense to theorise the model as an example of community governance.

Additional, substitute and oppositional

Across the book I introduced WRB discourses and practices that challenge and reproduce common sense. WRB cannot be treated as a singular, unified alternative given its hybridity as a community-led UNESCO designation. WRB produces many alternatives, some more radical than others. This can be explained in relation to the 'alternative economic and political spaces created by community initiatives'.[8] Alternatives can be 'additional', 'substitute' or 'oppositional'. The additional-alternative denotes activities that exist alongside and do not threaten hegemonic institutions. The substitute-alternative replaces established relations, especially when the hegemonic has failed to provide for specific groups. Finally, the oppositional-alternative challenges the hegemonic with 'defiant intent'.[9] WRB has embodied all three in different ways.

In the first instance, I would argue BR designation is an 'additional-alternative' because it is layered on top of hegemonic conservation logics and can be a 'cherry on top' that legitimises the status quo.[10] The BR zoning in Wester Ross for example adopted a hegemonic narrative of core areas as 'remote' and 'wild' – although importantly this did not create any new exclusions of people from nature as has occurred elsewhere (Chapter 2). The substitute-alternative then comes to the fore when the BR is constructed by local actors as a replacement for the hegemonic conservation that has come before in Wester Ross. Thereafter, the creation of a community Biosphere organisation embodies the oppositional-alternative challenging the hegemony of the nature–culture dichotomy and centring people and culture in community-led, place-based governance (Chapters 2, 3, 4 and 5). WRB as an actor does not reproduce the Myth of the Highlands, but instead advocates for tackling regional unsustainability and sees the region holistically (see Chapter 4), unlike BRs that only focus on conservation of core areas. As such, WRB is also an example of shifting from mainstream conservation's focus on the 'spectacular' towards convivial conservation's focus on everyday environmentalisms and celebrating rather than 'saving' nature.[11] Whilst some locals do interpret the BR designation more narrowly as a mechanism for environmental protection (Chapter 2), WRB's focus on regional development and livelihoods is clear (Chapters 4 and 8). As a substitute and oppositional alternative, WRB move beyond the protected area model towards convivial conservation's 'promoted area' – places where people are welcome and the focus is on building long-lasting relationships between humans and non-humans/ecologies[12] (see Chapters 2 and 5). WRB also challenge the Myth of the Highlands by emphasising that the BR must be sustained as a living and working area and by recognising that landscapes have always been shaped by people and culture. WRB actors also rarely emphasise 'privatised expert technocracy' in the BR, but instead advance 'common democratic engagement' – prioritising the views of local residents in decision-making whilst seeking to build regional collaboration (Chapters 2, 3, 4, 5 and 9).

Additional-alternatives seem most relevant when WRB reproduce hegemonic approaches to sustainable development. For example, translating global agendas into local practice through the SDGs without critically questioning the legitimacy of a goal supporting continued economic growth (Chapter 8). Here WRB has aligned with Scottish Government who similarly support and translate the SDGs into the Scottish context. This is problematic if we accept the argument that BRs must go beyond mainstream sustainable development towards alternatives, such as regenerative development (Chapter 4) and biocultural heritage (Chapter 6). Such alternatives do seem to align with much of WRB's approach to sustainability issues in the BR, which besides the SDGs, has embodied more of the substitute or oppositional alternative. For example, WRB challenges the hegemony of unsustainable tourism through narratives like 'good places to visit must first be good places to live' (Chapter 3). This goes against neoliberal narratives about growing the tourist economy and leads to alternative place trajectories for regional sustainability that prioritise the needs of local communities and BR landscapes. WRB place-making also problematises structural conditions not of their own making as barriers to sustainable tourism (Chapter 3) and sustainable land management (Chapter 10). WRB seem to defiantly challenge the global capitalist food system when they advocate for local systems that value small-scale agriculture and cultural heritage practices for sustainable livelihoods (Chapters 3, 5 and 8). Perhaps most significant, though, is how WRB embody the oppositional alternative by resisting the hegemonic separation of nature and culture (Chapters 2 and 4). WRB is a great example of a biocultural model although they themselves do not use the language. I return to this below.

The biocultural lens includes drawing attention to the loss of culturally specific nature–cultures (Chapter 5) including Gaelic (Chapter 7). The focus on everyday heritages in the BR that are at risk of being lost, such as local cultural knowledges, skills and practices (Chapters 5, 6 and 7) helps to broaden the scope of heritage. In seeking to manage change and respond to such loss, we see the substitute-alternative where WRB projects step in to conserve heritages that are not well served by hegemonic heritage conservation policy and practice in Scotland. Where WRB could be more oppositional is in challenging the processes through which local communities are excluded from decisions about conserving their own heritage and where heritage-making is driven by external actors and purposes. Substitute-alternatives also arise in Wester Ross in spaces of state or market failure where community groups alongside WRB step in as service deliverers to meet local or regional needs. For WRB, this has been about forming a community-led tourism partnership (Chapter 3); engaging in Gaelic development work (Chapter 7); advocating for a regional sustainable development plan and a local food hub (Chapter 8). For other groups in Wester Ross this tends to be about managing assets for the benefit of local people as a way to maintain living, working communities (Chapters 3, 9 and 10). These examples often reflect that as a sparsely populated 'remote' rural region, the BR is not prioritised by hegemonic actors (Chapters 8 and 9) and national agendas are rarely tailored to conditions in rural communities (Chapter 4).

Each example I would argue is a case of communities responding to the outcomes of uneven capitalist development. There is a perceived necessity to act, that embodies mutual aid – collective action beyond the state for the benefit of local economies and communities.[13] Anarchists argue that working beyond the state is desirable and indeed Phoebe suggested that for WRB this meant more freedom (Chapter 8). However, community action is nonetheless mired in complex local politics that can make it challenging to define and act for common interests (Chapters 3, 10). Additionally, concerns about lack of capacity and expertise in communities are part of wider narratives that state actors should still hold responsibilities rather than placing the burden fully onto communities (Chapter 9).

As a UNESCO BR, WRB construct an organisational identity around neutrality and inclusivity which shapes how alternatives are negotiated and produced. As such, some oppositional-alternatives that defiantly challenge hegemony are conveyed only implicitly or by individual actors and not part of the BR's organisational identity. For example, Coinneach uses explicit discourses of colonialism when speaking of national parks, Gaelic and community-land relationships (Chapters 7, 9 and 10), but this is not reflected in WRB organisational discourse. Similarly, Norman is critical of how crofts and land in the BR are treated as commodities to be bought and sold (Chapter 6), and Michael and Robert advocate strong action on landownership (Chapter 10). However, as a collective under the banner of UNESCO, WRB tends to be more cautious about how to approach political and contentious issues in practice. How and whether to act is a source of ongoing deliberation and WRB alternatives are a product of changing internal social relations and wider regional, national and international contexts. Whilst WRB have been challenging capitalist relations from my perspective, it is important to note the organisation has never self-identified as anti-capitalist. WRB is not a campaign group but rather a mechanism to facilitate processes of change and they rarely try to define the outcomes of such change (Chapters 2, 4 and 9). Instead WRB is open to multiple possibilities and alternatives that arise from collaborative working across sectors and actors, albeit always prioritising communities.

The many alternatives of WRB should help us to think more critically about BRs as part of a global sustainability agenda. It would be useful to examine more contexts to see how BRs globally reproduce, replace or challenge hegemonic nature–culture relations. This would offer a critical assessment of the value of different BR governance models as a means of producing specific kinds of sustainability transitions, whether business as usual, or representing socioecological transformations beyond common sense.

Prefiguring utopias

I turn now to theorising WRB in relation to non-hegemonic politics using assemblage theory and anarchism. WRB as an organisation is held together through social relations among community members working collectively for the benefit of their region under the UNESCO remit (Chapter 2). As an assemblage, WRB is a rhizome but it is a hybridisation of local community activism with UNESCO. In UNESCO World Heritage settings, usually UNESCO is associated with arborescent assemblages which conflict with rhizomic community activism. When arborescent and rhizome (UNESCO and community) meet, the power of the latter can be co-opted into rigid forms of co-management that are globally promoted yet locally inappropriate.[14] The 'creative friction' between UNESCO World Heritage and indigenous ontologies has encouraged a rethinking of heritage through dialogical, relational models.[15] In the same way, the community Biosphere pushes towards more dialogical and relational models of sustainability and non-hierarchal nature–culture relations. WRB as a rhizome is always in a state of becoming, and has a non-hierarchical form with elements that link 'horizontally on an equal footing'.[16] This is reflected in organisational decision-making, governance and in the relationality and multiplicity of nature–culture. WRB being like a spider's web (Chapter 9) captures the sense of the BR as opening up 'infinite possible trajectories' but which remain interwoven.[17]

I would also theorise WRB in relation to anarchist praxis, another form of non-hegemonic politics for alternative futures. For anarchists, new societies are built 'in the shell of the old'[18] through prefiguration: 'the deliberate experimental implementation of desired future social relations and practices in the here and now to create alternatives in the here and now'.[19] This kind of utopian politics involves direct action, horizontal decision-making[20] and 'inclusive and equitable forms of organisation' or 'social relations without coercion'.[21] This is because means are equal to ends; hierarchical means create hierarchical ends. WRB practises prefiguration through their process-driven approach to sustainability. The focus is not on a specific outcome and how to implement it by any means, but rather an inclusive process for building sustainable futures collaboratively without relations of domination or coercion. This is especially important for local communities who must be directly involved in decision-making and practices producing alternatives in the here and now. I see this ethos arising in both the smallest ideas such as community photographic archives (Chapter 5) and in larger efforts of regional collaboration to tackle unsustainable tourism (Chapter 3).

However, WRB could embrace a prefigurative approach to social change in other contexts. Rather than relying on external powers and national legislative action, WRB could help to create alternative political structures in the here and now for crofting and land management (Chapters 6 and 10). Adopting a prefigurative approach makes sense given the challenges WRB have had working with state actors (Chapters 3, 8 and 9). It opens up a new avenue for BR as an actor for advancing sustainability by working within, beyond or against the state. WRB as a BR might move beyond mainstream sustainable development towards prefiguring utopias. Namely, creating 'desired alternatives or utopian visions for a fairer, freer and more sustainably-balanced world through the actions, practices and social relationships they build in the here and now'.[22]

Utopianism helps to resist the idea that rigid blueprints, like the SDGs, must be implemented top down as the only 'realistic' action on sustainability challenges.[23] Utopian thinking offers an open and emancipatory approach to the future, where sustainability is an orientation or mentality. Rather than asking 'what works', utopias challenge common sense and the world as we know it.[24] This already aligns with WRB's approach to sustainability (Chapters 2 and 9) and utopian thinking brings out further radical potential. Rather than seeing BRs as learning places for sustainable development, we could consider them as places for prefiguring sustainability utopias. Utopianism is already part of thinking about the future of rural Scotland, with the idea of a 'Good Countryside' challenging the hegemony of a backward looking and middle-class 'rural idyll'.[25] Utopianism goes hand in hand with notions of networked rural development creating 'possibilities for social actors to collectively and deliberatively imagine their future and the future of their places'.[26] Whilst such thinking is already part of how WRB approach placemaking and rural development in the BR (Chapters 3, 4, 5 and 8), enacting this in practice is limited by regional spatial injustice – the lack of ability to collectively self-determine sustainable futures.

Biocultural heritage

A biocultural approach is central to WRB as an alternative to commonsense nature–culture relations. Throughout the book, I highlighted biocultural heritage (BCH) as part of the implicit and explicit approach of WRB actors. In academic research, BCH is constituted by five elements: ecosystem memories, landscape memories, place-based memories, integrated landscapes analysis and stewardship and change.[27] Alternatively as a decolonial model, the International Institute of Environment and Development BCH framework positions resilient livelihoods as a product of interactions between biodiversity, traditional knowledge, customary laws, cultural and spiritual values and landscapes.[28] Both models overcome the separation of conservation and development, although the latter is more valuable given its focus on indigenous governance through Biocultural Heritage Territories (BCHTs). I have used elements of each to make sense of nature–culture relations in Wester Ross, such as in relation to: the integration of natural and cultural heritage (Chapter 4); livelihoods, traditional knowledges and skills (Chapter 5); cultural heritage in the landscape (Chapters 5, 6 and 7); food systems (Chapters 6 and 8) and conservation (Chapter 9). WRB's Gaelic work was designed with BCH in mind, with Gaelic placenames and *dùthchas* presenting the important connections between cultural and biological diversity as part of culturally specific relations to place. In Portuguese BRs, BCH contributes to environmental governance rooted in lived experience.[29] I see WRB's approach similarly; centring communities and their heritage as part of sustainability action beyond the nature–culture dichotomy.

However, in Scotland, and indeed globally, BCH is marginalised in mainstream sustainability policies and practices shaped by commonsense hegemonic capitalist and colonial ideologies. Part of the problem is the perception of BCH as applying only to specific indigenous groups or cultural practices, rather than being seen as relevant to all societies.[30] By outlining WRB's approach in the Scottish Highlands, I highlighted the relevance of BCH not only for specific issues such as Gaelic and crofting, but as a wider lens for nature–culture relations in a context of declining biocultural diversity. Another part of the problem is the siloed nature of policies, for example how Gaelic and crofting are treated largely as separate – linguistic and agricultural – issues. Separate national bodies are set up to manage these alongside separate bodies for development (Highlands and Islands Enterprise), nature conservation (NatureScot) and cultural heritage conservation (Historic Environment Scotland). Working beyond such siloes is important not only in Scotland, but in the UK and globally. Such thinking is already present in the Highlands and Islands where it is argued, for example, that Gaelic should exist alongside other natural and cultural assets and inform decision-making, land management and economic development.[31] WRB as a community Biosphere can deliver this kind of approach, and thinking with BCH is one way to do so.

To further evidence the value of BCH as an approach to nature–culture relations in the Scottish Highlands, I propose an adapted BCH framework which is also relevant to the UK as a whole (see Figure 11.1). This should help to map the condition of BCH as a whole and its components in specific contexts and at different scales. Alongside it, Figure 11.2 conveys that actions around BCH will occur on a spectrum in Wester Ross and beyond. For example, different practices, knowledges and relations in different places will be shaped by differing degrees of loss.

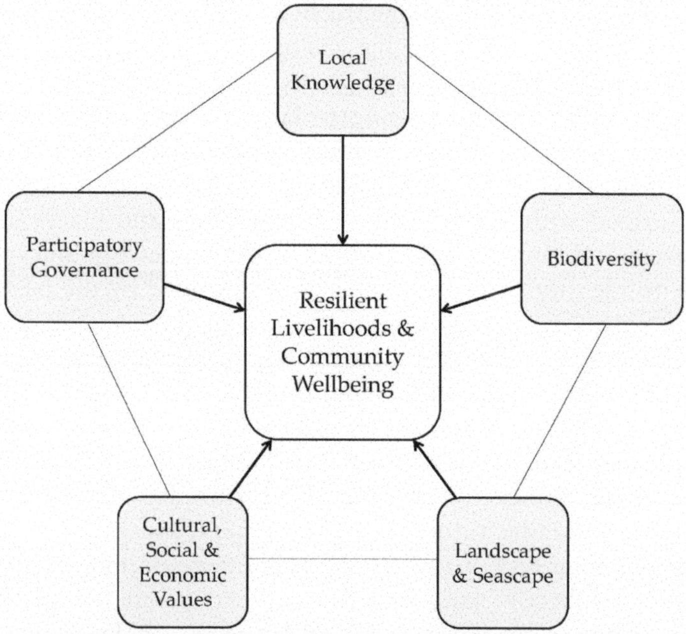

Figure 11.1 Biocultural heritage framework, adapted from Swiderska and Argumedo 2017 by author.

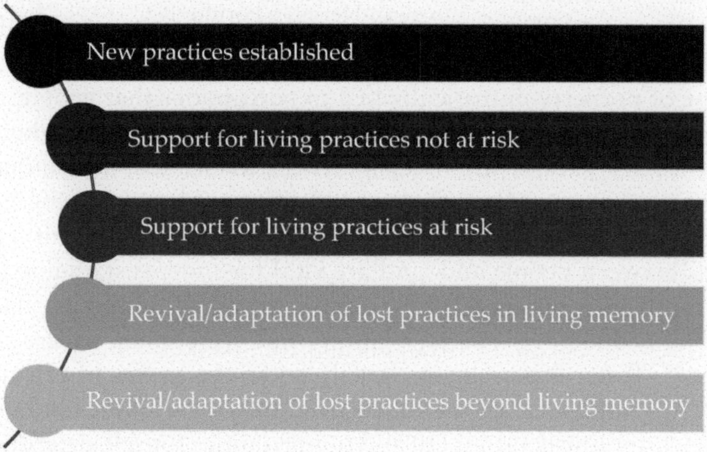

Figure 11.2 Biocultural heritage spectrum.

As such, what it means to safeguard BCH will differ, invoking diverse actions for adaptation, managing change and revival. For example, cultural practices like dyeing with plants, use of seaweed as a fertiliser, droving and thatching, or relating to land through *dùthchas* may be lost in some communities and thriving in others. Importantly, there is scope to create new BCH, recognising that unsustainable relations must be transformed with alternatives as communities and places adapt to meet current and future needs. Ultimately, the framework and spectrum are tools to identify BCH and take action informed by the past, in the present, for the future. WRB could use them as part of funding proposals to emphasise where projects contribute to specific elements of BCH and/or respond to significant loss and threatened heritages.

BCHTs can also act as sources of inspiration for WRB and BRs generally. As models of governance, they offer learning about how communities can engage in collective action, which is needed in Wester Ross to create more sustainable futures in crofting, food, conservation and land in the BR (Chapter 6, 8, 9 and 10). BCHTs offer a decolonial approach, strengthening collective land rights in contexts where colonialism and capitalism threaten the livelihoods and heritage of indigenous peoples. Therein, land stewardship shaped by BCH is about 'collective, rather than individual rights, within a framework of heritage, rather than property'.[32] This speaks directly to *dùthchas* which although eroded over time,[33] is experiencing a revival and is part of how people in Wester Ross and WRB frame relations with each other and with land (Chapter 7). *Dùthchas* is already shaped by a heritage sensibility rather than one of property, historically tied to perceptions that people are not owners of land, but are part of it. BCHTs provide examples where such mentalities are part of the living practices associated with indigenous sovereignty. Learning from them could offer insights to strengthen the practice of collective claims to land. Systems based on deep cultural connections between people and land are vital for more sustainable futures in the Scottish Highlands. Whilst community land ownership has been disrupting neoliberal property relations and overcoming nature–culture binaries,[34] Wester Ross remains largely under the power of private land owners. Communities are excluded from decisions about land and the region lacks political autonomy and opportunities for self-determination (Chapters 2, 3 and 10). BCHTs as models for self-determination could inspire new thinking about land futures in Scotland. WRB and other BRs in the World Network could engage in knowledge exchange with local communities and indigenous peoples managing BCHTs. Alongside learning about participatory governance, this would bring to the fore learning on community adaptations to challenging environmental, social and political conditions: from climate change to the devaluing of small-scale agriculture and extractive, colonial conservation models.[35] WRB are already learning from other BRs in the Global North, and a move towards BCH could lead to new relationships with indigenous communities globally, both within and beyond the MAB programme.

Planetary thinking

Multi-scalar relations are at the heart of WRB, part of the multiplicity and complexity of BRs as adapting to specific local, regional, national and global contexts. I explained how WRB discourses and practices are shaped by the local–global nexus; a community Biosphere in a World Network with responsibility to address both regional and global sustainability challenges (Chapter 8). Additionally, I outlined how the MAB programme was acting as a mechanism for building relations of solidarity between BRs in the World Network. Whilst I cannot speak to MAB as a whole, I argued there was an ethos of 'unity-in-diversity'[36] in WRB's relations with other BRs. Arguably, this ethos is an important aspect of recognising that development is context dependent.[37] WRB actors take local knowledge, practices and values seriously as part of their understandings of what development means for Wester Ross (Chapters 5 and 7). However, whether unity-in-diversity would also apply to global North–South relations remains unclear. So far, WRB has largely only created relations of solidarity with other actors in the Global North, despite desire to take global responsibility and be international in outlook.

From the perspective of post-colonialism, I would argue BRs are places to reject the universal planetary sameness embodied in the concept of the Anthropocene and engage in 'planetary thinking', which, like unity-in-diversity, is about acknowledging and embracing difference.[38] This is important because the Anthropocene is a colonial discourse that places the blame for current global sustainability crises on humanity as a whole, failing to distinguish nature–culture relations based in reciprocity, and those which are colonial interventions.[39] Moreover, the Anthropocene concept erases the historical and contemporary experience of most of the world's inhabitants.[40] Diverse peoples and their relationships with nature are 'othered' in the Anthropocene 'master narrative'.[41] I would consider this to include the Gaelic ontologies and cultural practices of local people in Wester Ross. As an alternative to the Anthropocene, planetary thinking, such as Spivak's concept of 'planetarity', opens up space to know the world from categories outside of western thought and acknowledge difference without otherness.[42] The African concept of Ubuntu for instance is a relational understanding of humanity as affirmed through relatedness to human and non-human others. Here, there are parallels in Gaelic and *dùthchas*.[43] Planetary thinking in BRs is therefore about identifying local and regionally specific ways of knowing and embracing difference within and across BRs in the World Network. There are currently 759 BRs globally, with huge potential to showcase and strengthen alternative ways of knowing the world and to embrace planetary diversity.

At present the Anthropocene concept is often drawn on uncritically; it is said that BRs have a role to play in addressing the 'challenges of the Anthropocene'.[44] Over time, MAB has institutionalised the Anthropocene narrative alongside its conservation and sustainable development logics, albeit in disjointed ways.[45] However, I would argue for reframing BRs as places to destabilise the hegemony and colonialism of the Anthropocene master narrative. We must also consider how individual BRs, and MAB as a whole, reproduce or challenge relations of colonial modernity in sustainability transitions.[46] For Wester Ross, this requires further analysis of contemporary industries and modes of living, building on existing knowledge of how the region and its communities were affected by, and implicated in, colonialism. WRB can play a part by supporting research and broadening their global networks, building solidarities with marginalised indigenous communities.

Finally, MAB embodies a vision for societies living in harmony with nature and some see BR's as places to 'become aware that we are part of a planetary citizenship and a community of life' where 'all beings are connected'.[47] Following anarchist geographer Elisée Reclus, 'unity-in-diversity' requires a planetary consciousness that is not only about interconnection, but moving beyond the domination of all living beings on the planet.[48] Whilst the complex topic of undoing human supremacy[49] has not been discussed in this book, during my research I was part of many conversations about sustainable futures for Wester Ross and Scotland involving human–animal relations. For example, mass culling of deer for conservation is seen by many as necessary and desirable whilst animal agriculture is normalised in everyday life. Hence, to theorise BRs as radical alternatives for more sustainable futures, requires further attention to the domination and exploitation of animals. Domination ideology and the ethos of capital accumulation are fundamental drivers of globally destructive human–animal relations[50] and these must be examined in BRs across the World Network.

CONCLUSION

This chapter has explored the notion of the BR as an alternative for more just and sustainable futures drawing together examples from across the book to theorise WRB through hegemonic and non-hegemonic critical theories. I first argued that WRB produce 'many alternatives' drawing on the typology of additional, substitute or oppositional alternatives in community initiatives. I emphasised that we must think critically about how and whether BRs reproduce or move beyond common sense. Thereafter, I drew on the non-hegemonic politics of assemblages and anarchism to make sense of WRB as an alternative. I argued that WRB are a hybrid rhizome characterised by horizontal and non-hierarchical relations. Moreover, I argued that WRB embodies prefiguration in their process-driven approach to creating alternatives in the here and now through inclusive relations. Embracing this more fully might allow WRB and BRs to move beyond sustainable development towards prefiguring sustainability utopias. Importantly, this helps to transcend the limitations of thinking about 'what works' by allowing for a more open and collective imagining and enacting of utopian futures.

I have also consolidated arguments about WRB's biocultural approach and biocultural heritage. I presented a framework and spectrum to mobilise action in Wester Ross and Scotland alongside encouraging learning from BCHTs as a way of rethinking governance and land futures. I argued that WRB and BRs must contribute to decolonising sustainability by challenging colonial modernity in sustainability transitions. This requires planetary thinking to support alternative ways to know the world and challenge the common sense of the Anthropocene master narrative. In my final chapter, having summarised book themes here, I conclude with two remaining arguments: the necessity of critical, ethnographic approaches to sustainability and the need to value the BR model in Scotland.

NOTES

1. Christa Wichterich, 'Contesting Green Growth: Connecting Care, Commons and Enough,' in *Practising Feminist Political Ecologies: Moving Beyond the Green Economy*, ed. W. Harcourt and I. Nelson (Zed Books, 2015), 83.
2. Mark Purcell, 'Gramsci is Not Dead: For a "Both/And" Approach to Radical Geography,' *ACME: An International E-Journal for Critical Geographies* 11, no. 3 (2012): 512–24.
3. Schmid et al., 'Governing Through Community.'

4. Schmid et al., 'Governing Through Community.'
5. Susanne Stoll-Kleemann, Anne Cristina De La Vega-Leinert and Lisen Schultz, 'The Role of Community Participation in the Effectiveness of UNESCO Biosphere Reserve Management: Evidence and Reflections From Two Parallel Global Surveys,' *Environmental Conservation* 37, no. 3 (2010): 227–38.
6. Stoll-Kleemann et al., 'The Role of Community Participation.'
7. Stoll-Kleemann et al., 'The Role of Community Participation.'
8. Schmid et al., 'Governing Through Community,' 155.
9. Schmid et al., 'Governing Through Community.'
10. Raphaël Mathevet and Catherine Cibien, 'The French Biosphere Reserves: Looking For Ecological Solidarity and Stewardship,' in *UNESCO Biosphere Reserves: Supporting Biocultural Diversity, Sustainability and Society*, ed. M. Reed and M. F. Price (Routledge, 2020), 114–24; Zoe Russell, 'The Isle of Man Biosphere Reserve: An Entire Nation Approach to Sustainable Development,' *Environmental Policy and Planning* 25, no. 3 (2022): 273–86.
11. Bram Büscher and Robert Fletcher, *The Conservation Revolution: Ideas For Saving Nature Beyond the Anthropocene* (Verso, 2020).
12. Büscher and Fletcher, *The Conservation Revolution.*
13. Jeff Shantz, *Commonist Tendencies: Mutual Aid Beyond Communism* (Punctum Books, 2013), 7.
14. Leah S. Horowitz, 'Rhizomic Resistance Meets Arborescent Assemblage: UNESCO World Heritage and the Disempowerment of Indigenous Activism in New Caledonia,' *Annals of the American Association of Geographers* 106, no. 1 (2016): 1.
15. Rodney Harrison, *Heritage: Critical Approaches.*
16. Purcell, 'Gramsci is Not Dead,' 520.
17. Horowitz, 'Rhizomic Resistance.'
18. Anthony Ince, 'In the Shell of the Old: Anarchist Geographies of Territorialisation,' *Antipode* 44, no. 5 (2012): 5.
19. Paul Raekstad and Sofa S. Gradin, *Prefigurative Politics: Building Tomorrow Today* (Polity Press, 2019), 10.
20. Ruth E. Kinna, 'Utopianism and Prefiguration,' in *Political Uses of Utopia: New Marxist, Anarchist, and Radical Democratic Perspectives*, ed. S. Chrostowska and J. Ingram (Columbia University Press, 2016), 198–218.
21. Angela Wigger, 'Anarchism as Emancipatory Theory and Praxis: Implications for Critical Marxist Research,' *Capital and Class*, 40, no. 1 (2016), 135.
22. Anja Habersang, 'Utopia, Future Imaginations and Prefigurative Politics in the Indigenous Women's Movement in Argentina,' *Social Movement Studies* 23, no. 4 (2024): 481.
23. Fabio Rubio Scarano, 'Deep Sustainability Utopia,' in *Regenerative Dialogues for Sustainable Futures* (Springer International Publishing, 2024), 157–63.

24. Scarano, 'Deep Sustainability Utopia.'
25. Mark Shucksmith, 'Re-Imagining the Rural: From Rural Idyll to Good Countryside,' *Journal of Rural Studies* 59 (April 2018): 171.
26. Shucksmith, 'Re-Imagining the Rural.'
27. Karl-Johan Lindholm and Anneli Ekblom, 'A Framework for Exploring and Managing Biocultural Heritage,' *Anthropocene* 25 (March 2019): 1–11.
28. Krystyna Swiderska and Alejandro Argumedo, 'What is Biocultural Heritage?,' *International Institute for Environment and Development*, 2017, https://pubs.iied.org/g04151.
29. Maria F. Rollo, 'Interconnected Nature and People: Biosphere Reserves and the Power of Memory and Oral Histories as Biocultural Heritage for a Sustainable Future,' *Sustainability* 17, no. 9 (2025): 1–33.
30. Michelle L. Cocks, 'Biocultural Diversity: Moving Beyond the Realm of "Indigenous" And "Local" People,' *Human Ecology* 34, no. 2 (2006): 185–200.
31. Gòrdan Camshron, 'Resisting Dismissal in the Gàidhealtachd,' *Scottish Affairs* 30, no. 2 (2021): 244.
32. Krystyna Swiderska, 'Protecting Traditional Knowledge: A Holistic Approach Based on Customary Laws and Bio-Cultural Heritage,' in *Conserving and Valuing Ecosystem Services and Biodiversity: Economic, Institutional and Social Challenges*, ed. K. N. Ninan (Earthscan, 2009), 339.
33. Iain MacKinnon, '"Decommonising the Mind": Historical Impacts of British Imperialism on Indigenous Tenure Systems and Self-Understanding in the Highlands and Islands of Scotland,' *International Journal of the Commons* 12, no. 1 (2018): 278–300.
34. Fiona Mackenzie, *Places of Possibility: Property, Nature and Community Land Ownership* (John Wiley Sons, 2013).
35. T. Garrett Graddy, 'Regarding Biocultural Heritage: In Situ Political Ecology of Agricultural Biodiversity in the Peruvian Andes,' *Agriculture and Human Values* 30, no. 4 (2013): 587–604; Matthew Sayre et al., 'You Can't Grow Potatoes in the Sky: Building Resilience in the Face of Climate Change in the Potato Park of Cuzco, Peru,' *Culture, Agriculture, Food and Environment* 39, no. 2 (2017): 103; Krystyna Swiderska et al., 'Indigenous Peoples' Food Systems and Biocultural Heritage: Addressing Indigenous Priorities Using Decolonial and Interdisciplinary Research Approaches,' *Sustainability* 14, no. 18 (2022): 11311.
36. John Clark, ed., *Anarchy, Geography, Modernity: Selected Writings of Elisée Reclus* (PM Press, 2016).
37. Manuel Peters, 'Culture, Heritage and Solidarity in the Context of Sustainable Development,' in *Perceptions of Sustainability in Heritage Studies*, ed. M. T. Albert (DeGruyter, 2015), 137–44.
38. Cheryl McEwan, 'Decolonizing the Anthropocene,' in *International Relations in the Anthropocene*, ed. David Chandler et al. (Springer International Publishing, 2021).

39. Kyle Whyte, 'Indigenous Climate Change Studies: Indigenizing Futures, Decolonizing the Anthropocene,' *English Language Notes* 55, nos. 1–2 (2017): 153–62.
40. McEwan, 'Decolonizing the Anthropocene.'
41. Stefania Barca, *Forces of Reproduction: Notes for a Counter-hegemonic Anthropocene* (Cambridge University Press, 2020).
42. McEwan, 'Decolonizing the Anthropocene.'
43. Mackenzie, *Places of Possibility*; Paul J. Meighan, 'Dùthchas, a Scottish Gaelic Methodology to Guide Self-Decolonization and Conceptualize a Kincentric and Relational Approach to Community-Led Research,' *International Journal of Qualitative Methods* 21 (2022): 16094069221142451.
44. Susanne Stoll-Kleemann and Tim O'Riordan, 'The Challenges of the Anthropocene for Biosphere Reserves,' *Parks* 23 (March 2017): 93.
45. Desirée Fiske, 'Towards an Anthropocene Narrative and a New Philosophy of Governance: Evolution of Global Environmental Discourse in the Man and the Biosphere Programme,' *Journal of Environmental Policy and Planning* 24, no. 1 (2022): 1.
46. Saurabh Arora and Andy Stirling, 'Colonial Modernity and Sustainability Transitions: A Conceptualisation in Six Dimensions,' *Environmental Innovation and Societal Transitions* 48 (2023): 100733.
47. Tania Moreno-Ramos and Eduard Müller, 'Biosphere Reserves, Ideal Sites to Implement Holistic Approaches in Regenerative Development,' in *UNESCO Biosphere Reserves: Supporting Biocultural Diversity, Sustainability and Society*, ed. M. Reed and M. F. Price (Routledge, 2020), 254–69.
48. Clark, *Anarchy, Geography, Modernity.*
49. Simon Springer et al., *Undoing Human Supremacy: Anarchist Political Ecology in the Face of Anthroparchy* (Rowman & Littlefield, 2021).
50. Diana Stuart and Ryan Gunderson, 'Human–Animal Relations in the Capitalocene: Environmental Impacts and Alternatives,' *Environmental Sociology* 6, no. 1 (2020): 68–81.

12

Conclusion: Moving Beyond Common Sense

THIS BOOK TOLD THE story of a community Biosphere in the North-West Highlands of Scotland from the perspective of critical ethnographic research. It answered four key questions across eleven chapters: first, what does the community Biosphere in Wester Ross mean in discourse and practice according to local actors? Second, how do actors involved in the community Biosphere negotiate nature–culture relations? Third, how are these relations shaped by the politics of scale, governance and land ownership? Finally, to what extent does the community Biosphere represent an alternative for more just and sustainable futures? What the Biosphere means as designation, organisation and place-making is discussed in Chapters 2 and 3. How actors negotiate nature–culture relations in discourse and practice is addressed in Chapters 4, 5, 6 and 7, covering a breadth of issues from regional unsustainability and green jobs to traditional skills and cultural practices, alongside more in-depth discussion of crofting and Gaelic. The politics of scale, governance and landownership are the focus of Chapters 8, 9 and 10, which in turn cover the local–global nexus, nature conservation and land use and ownership in the BR. Chapter 11 synthesised examples from across the book to critically theorise WRB as an alternative for more just and sustainable futures. In this final chapter, I reflect on two themes of the book with theoretical, methodological and practical significance. First, the need for critical approaches to sustainability challenges involving collaboration with communities and second, the need to better value the BR in Scotland. I conclude with a final argument to move beyond the common sense of hegemonic nature–culture relations.

A CRITICAL APPROACH TO SUSTAINABILITY CHALLENGES

Critical theory (encompassing a wide range of approaches) is about analysing the world in accordance with an ontological commitment for 'a more just and egalitarian society'.[1] This requires questioning the world as we know it. Rather than taking the existing social order for granted, we must ask how it came to be as it is and open up possibilities for alternatives in the present and for the future. Using critical theory to study the Wester Ross BR has meant not taking the concept of a Biosphere, of community, heritage or sustainability as given, but unpacking what they mean in discourse and practice. It has meant questioning the conditions surrounding common-sense nature–cultures in Scotland and considering the power relations and scalar politics that are often obscured in mainstream sustainability policies and research. Critical approaches help to situate contemporary relations in historical context and wider capitalist and colonial dynamics. Critical ethnography, following such logics, is not only about what is, but about what could be.[2]

Across the book I used critical theory as a bridge between diverse disciplinary contexts, allowing me to bring together siloed, yet complementary areas of research about: nature and heritage conservation, BRs and the Scottish Highlands. Critical thinkers in each of these areas have drawn attention to the importance of overcoming the nature–culture dichotomy, and adopting decolonial and relational approaches that consider temporalities (pasts, present and futures) and scales (local, regional, national, global). I have drawn on Gramscian, Marxian, anarchist, feminist and postcolonial thinking, and see value in 'both/and'[3] approaches that unite critical theorists and movements in networks of action for societal transformation. Whilst my focus was an ethnographic study of a community sustainability initiative in the Scottish Highlands, I situated this in a wider agenda for more just and sustainable futures globally. This recognises that the Scottish Highlands face the same challenges as other regions in the world, namely, interrelated crises of contemporary capitalism and cultural and ecological loss. There is much to be gained from this cross-world dialogue including the building of global solidarities and collective interests to move beyond the status quo. WRB is a community actor fundamentally shaped by a specific cultural context, but as an example it resonates with multiple community initiatives for sustainability elsewhere. Such initiatives importantly enable us to move beyond neoliberal individualism and embrace how 'collective action and community-led organising can be a powerful tool for achieving transformation'.[4]

This book was a product of a long, slow and critical ethnography, which felt at times to be a process of knowledge generation at odds with the world around me. For example, I have witnessed the unrelenting rise of AI – processing masses of information in an instant – and a recurrent, uncritical emphasis on technologies as the solution to global unsustainability. Ethnographic and critical theory approaches, especially those involving collaboration with communities are not common in mainstream sustainability science or within government agendas but are vital for prefiguring more just and sustainable futures. They not only enable us to account for the complexity of nature–culture relations and do the slow work of building change from the bottom-up, but they help to empower those who are so often the subject, but not the active beneficiaries of research. Whilst attending a Biosphere workshop in Gairloch, Seumas said my involvement with WRB was an exception to many years where Wester Ross and its communities have never directly benefitted from any research carried out there. His comment captures an ongoing problem, that much research is *on* communities rather than *with* them, and is fundamentally extractive.

I sought to use my (limited) power and expertise to support the goals of WRB as an academic activist, and I hope to continue to do this in the future. Currently, however, it seems mainstream sustainability policy and research agendas are not well tailored to allowing for genuine community-led or critical approaches. Instead, hegemonic concepts like natural capital, ecosystem services and net zero are prioritised alongside tokenistic community involvement. There is a need for more meaningful community-led research and a focus on producing contextually and culturally rich knowledge about enacting more sustainable nature–culture relations in practice. I have discussed regional spatial justice for Wester Ross, and there is also a need for research justice. Research justice means transforming structural inequities in research and centring the voices of communities for social change.[5] For Wester Ross BR, research justice would mean the ability to self-determine regional priorities and utilise research in local decision-making and practice. BRs have a remit for education and research, and although I tried to support WRB in this, community-led research is sorely underdeveloped and there are structural inequalities in relationships with universities. Establishing an interdisciplinary community-led research centre is one future possibility for WRB, following in the footsteps of BRs such as Mount Arrowsmith in Canada.[6] Therein students and academics could work productively with communities in Wester Ross and with WRB to produce locally driven, place-based knowledges for sustainability action. However, a key challenge will be funding such collaborations, especially given how universities, including my own, are embarking on renewed programmes of austerity and neoliberal reforms.

VALUING THE COMMUNITY BIOSPHERE

WRB is still building legitimacy among different local, regional and national actors, some of whom do not understand or value the model. Whilst this is true of many BRs globally, I would argue that WRB in particular has been let down by the failure of more powerful Scottish actors to take the BR seriously. Despite supporting nomination to UNESCO, the Scottish Government has not invested in the BR and NatureScot has not taken much interest in the community-led model. Whilst HIE has funded tourism work in the BR, and Highland Council some planning work, the BR region has a scale and population that has been perceived as insignificant. Additionally, HES has had a minimal working relationship with WRB surrounding heritage, meaning there is much scope to improve how the BR is supported to advance a place-based approach to integrating cultural heritage and sustainability.

WRB has been doing amazing things with very little resource, capacity and support. They could do significantly more for sustainability in Scotland with proper resourcing. Whilst WRB are taking this into their own hands by becoming more entrepreneurial, they have been struggling for nearly a decade with financial precarity. This is a failure in Scottish policy and politics to invest in community-driven sustainability transformations. WRB has applied for funding for numerous projects, often to no avail, but continue nonetheless to advance the UNESCO BR remit in whatever way they can, including overcoming the nature–culture dichotomy and advocating for inclusive place-based sustainability governance. WRB could do much more, with financial support and through collaborative relationships with actors across scales to tackle the region's most pressing problems related to communities, land and heritage.

The lack of regional spatial justice in Scotland between our two BRs is also stark. Galloway and Southern Ayrshire BR in the south of the country has been well funded; in contrast, WRB in the Highlands has received only approximately 1 per cent of the funding of their lowland neighbour (see Chapter 8). Financial precarity shows no signs of abating, and in 2025 WRB was forced to launch a crowdfunder to try to raise £59,000 to resolve a cash flow problem to prevent staff redundancies. This came at a time when WRB was entering its ten year periodic review with UNESCO – a process that could secure the designation for the next ten years, or result in the loss of the designation. The same process is underway in the Isle of Man, also designated in 2016, and the government there are supporting the BR to engage in an extensive process of review and strategy building to create a more sustainable future on the island. Meanwhile, WRB reached out to NatureScot, HIE and the Scottish Government to support their periodic review and secure the designation in Wester Ross, but all parties initially declined to help. At the last minute, NatureScot funding was secured, on the premise that Phoebe would produce the periodic review in a three-month window, alongside other deliverables. Whilst better than nothing, as discussed previously, short-term funding does not help to secure the long-term future of WRB. As a highly valuable mechanism to advance new ways of living sustainably and address the twin cultural and ecological crises of the Scottish Highlands, losing this designation would be a huge blow.

As well as support for WRB, UNESCO BRs should be better valued across the UK as a whole. Although the UK BR network is active, with committed BR managers, the designation is not well known or valued in national policy contexts.[7] The UK's seven BRs are less explored in critical social research too, with some exceptions in North Devon BR,[8] Galloway and Southern Ayrshire BR[9] and the Isle of Man BR.[10] By focusing on the UK's only community Biosphere, I offered insights into this governance model specifically and sustainability in the Scottish Highlands. The book thus contains valuable learning about nature–culture relations and sustainability governance that could shape approaches elsewhere in the UK. At the very least, I hope the book will increase awareness of, and interest in, BRs among residents, researchers and policymakers.

Evidence that WRB and BRs generally are undervalued is not only drawn from perspectives of those involved, but my experiences of the wider Scottish policy and research landscape, including interactions with policymakers and academics. WRB is often marginalised because hegemonic and common-sense narratives do not emphasise the need to change our relationships with each other and with non-human nature. As aforementioned, they focus instead on growing and greening the capitalist economy through technological and market fixes. Meaningful societal change for sustainability requires moving beyond this narrow focus. BRs offer culturally specific models for just and sustainable nature–culture relationships and can enact alternatives to the common sense of neoliberal policies. WRB are already doing this in many ways, and represent a vital source of inspiration for moving beyond the common-sense nature–culture dichotomy. However, this should never be taken for granted, it does not simply arise out of the BR model, but is rooted in WRB's process-oriented, community-led approach to sustainability.

These approaches are needed to think beyond the mainstream of top-down blueprints such as the SDGs. In Scotland, and elsewhere, we need to expand our imagination and recognise that there are many alternatives – alternatives that reject the continuation of unsustainable economic growth in favour of pursuing collective wellbeing.[11] Whilst my arguments above are a direct call for public bodies and government to act, at the same time, being influenced by anarchism, I am not optimistic that this will happen, or convinced that states are the legitimate actors to foster change. Instead, I find hope in the idea that a community Biosphere like WRB can create new societies in the shell of the old, prefiguring more sustainable nature–culture relations in the here and now. As critical researchers we can also help to make this happen. We can do so practically by channelling research power and funding into community sustainability initiatives and reshaping our practices towards research justice. Moreover, we can do so conceptually, rejecting the narrow parameters of common-sense ideologies and working for radical change in nature–culture relationships.

NOTES

1. Angela Wigger, 'Anarchism as Emancipatory Theory and Praxis: Implications for Critical Marxist Research,' *Capital and Class* 40, no. 1 (2016), 132.
2. Jim Thomas, *Doing Critical Ethnography* (Sage, 1993), 4.
3. Mark Purcell, 'Gramsci is Not Dead: For a "Both/And" Approach to Radical Geography,' *ACME: An International E-Journal for Critical Geographies* 11, no. 3 (2012): 512–24.
4. Benedikt Schmid, Thomas S. J. Smith and Gerald Taylor Aiken, 'Governing Through Community: Transformative Geographies From the Bottom Up,' *Environmental Policy and Governance* 31, no. 3 (2021): 155–8.
5. See Andrew J. Jolivétte, *Research Justice: Methodologies for Social Change* (Policy Press, 2025).
6. Vancouver Island University, Mount Arrowsmith Biosphere Region Research Institute (last accessed 5 September 2025), https://research.viu.ca/mount-arrowsmith-biosphere-region-research-institute.
7. Martin F. Price, 'The Evolution of the Biosphere Reserve Network in the United Kingdom,' in *UNESCO Biosphere Reserves: Supporting Biocultural Diversity, Sustainability and Society*, ed. M. Reed and M. F. Price (Routledge, 2020), 89–101.
8. Nick Kirsop-Taylor, Duncan Russel and Michael Winter, 'The Contours of State Retreat From Collaborative Environmental Governance Under Austerity,' *Sustainability* 12, no. 7 (2020): 1–16.
9. Maya I. Hernes and Marc J. Metzger, 'Understanding Local Community's Values, Worldviews and Perceptions in the Galloway and Southern Ayrshire

Biosphere Reserve, Scotland,' *Journal of Environmental Management* 186, no. 1 (2017): 12–23.

10. Zoe Russell, 'The Isle of Man Biosphere Reserve: An Entire Nation Approach to Sustainable Development,' *Environmental Policy and Planning* 25, no. 3 (2022): 273–86.
11. Janet Newman and J. Clarke, 'States of Imagination,' in *After Neoliberalism? The Kilburn Manifesto*, ed. S. Hall, D. Massey and M. Ruskin (Soundings, 2015), 109.

Appendix: Participant List

Pseudonym	Age/Gender	Roles
Adaira	Under 50/Female	Staff member WRB
Alan	Over 50/Male	Volunteer director WRB
Alison	Over 50/Female	Staff member NatureScot, co-opted advisor WRB
Anndra	Over 50/Male	Volunteer director WRB (Gaelic speaker)
Brian	Over 50/Male	Volunteer director WRB
Carla	Under 50/Female	Staff member NatureScot, co-opted advisor WRB
Callum	Under 50/Male	Forest planner, Forestry Land Scotland
Catherine	Over 50/Female	Wester Ross estate owner
Chris	Under 50/Male	Local resident, Gairloch
Coinneach	Under 50/Male	Volunteer director WRB (Gaelic speaker)
Elisabeth	Over 50/Female	Volunteer director WRB (Gaelic speaker)
Fionnlagh	Under 50/Male	Local resident, Applecross (Gaelic speaker)
Graham	Under 50/Male	Wester Ross estate owner, male, under 50
Jane	Under 50/Female	Former volunteer director WRB (Gaelic speaker)
Keith	Over 50/Male	Wester Ross estate owner
Shannon	Under 50/Female	Wester Ross estate owner
Mairi	Over 50/Female	Volunteer director WRB
Matthew	Under 50/Male	Conservation charity CEO
Michael	Over 50/ Male	Volunteer director WRB
Molly	Under 50/Female	Staff member, then volunteer director WRB
Norman	Over 50/ Male	Volunteer director WRB/ Staff member National Trust for Scotland
Phoebe	Under 50/Female	Staff member WRB
Robert	Over 50/Male	Highland Councillor, co-opted advisor WRB
Seumas	Over 50/Male	Volunteer director WRB
Thomas	Over 50/Male	Highland Councillor, co-opted advisor WRB
Uilleam	Over 50/Male	Highland Councillor, co-opted advisor WRB

References

Adams, William M., and Martin Mulligan, eds. *Decolonizing Nature: Strategies for Conservation in a Post-Colonial Era*. Earthscan from Routledge, 2003.

Adloff, Frank. 'Sustainability.' In *Critical Terms in Futures Studies*, edited by P. Heike. Springer International Publishing, 2019.

Ahenakew, Cash. 'Grafting Indigenous Ways of Knowing onto Non-Indigenous Ways of Being: The (Underestimated) Challenges of a Decolonial Imagination.' *International Review of Qualitative Research* 9, no. 3 (2016): 3.

Albertus, Michael. *Land Power: Who Has It, Who Doesn't and How That Determines the Fate of Societies*. Basic Books, 2025.

Alonso Gonzalez, Pablo. 'From a Given to a Construct: Heritage as a Commons.' *Cultural Studies* 28, no. 3 (2014): 359–90. https://doi.org/10.1080/09502386.2013.789067.

Alston, David. *Slaves and Highlanders: Silenced Histories of Scotland and the Caribbean*. Edinburgh University Press, 2021.

Apostolopoulou, Evangelia, and William M. Adams. 'Neoliberal Capitalism and Conservation in the Post-Crisis Era: The Dialectics of "Green" and "Un-Green" Grabbing in Greece and the UK: The Dialectics of "Green" and "Un-Green" Grabbing.' *Antipode* 47, no. 1 (2015): 15–35. https://doi.org/10.1111/anti.12102.

Armstrong, Timothy et al. 'Gaelic and Identity: A Response to Iain MacKinnon.' *Scottish Affairs* 31, no. 1 (2022): 1.

Arora, Saurabh, and Andy Stirling. 'Colonial Modernity and Sustainability Transitions: A Conceptualisation in Six Dimensions.' *Environmental Innovation and Societal Transitions* 48 (September 2023): 100733. https://doi.org/10.1016/j.eist.2023.100733.

Aschenbrand, Erik, and Thomas Michler. 'Why Do UNESCO Biosphere Reserves Get Less Recognition than National Parks? A Landscape Research Perspective on Protected Area Narratives in Germany.' *Sustainability* 13, no. 24 (2021): 13647. https://doi.org/10.3390/su132413647.

Baird, Julia, Ryan Plummer, Lisen Schultz, Derek Armitage and Örjan Bodin. 'Integrating Conservation and Sustainable Development Through Adaptive Co-Management in UNESCO Biosphere Reserves.' *Conservation and Society* 16, no. 4 (2018): 409–19. https://doi.org/10.4103/cs.cs_17_58.

Baldwin, J., ed. *Peoples and Settlement in North-West Ross*. Scottish Society for Northern Studies, 1994.

Bannister, John. 'Death of a Crofting Community?' *The Crofter* 117: 7. https://www.crofting.org/wp-content/uploads/2020/03/crofter117.pdf.

Barca, Stefania. *Forces of Reproduction: Notes for a Counter-Hegemonic Anthropocene*. Cambridge University Press, 2020. https://doi.org/10.1017/9781108878371.

Bargheer, Stefan. 'Conserving the Future: UNESCO Biosphere Reserves as Laboratories for Sustainable Development.' In *Endangerment, Biodiversity and Culture*, edited by F. Vidal and N. Dias. Routledge, 2015.

Barker, Adam, and Aileen Stockdale. 'Out of the Wilderness? Achieving Sustainable Development within Scottish National Parks.' *Journal of Environmental Management* 88, no. 1 (2008): 181–93. https://doi.org/10.1016/j.jenvman.2007.04.007.

Barraclough, Alicia D., Maureen G. Reed, Kaera Coetzer et al. 'Global Knowledge–Action Networks at the Frontlines of Sustainability: Insights from Five Decades of Science for Action in UNESCO's World Network of Biosphere Reserves.' *People and Nature* 5, no. 5 (2023): 1430–44. https://doi.org/10.1002/pan3.10515.

Bartolini, Nadia. 'Fixing Naturecultures: Spatial and Temporal Strategies For Managing Heritage Transformation and Entanglement.' In *Heritage Futures: Comparative Approaches to Natural and Cultural Heritage Practices*, edited by Rodney Harrison, C. DeSilvey, C. Holtorf, S. MacDonald, N. Bartolini, H. Fredheim, A. Lyons, S. May, J. Morgan and S. Penrose. UCL Press, 2020.

Bartolini, Nadia, and Caitlin DeSilvey. "Transforming Loss." In *Heritage Futures: Comparative Approaches to Natural and Cultural Heritage Practices*, edited by R. Harrison, C. DeSilvey, C. Holtorf, S. MacDonald, N. Bartolini, H. Fredheim, A. Lyons, S. May, J. Morgan and S. Penrose. UCL Press, 2020, 347–56.

Bateman, Meg. 'The Landscape of the Gaelic Imagination.' *International Journal of Heritage Studies* 15, nos. 2–3 (2009): 2–3. https://doi.org/10.1080/13527250902890613.

Baumgartner, Julia, Elisa Kuntner, Johannes Melchert et al. 'Biosphere Reserves as Drivers of Regional Governance? Communication Challenges within the UNESCO Biosphere Reserves Engiadina Val Müstair (Switzerland) and Schwäbische Alb (Germany).' *Eco.Mont (Journal on Protected Mountain Areas Research)* 15 (January 2022): 4–10. https://doi.org/10.1553/eco.mont-15-1s4.

Bechhofer, Frank, and David McCrone. 'What Makes a Gael? Identity, Language and Ancestry in the Scottish Gàidhealtachd.' *Identities* 21, no. 2 (2014): 2. https://doi.org/10.1080/1070289X.2014.878249.

Bennett, Sammi, and Krystyna Swiderska. 'Sumaq Kawsay: Alternative Development Rooted in the Wellbeing of Humans and Nature,' 2023. https://biocultural.iied.org/sumaq-kawsay-alternative-development-rooted-wellbeing-humans-and-nature.

Berghoefer, Uta, Ricardo Rozzi and Kurt Jax. 'Many Eyes on Nature: Diverse Perspectives in the Cape Horn Biosphere Reserve and their Relevance for Conservation.' *Ecology and Society* 15, no. 1 (2010): 18. https://doi.org/10.5751/ES-03316-150118.

Bogert, Jeanne M., Jacintha Ellers, Stephan Lewandowsky, Meena M. Balgopal and Jeffrey A. Harvey. 'Reviewing the Relationship Between Neoliberal

Societies and Nature: Implications of the Industrialized Dominant Social Paradigm For a Sustainable Future.' *Ecology and Society* 27, no. 2 (2022). https://doi.org/10.5751/ES-13134-270207.

Bohnet, Iris C., Rosalind Bryce, Inger E Måren et al. 'Co-Creating Cultural Narratives for Sustainable Rural Development: A Transdisciplinary Learning Framework for Guiding Place-Based Social-Ecological Research.' *Current Opinion in Environmental Sustainability* 73 (April 2025): 101506. https://doi.org/10.1016/j.cosust.2024.101506.

Boym, Svetlana. *The Future of Nostalgia*. Basic Books, 2001.

Breglia, Lisa. *Monumental Ambivalence: The Politics of Heritage*. University of Texas Press, 2006.

Bridgewater, Peter. 'Biosphere Reserves: Special Places for People and Nature.' *Environmental Science and Policy* 5, no. 1 (2002): 9–12. https://doi.org/10.1016/S1462-9011(02)00018-7.

Bridgewater, Peter, and Ian D. Rotherham. 'A Critical Perspective on the Concept of Biocultural Diversity and its Emerging Role in Nature and Heritage Conservation.' *People and Nature* 1, no. 3 (2019): 291–304. https://doi.org/10.1002/pan3.10040.

Brokaw, M. S. 'Solving the "Highland Problem": Frank Fraser Darling and the West Highland Survey, 1943–1955.' MPhil thesis, University of St Andrews, 2004.

Brossette, Florian, Claudia Bieling and Marianne Penker. 'Adapting Common Resource Management to Under-Use Contexts: The Case of Common Pasture Organizations in the Black Forest Biosphere Reserve.' *International Journal of the Commons* 16, no. 1 (2022): 1. Common pasture organizations. https://doi.org/10.5334/ijc.1138.

Brown, Katrina Myrvang. 'New Challenges for Old Commons: The Role of Historical Common Land in Contemporary Rural Spaces.' *Scottish Geographical Journal* 122, no. 2 (2006): 2. https://doi.org/10.1080/00369220600917412.

Brown, Katrina Myrvang. 'Understanding the Materialities and Moralities of Property: Reworking Collective Claims to Land.' *Transactions of the Institute of British Geographers* 32, no. 4 (2007): 4.

Burnett, John. *The Making of the Modern Scottish Highlands*. Four Courts Press, 2011.

Büscher, Bram. 'Reassessing Fortress Conservation? New Media and the Politics of Distinction in Kruger National Park.' *Annals of the American Association of Geographers* 106, no. 1 (2016): 114–29. https://doi.org/10.1080/00045608.2015.1095061.

Büscher, Bram, and Robert Fletcher. *The Conservation Revolution: Ideas for Saving Nature Beyond the Anthropocene*. Verso, 2020. https://www.versobooks.com/en-gb/products/856-the-conservation-revolution.

Büscher, Bram, Sian Sullivan, Katja Neves, Jim Igoe and Dan Brockington. 'Towards a Synthesized Critique of Neoliberal Biodiversity Conservation.' *Capitalism Nature Socialism* 23, no. 2 (2012): 4–30. https://doi.org/10.1080/10455752.2012.674149.

Byrne, Dennis, Sally Brockwell and Sue O'Connor. 'Introduction: Engaging Culture and Nature.' In *Transcending the Culture–Nature Divide in Cultural Heritage Views From the Asia-Pacific Region*. ANU E Press, 2013.

Cameron, Ewen A. 'The Scottish Highlands as a Special Policy Area, 1886 to 1965.' *Rural History* 8, no. 2 (1997): 195–215. https://doi.org/10.1017/S0956793300001278.

Camshron, Gòrdan. 'Resisting Dismissal in the *Gàidhealtachd*.' *Scottish Affairs* 30, no. 2 (2021): 240–50. https://doi.org/10.3366/scot.2021.0363.

Clapp, Jennifer, and William G. Moseley. 'This Food Crisis Is Different: COVID-19 and the Fragility of the Neoliberal Food Security Order.' *Journal of Peasant Studies* 47, no. 7 (2020): 1393–417. https://doi.org/10.1080/03066150.2020.1823838.

Clark, John, ed. *Anarchy, Geography, Modernity: Selected Writings of Elisée Reclus*. Translated by Camille Martin. PM Press, 2016. http://www.tandfonline.com/doi/full/10.1080/2325548X.2016.1146000.

Clement, Charles R., Carolina Levis, Joana Cabral de Oliveira et al. 'Naturalness Is in the Eye of the Beholder.' *Frontiers in Forests and Global Change* 4 (December 2021). https://doi.org/10.3389/ffgc.2021.800294.

Cocks, Michelle L. 'Biocultural Diversity: Moving Beyond the Realm of "Indigenous" and "Local" People.' *Human Ecology* 34, no. 2 (2006): 185–200.

Cocks, Michelle, Susanne Vetter and K. Freerk Wiersum. 'From Universal to Local: Perspectives on Cultural Landscape Heritage in South Africa.' *International Journal of Heritage Studies* 24, no. 1 (2018): 35–52. https://doi.org/10.1080/13527258.2017.1362573.

Coetzer, Kaera L., Edward T. F. Witkowski and Barend F. N. Erasmus. 'Reviewing Biosphere Reserves Globally: Effective Conservation Action or Bureaucratic Label?' *Biological Reviews of the Cambridge Philosophical Society* 89, no. 1 (2014): 82–104. https://doi.org/10.1111/brv.12044.

Cole, Stroma. 'A Gendered Political Ecology of Tourism And Water.' In *Political Ecology of Tourism: Community, Power and the Environment*, edited by M. Mostafanezhad, R. Norum, E. Shelton and A. Thompson-Carr. Routledge, 2016.

Combe, Malcolm Jayne Glass and Annie Tindley. *Land Reform in Scotland: History, Law and Policy*. Edinburgh University Press, 2020.

Convention on Biological Diversity Aichi Target Pages. Aichi Target 18. Accessed 12 June 2025, https://www.cbd.int/aichi-targets/target/18.

Corson, Catherine, and Kenneth Iain MacDonald. 'Enclosing the Global Commons: The Convention on Biological Diversity and Green Grabbing.' *Journal of Peasant Studies* 39, no. 2 (2012): 263–83. https://doi.org/10.1080/03066150.2012.664138.

Costello, Eugene. 'Hill Farmers, Habitats and Time: The Potential of Historical Ecology in Upland Management and Conservation.' *Landscape Research* 45, no. 8 (2020): 8. https://doi.org/10.1080/01426397.2020.1798367.

Course, Magnus. 'Houses of Uist: Memory and Dwelling in the Outer Hebrides: Houses of Uist.' *Journal of the Royal Anthropological Institute* 25, no. 1 (2018): 1. https://doi.org/10.1111/1467-9655.12962.

Crofting Commission, Appointment of Common Grazings Committees. Accessed 11 June 2025, https://www.crofting.scotland.gov.uk/common-grazings/appointment-of-grazings-committees/.

Cronon, William. 'The Trouble with Wilderness: Or, Getting Back to the Wrong Nature.' *Environmental History* 1, no. 1 (1996): 7–28. https://doi.org/10.2307/3985059.

Cusens, Jarrod, Alicia M. D. Barraclough and Inger Elisabeth Måren. 'Participatory Mapping Reveals Biocultural and Nature Values in the Shared Landscape of a Nordic UNESCO Biosphere Reserve.' *People and Nature* 4, no. 2 (2022): 365–81. https://doi.org/10.1002/pan3.10287.

Dabard, Caroline Hélène, Carsten Mann and Berta Martín-López. 'Biosphere Reserves as Catalysts for Sustainability Transformations: Five Strategies to Support Place-Based Innovation.' *Current Opinion in Environmental Sustainability* 73 (April 2025): 101508. https://doi.org/10.1016/j.cosust.2025.101508.

Deleuze, Gilles, and Félix Guattari. *A Thousand Plateaus: Capitalism and Schizophrenia*. University of Minnesota Press, 1987.

DeSilvey, Caitlin, and Rodney Harrison. 'Anticipating Loss: Rethinking Endangerment in Heritage Futures.' *International Journal of Heritage Studies* 26, no. 1 (2020): 1–7. https://doi.org/10.1080/13527258.2019.1644530.

Devine, Tom. *Clanship to Crofters' War: The Social Transformation of the Scottish Highlands*. Manchester University Press, 1994.

Doyle, Carey. 'Rethinking Communities, Land and Governance: Land Reform in Scotland and the Community Ownership Model.' *Planning Theory and Practice* 24, no. 3 (2023): 429–41. https://doi.org/10.1080/14649357.2023.2225322.

The Economist. 'Scotland's outdated land laws threaten the future of rural towns.' May 2025, last accessed 4 September 2025, https://www.economist.com/britain/2025/05/01/scotlands-outdated-land-laws-threaten-the-future-of-rural-towns.

Ekblom, Anneli, Anna Shoemaker, Lindsey Gillson, Paul Lane and Karl-Johan Lindholm. 'Conservation through Biocultural Heritage – Examples from Sub-Saharan Africa.' *Land* 8, no. 1 (2019): 1–15. https://doi.org/10.3390/land8010005.

Falzon, Mark-Anthony. *Multi-Sited Ethnography: Theory, Praxis and Locality in Contemporary Research*. Routledge, 2009. https://www.routledge.com/Multi-Sited-Ethnography-Theory-Praxis-and-Locality-in-Contemporary-Research/Falzon/p/book/9780367603168.

Federici, Silvia. *Re-enchanting the World: Feminism and the Politics of the Commons*. PM Press, 2018.

Fernández-Llamazares, Álvaro, and Mar Cabeza. 'Rediscovering the Potential of Indigenous Storytelling for Conservation Practice.' *Conservation Letters* 11, no. 3 (2018): 3. https://doi.org/10.1111/conl.12398.

Ferreira, Ana Filipa, Heike Zimmermann, Rui Santos and Henrik von Wehrden. 'Biosphere Reserves' Management Effectiveness – A Systematic Literature

Review and a Research Agenda.' *Sustainability* 12, no. 14 (2020): 14. https://doi.org/10.3390/su12145497.

Fiske, Desirée. 'Towards an Anthropocene Narrative and a New Philosophy of Governance: Evolution of Global Environmental Discourse in the Man and the Biosphere Programme,' *Journal of Environmental Policy and Planning* 24, no. 1 (2022): 109–22.

Flexner, James L. 'Doing Archaeology in Non-State Space.' *Journal of Contemporary Archaeology* 5, no. 2 (2018): 254–9. https://doi.org/10.1558/jca.33431.

Fraser Darling, Frank. *Natural History in the Highlands and Islands*. London, 1947.

Fraser Darling, Frank. ed. *West Highland Survey: An Essay in Human Ecology*. London, 1955.

Gonzalez-Tennant, Edward. 'Anarchism, Decolonization, and Collaborative Archaeology.' *Journal of Contemporary Archaeology* 5, no. 2 (2018): 238–44. https://doi.org/10.1558/jca.33487.

Gordon, Uri. 'Power and Anarchy: In/equality + In/visibility in Autonomous Politics.' In *New Perspectives on Anarchism*, edited by N. Jun and S. Wahl. Lexington Books, 2010.

Graddy, T. Garrett. 'Regarding Biocultural Heritage: In Situ Political Ecology of Agricultural Biodiversity in the Peruvian Andes.' *Agriculture and Human Values* 30, no. 4 (2013): 587–604.

Graham, Helen. 'Horizontality: Tactical Politics for Participation and Museums.' In *Engaging Heritage, Engaging Communities*, edited by Bryony Onciul, Michelle L. Stefano and Stephanie Hawke. Boydell and Brewer, 2017.

Graham, Helen. 'Publics and Commons: The Problem of Inclusion for Participation.' *ARKEN Bulletin* 7 (2017): 150–68.

Gramsci, Antonio. *Selections from the Prison Notebooks*. Translated by Quinton Hoare and Geoffrey Nowell-Smith. Lawrence and Wishart, 1998.

Gray, Malcolm. 'Crofting and Fishing in the North-West Highlands, 1890–1914.' *Northern Scotland* 1, no. 1 (1972): 89–114.

Gullion, Jessica Smartt. 'Assemblages and Entanglements.' In *Diffractive Ethnography*. Routledge, 2018.

Habersang, Anja. 'Utopia, Future Imaginations and Prefigurative Politics in the Indigenous Women's Movement in Argentina.' *Social Movement Studies* 23, no. 4 (2024): 479–94. https://doi.org/10.1080/14742837.2022.2047639.

Hains, Bryan, Ronald Hustedde and Kristina Ricketts. '21st Century Crofting: Strengths and Opportunities for Community Development.' *Journal of Agriculture, Food Systems, and Community Development*, 8 May 2013: 47–60. https://doi.org/10.5304/jafscd.2013.033.002.

Hall, Stuart, and Alan O'Shea. Soundings. https://doi.org/10.3898/136266213809450194.

Hanspach, Jan, Lisbeth Jamila Haider, Elisa Oteros-Rozas et al. 'Biocultural Approaches to Sustainability: A Systematic Review of the Scientific Literature.' *People and Nature* 2, no. 3 (2020): 643–59. https://doi.org/10.1002/pan3.10120.

Harrison, Rodney. *Heritage: Critical Approaches*. Routledge, 2013.

Harrison, Rodney. 'Beyond "Natural" and "Cultural" Heritage: Toward an Ontological Politics of Heritage in the Age of Anthropocene.' *Heritage and Society* 8, no. 1 (2015): 24–42. https://doi.org/10.1179/2159032X15Z.00000000036.

Harrison, Rodney, Caitlin DeSilvey, Cornelius Holtorf et al., eds. *Heritage Futures: Comparative Approaches to Natural and Cultural Heritage Practices*. UCL Press, 2020.

Harrison Rodney et al. 'For Ever, For Everyone.' In *Heritage Futures: Comparative Approaches to Natural and Cultural Heritage Practices*, edited by Rodney Harrison, C. DeSilvey, C. Holtorf, S. MacDonald, N. Bartolini, H. Fredheim, A. Lyons, S. May, J. Morgan and S. Penrose. UCL Press, 2020.

Harvey, David. 'The "New" Imperialism: Accumulation by Dispossession.' *The Socialist Register*, 2004.

Harvey, David C. 'Heritage and Scale: Settings, Boundaries and Relations.' *International Journal of Heritage Studies* 21, no. 6 (2015): 577–93. https://doi.org/10.1080/13527258.2014.955812.

Hernes, Maya I., and Marc J. Metzger. 'Understanding Local Community's Values, Worldviews and Perceptions in the Galloway and Southern Ayrshire Biosphere Reserve, Scotland.' *Journal of Environmental Management* 186 (January 2017): 12–23. https://doi.org/10.1016/j.jenvman.2016.10.040.

Hockings, Marc, Ian Lilley, Diane Matar, Nigel Dudley and Robert Markham. 'Integrating Science and Local Knowledge to Strengthen Biosphere Reserve Management.' In *UNESCO Biosphere Reserves: Supporting Biocultural Diversity, Sustainability and Society*, edited by Maureen Reed and Martin F. Price. Routledge, 2020.

Matthew Hoffman, 'Private Property in the Context of Community: Property and Community.' *American Journal of Economics and Sociology* 77, no. 1 (2018): 125–48.

Horowitz, Leah S. 'Rhizomic Resistance Meets Arborescent Assemblage: UNESCO World Heritage and the Disempowerment of Indigenous Activism in New Caledonia.' *Annals of the American Association of Geographers* 106, no. 1 (2016): 1. https://doi.org/10.1080/00045608.2015.1090270.

Hunter, James. *The Claim of Crofting: The Scottish Highlands and Islands, 1930–1990*. Mainstream Publishing, 1991.

Hunter, James. *The Making of the Crofting Community*. Birlinn, 2000.

Hunter, James. *Last of the Free: A Millennial History of the Highlands and Islands of Scotland*. Reprinted. Mainstream, 2003.

Hunter, James. *On the Other Side of Sorrow: People and Nature in the Highlands* (Birlinn, 2014).

Ince, Anthony. 'In the Shell of the Old: Anarchist Geographies of Territorialisation.' *Antipode* 44, no. 5 (2012): 5. https://doi.org/10.1111/j.1467-8330.2012.01029.x.

Ingold, Tim. 'Globes and Spheres: The Topology of Environmentalism.' In *The Perception of the Environment*. Routledge, 2021.

Ireland, Tracy, Steve Brown, Kate Bagnall, Jane Lydon, Tim Sherratt and Sharon Veale. 'Engaging the Everyday: The Concept and Practice of "Everyday

Heritage".' *International Journal of Heritage Studies* 31, no. 2 (2025): 192–215. https://doi.org/10.1080/13527258.2024.2417066.

Jamie, Kathleen. 'A Lone Enraptured Male'. Review of *The Wild Places*, by Robert Macfarlane. Psychology and Anthropology. *London Review of Books*, 6 March 2008. https://www.lrb.co.uk/the-paper/v30/n05/kathleen-jamie/a-lone-enraptured-male.

Jędrej, Charles, and Mark Nuttall. *White Settlers: The Impact of Rural Repopulation in Scotland*. Harwood Academic Publishers, 1996.

Jones, Rhys. 'Governing the Future and the Search for Spatial Justice: Wales' Wellbeing of Future Generations Act.' *Fennia* 197, no. 1 (2019): 8–24.

Jones, Rhys, Bryonny Goodwin-Hawkins and Michael Woods. 'From Territorial Cohesion to Regional Spatial Justice: The Well-Being of Future Generations Act in Wales.' *International Journal of Urban and Regional Research* 44, no. 5 (2020): 894–912. https://doi.org/10.1111/1468-2427.12909.

Jones, Siân. 'Making Place, Resisting Displacement: Conflicting National and Local Identities in Scotland.' In *The Politics of Heritage: The Legacies of Race*, edited by Jo Littler and Roshi Naidoo. Routledge, 2005.

Jones, Siân. '"Thrown like Chaff in the Wind": Excavation, Memory and the Negotiation of Loss in the Scottish Highlands.' *International Journal of Historical Archaeology* 16, no. 2 (2012): 346–66. https://doi.org/10.1007/s10761-012-0181-2.

Jones, Siân, and Thomas Yarrow. *The Object of Conservation: An Ethnography of Conservation Practice*. Routledge, Taylor and Francis Group, 2022.

Jolivétte, Andrew J. *Research Justice: Methodologies for Social Change*. Policy Press, 2025.

Kallis, Georgis. *Degrowth*. Agenda Publishing, 2018.

Karez, Cládia, Juan Hernández Faccio, Elke Schüttler et al. 'Learning Experiences about Intangible Heritage Conservation for Sustainability in Biosphere Reserves.' *Material Culture Review* 82–3 (2015): 84–96.

Kehoe, S. Karly, and Chris Dalglish, 'History, Heritage and Sustainable Development: A Position Statement on the Scottish Highlands,' *Northern Scotland* 9, no. 1 (2018): 1–16.

Kelly, Alice B. 'Conservation Practice as Primitive Accumulation.' *Journal of Peasant Studies* 38, no. 4 (2011): 683–701. https://doi.org/10.1080/03066150.2011.607695.

Kenterelidou, Clio, and Fani Galatsopoulou. 'Sustainable Biocultural Heritage Management and Communication: The Case of Digital Narrative for UNESCO Marine World Heritage of Outstanding Universal Value.' *Sustainability* 13, no. 3 (2021): 1449. https://doi.org/10.3390/su13031449.

Kinna, Ruth E. 'Utopianism and Prefiguration.' In *Political Uses of Utopia: New Marxist, Anarchist, and Radical Democratic Perspectives*, edited by S. Chrostowska and J. Ingram. Columbia University Press, 2016.

Kirsop-Taylor, Nick, Duncan Russel and Michael Winter. 'The Contours of State Retreat from Collaborative Environmental Governance under Austerity.' *Sustainability* 12, no. 7 (2020): 1–16. https://doi.org/10.3390/su12072761.

Konsa, Kurmo. 'Natural and Cultural Heritage: Framing Meanings and Practices.'

International Journal of Sustainability in Economic, Social, and Cultural Context 12, no. 4 (2016): 9–18.

Kothari, Ashish, Federico Demaria and Alberto Acosta. 'Buen Vivir, Degrowth and Ecological Swaraj: Alternatives to Sustainable Development and the Green Economy.' *Development* 57, nos. 3–4 (2014): 3–4. https://doi.org/10.1057/dev.2015.24.

Leibenath, Markus, Nadja Diemunsch, Myriam Pregizer and Jannou Catrin Bergsträßer. 'Biosphere Reserves as Landscape Laboratories for Sustainability Transitions.' *Landscape Research* 50, no. 3 (2025): 491–504. https://doi.org/10.1080/01426397.2024.2421336.

Lindholm, Karl-Johan, and Anneli Ekblom. 'A Framework for Exploring and Managing Biocultural Heritage.' *Anthropocene* 25 (March 2019): 1–11. https://doi.org/10.1016/j.ancene.2019.100195.

Local Voices CIC. *Mapping Intangible Cultural Heritage Assets and Collections in Scotland*. 2021.

Lopes De Souza, Marcelo. 'Whose Environment? Epistemic-Political Disputes over a Concept and its Uses.' In *Undoing Human Supremacy: Anarchist Political Ecology in the Face of Anthroparchy*, edited by Simon Springer et al. Rowman and Littlefield, 2021.

McCullough, Katie Louise. 'Resolving the "Highland Problem": The Highlands and Islands of Scotland and the European Union.' *Local Economy* 33, no. 4 (2018): 421–37. https://doi.org/10.1177/0269094218779516.

MacDonald, Fraser. 'Viewing Highland Scotland: Ideology, Representation and the "Natural Heritage".' *Area* 30, no. 3 (1998): 3. https://doi.org/10.1111/j.1475-4762.1998.tb00068.x.

MacDonald, Fraser. 'Wild Beasts.' *London Review of Books* 43, no. 18 (2021): 44–5.

Macdonald, Sharon. 'The Gaelic Renaissance and Scotland's Identities.' *Scottish Affairs* 26 (First Series), no. 1 (1999): 100–18. https://doi.org/10.3366/scot.1999.0009.

Macdonald, Sharon. *Difficult Heritage: Negotiating the Nazi Past in Nuremberg and Beyond*. Routledge, 2009.

Macdonald, Patricia, and Angus Macdonald. 'Marginal Lands? An Overview of the Environmental Contexts of Cultural Landscapes in the Highlands and Islands of Scotland.' *International Journal of Heritage Studies* 15, nos. 2–3 (2009): 108–41. https://doi.org/10.1080/13527250902890605.

McEwan, Cheryl. 'Decolonizing the Anthropocene.' In *International Relations in the Anthropocene*, edited by David Chandler, Franziska Müller and Delf Rothe. Springer International Publishing, 2021. https://doi.org/10.1007/978-3-030-53014-3_5.

McFadyen, Mairi, and Raghnaid Sandilands. 'On "Cultural Darning and Mending": Creative Responses to *Ceist an Fhearainn* / The Land Question in the *Gàidhealtachd*.' *Scottish Affairs* 30, no. 2 (2021): 157–77. https://doi.org/10.3366/scot.2021.0359.

McFadyen, Mairi, Chris Mackie, Elle Adams and Raghnaid Sandilands. *Integrating Intangible Cultural Heritage in Nature Recovery: A Place-Sensitive*

Approach in the Scottish Highlands. British Academy, 2025. https://www.thebritishacademy.ac.uk/documents/5971/00012_Nature_Recovery_Paper_7_-_McFadyen_Final.pdf.

McKee, Annie J. 'Legitimising the Laird? Communicative Action and the Role of Private Landowner and Community Engagement in Rural Sustainability.' *Journal of Rural Studies* 41 (October 2015): 23–36. https://doi.org/10.1016/j.jrurstud.2015.07.003.

Mackenzie, Fiona. *Places of Possibility: Property, Nature and Community Land Ownership*. John Wiley and Sons, 2013. https://doi.org/10.1002/978 1118278772.ch1.

MacKinnon, Danny. 'Regulating Regional Spaces: State Agencies and the Production of Governance in the Scottish Highlands.' *Environment and Planning A: Economy and Space* 33, no. 5 (2001): 5. https://doi.org/10.1068/a3346.

MacKinnon, Iain. 'Colonialism and the Highland Clearances.' *Northern Scotland* 8, no. 1 (2017): 22–48. https://doi.org/10.3366/nor.2017.0125.

MacKinnon, Iain. '"Decommonising the Mind": Historical Impacts of British Imperialism on Indigenous Tenure Systems and Self-Understanding in the Highlands and Islands of Scotland.' *International Journal of the Commons* 12, no. 1 (2018): 278–300. https://doi.org/10.18352/ijc.814.

MacKinnon, Iain. 'The Invention of the Crofting Community: Scottish History's Elision of Indigenous Identity, Ideology and Agency in Accounts of Land Struggle in the Modern Gàidhealtachd.' *Scottish Historical Review* 98, no. 1 (2019): 77–102. https://doi.org/10.3366/shr.2019.0380.

MacKinnon, Iain. 'Crofting Policy and Legislation: An Undemocratic and Illegitimate Structure of Domination?' In *Land Reform in Scotland: History, Law and Policy*, edited by Jayne Glass, Malcolm Combe and Annie Tindley. Edinburgh University Press, 2020.

MacKinnon, Iain. 'Recognising and Reconstituting Gàidheil Ethnicity.' *Scottish Affairs* 30, no. 2 (2021): 212–300. https://doi.org/10.3366/scot.2021.0361.

MacKinnon, Iain, and Andrew Mackillop. *Plantation Slavery and Landownership in the West Highlands and Islands: Legacies and Lessons*. Community Land Scotland, 2020.

MacKinnon, Iain, Lewis Williams and Arianna Waller. 'The Re-Indigenization of Humanity to Mother Earth: A Learning Platform for Cultivating Social-Ecological Resilience to Challenge the Anthropocene.' *Journal of Sustainability Education* 16 (January 2018).

Maclean, Roddy. 'Gaelic and Ecosystem Services: a Scoping Exercise,' NatureScot Report 1230, 2021, https://www.nature.scot/doc/naturescot-research-report-1230-ecosystem-services-and-gaelic-scoping-exercise.

Wilson McLeod, *Gaelic in Scotland: Policies, Movements, Ideologies*. Edinburgh University Press, 2022.

Macleod, Angus, and Geoff Payne. 'Locals and Incomers: Social and Cultural Identity in Late Twentieth Century Coigach.' In *Peoples and Settlement in North-West Ross*, edited by John R. Baldwin. Scottish Society for Northern Studies, 1994.

MacRae, Graeme. 'Universal Heritage Meets Local Livelihoods: "Awkward

Engagements" at the World Cultural Heritage Listing in Bali.' *International Journal of Heritage Studies* 23, no. 9 (2017): 846–59. https://doi.org/10.1080/13527258.2017.1339107.

Madison, D. Soyini. *Critical Ethnography: Method, Ethics, and Performance*. Third edition. SAGE, 2020.

Main, Rebecca, Richard Oram and Annie Tindley. 'Scotland's Environmental Histories: Mapping a Way Forward'. *Scottish Historical Review* 104, no. 2 (2025): 155–73. https://doi.org/10.3366/shr.2025.0717.

Makey, Leane. '"Thinking With Kaipara": A Decolonising Methodological Strategy to Illuminate Social Heterogenous Nature–Culture Relations in Place.' *Nature and Space* 0 (2022): 1–29.

Malcolm, Zoe, et al. 'Towards a Circular Economy and Just Transition to Net-Zero in Rural Scotland: Resident Perspectives on Policy and Practice,' *Journal of Rural Studies* 108 (May 2024): 103300.

Margulis, Matias, Nora Mckeon and Saturnino Borras. 'Land Grabbing and Global Governance: Critical Perspectives.' *Globalizations* 10 (February 2013). https://doi.org/10.1080/14747731.2013.764151.

Martin, Alison, Anke Fischer and Rob McMorran. 'Who Decides? The Governance of Rewilding in Scotland 'between the Cracks': Community Participation, Public Engagement, and Partnerships.' *Journal of Rural Studies* 98 (February 2023): 80–91. https://doi.org/10.1016/j.jrurstud.2023.01.007.

Matar, Diane and Brandon Anthony. 'Sense and Sustainability: the Story of Biosphere Reserves in Lebanon.' In *UNESCO Biosphere Reserves: Supporting Biocultural Diversity, Sustainability and Society*, edited by Maureen Reed and Martin F. Price. Routledge, 2020.

Mathevet, Raphaël, and Catherine Cibien. 'The French Biosphere Reserves: Looking for Ecological Solidarity and Stewardship.' In *UNESCO Biosphere Reserves: Supporting Biocultural Diversity, Sustainability and Society*, edited by Maureen Reed and Martin F. Price. Routledge, 2020.

Mathevet, Raphaël, Nancy Lee Peluso, Alexandre Couespel and Paul Robbins. 'Using Historical Political Ecology to Understand the Present: Water, Reeds, and Biodiversity in the Camargue Biosphere Reserve, Southern France.' *Ecology and Society* 20, no. 4 (2015): 17. https://doi.org/10.5751/ES-07787-200417.

Meighan, Paul J. 'Dùthchas, a Scottish Gaelic Methodology to Guide Self-Decolonization and Conceptualize a Kincentric and Relational Approach to Community-Led Research.' *International Journal of Qualitative Methods* 21 (April 2022): 16094069221142451. https://doi.org/10.1177/16094069221142451.

Meighan, Paul. 'Languages Do Not "Die", They Are Persecuted: A Scottish Gael's Perspective on Language "Loss".' *Bella Caledonia*, 19 July 2023. https://bellacaledonia.org.uk/2023/07/19/languages-do-not-die-they-are-persecuted-a-scottish-gaels-perspective-on-language-loss/.

Merçon, Juliana, Susanne Vetter, Maria Tengö et al. 'From Local Landscapes to International Policy: Contributions of the Biocultural Paradigm to Global Sustainability.' *Global Sustainability* 2 (2019): e7. https://doi.org/10.1017/sus.2019.4.

Meyfroidt, Patrick, Ariane De Bremond, Casey M. Ryan et al. 'Ten Facts about Land Systems for Sustainability.' *Proceedings of the National Academy of Sciences* 119, no. 7 (2022): e2109217118. https://doi.org/10.1073/pnas.2109217118.

Moreno-Ramos, Tania, and Eduard Müller. 'Biosphere Reserves, Ideal Sites to Implement Holistic Approaches in Regenerative Development.' In *UNESCO Biosphere Reserves: Supporting Biocultural Diversity, Sustainability and Society*, edited by Maureen Reed and Martin F. Price. Routledge, 2020.

Morgan, Colleen. 'Save the Date for Future Mourning: Prefiguration and Heritage.' *Forum Kritische Archäologie* 10 (2021): 1–5. https://doi.org/10.17169/REFUBIUM-29529.

Munro, Gillian and Keith Hart. *'The Highland Problem': State and Community in Local Development*. 2000, 49.

Munro, Jean. 'Ullapool and the British Fisheries Society.' In *Peoples and Settlement in North-West Ross*, edited by J. Baldwin. Scottish Society for Northern Studies, 1994.

Murray, John. *Reading the Gaelic Landscape: Leughadh Aghaidh na Tíre*. Whittles Publishing, 2014.

NatureScot. 'Our Approach to Community Empowerment', accessed 11 June 2025, https://www.nature.scot/about-naturescot/our-work/community-empowerment-and-scotlands-environment/our-approach-community-empowerment.

Newman, Janet, and John Clarke. 'States of Imagination.' In *After Neoliberalism? The Kilburn Manifesto*, edited by Stuart Hall, Doreen Massey and Michael Ruskin. Soundings, 2015.

Newton, Michael. *Warriors of the Word*. Birlinn Ltd, 2009.

Nicholls, Ron, Freya Higgins-Desbiolles and Grant Rigney. 'Ngarrindjeri Authority: a Sovereignty Approach to Tourism.' In *Political Ecology of Tourism: Community, Power and the Environment*, edited by M. Mostafanezhad, R. Norum, E. Shelton and A. Thompson-Carr. Routledge, 2016.

Nightingale, Andrea. 'Challenging the Romance With Resilience: Communities, Scale and Climate Change.' In *Practising Feminist Political Ecologies: Moving Beyond The Green Economy*, edited by W. Harcourt and I. Nelson. Zed Books, 2015.

Ní Mhathúna, Déirdre. 'Traditional Ecological Knowledge and the Relevance of *Dùthchas* in *Gàidhealtachd* Environmental Futures.' *Scottish Affairs* 30, no. 2 (2021): 2. https://doi.org/10.3366/scot.2021.0364.

Ó Giollagáin, Conchúr, Gòrdan Camshron, Pàdruig Moireach et al. *Gaelic Crisis in the Vernacular Community: A Comprehensive Sociolinguistic Survey of Scottish Gaelic*. Aberdeen University Press, 2020.

Onaindia, Miren, Cristina Herrero, Alberto Hernandez et al. 'Co-Creation of Sustainable Development Knowledge in Biosphere Reserves.' In *UNESCO Biosphere Reserves: Supporting Biocultural Diversity, Sustainability and Society*, edited by Maureen Reed and Martin F. Price. Routledge, 2020.

Orr, Raymond. 'The Nostalgic Native? The Politics and Terms of Heritage and Remembrance in Two Communities.' *International Journal of Heritage Studies* 23, no. 7 (2017): 7. https://doi.org/10.1080/13527258.2017.1300929.

Pacifico, David. 'Beyond the Property Paradigm: Fragments for an Anarchist Approach to Archaeological Heritage.' *Journal of Contemporary Archaeology* 5, no. 2 (2018): 283–302.

Parra, Constanza, and Frank Moulaert. 'The Governance of the Nature–Culture Nexus: Lessons Learned from the San Pedro de Atacama Case Study.' *Nature and Culture* 11, no. 3 (2016): 239–58. https://doi.org/10.3167/nc.2016.110302.

Peters, Manuel. 'Culture, Heritage and Solidarity in the Context of Sustainable Development.' In *Perceptions of Sustainability in Heritage Studies*, edited by M. T. Albert. DeGruyter, 2015.

Pickerill, Jenny. 'From Wilderness to WildCountry: The Power of Language in Environmental Campaigns in Australia.' *Environmental Politics* 17, no. 1 (2008): 95–104. https://doi.org/10.1080/09644010701811681.

Poole, Alexandria K. 'Where Is Goal 18? The Need for Biocultural Heritage in the Sustainable Development Goals.' *Environmental Values* 27 (February 2018): 55–80. https://doi.org/info:doi/10.3197/096327118X151446986375 22.

Posocco, Silvia. 'Zoning: Environmental Cosmopolitics in and Around the Maya Biosphere Reserve, Petén, Guatemala.' *Nature + Culture; New York* 3, no. 2 (2008): 206–24. http://dx.doi.org/10.3167/nc.2008.030204.

Price, Martin F. 'The Periodic Review of Biosphere Reserves: A Mechanism to Foster Sites of Excellence for Conservation and Sustainable Development.' *Environmental Science*, 2002, 6.

Price, Martin F. 'The Re-Territorialisation of Biosphere Reserves: The Case of Wester Ross, Northwest Scotland.' *Environmental Science and Policy* 72 (June 2017): 30–40. https://doi.org/10.1016/j.envsci.2017.02.002.

Price, Martin F. 'The Evolution of the Biosphere Reserve Network in the United Kingdom.' In *UNESCO Biosphere Reserves: Supporting Biocultural Diversity, Sustainability and Society*, edited by Maureen Reed and Martin F. Price. Routledge, 2020.

Purcell, Mark. 'Gramsci Is Not Dead: For a "Both/And" Approach to Radical Geography.' *ACME: An International E-Journal for Critical Geographies* 11, no. 3 (2012): 512–24.

Raekstad, Paul, and Sofa S. Gradin. *Prefigurative Politics: Building Tomorrow Today*. Polity, 2019.

Reed, Mark S. R., Kerry A. Waylen, Jayne Glass, J. P. G. Glendinning, R. McMorran, Leo Peskett, Hannah Rudman, D. B. S. Stevens, A. W. Williams. 'Land Use Partnerships Using a National Capital Approach: Lessons for Scotland', 2022, http://dx.doi.org/10.7488/era/2229.

Reed, Maureen. 'Conceptual Origins and First-Generation Biosphere Reserves.' In *UNESCO Biosphere Reserves: Supporting Biocultural Diversity, Sustainability and Society*, edited by Maureen Reed and Martin F. Price. Routledge, 2020.

Reed, Maureen and Martin F. Price. 'Unfinished Business: The Present and Future Contributions of Biosphere Reserves to Sustainability Science.' In *UNESCO Biosphere Reserves: Supporting Biocultural Diversity, Sustainability and Society*. Routledge, 2020.

Reed, Maureen, and Martin F. Price. 'Introducing UNESCO Biosphere Reserves.' In *UNESCO Biosphere Reserves: Supporting Biocultural Diversity, Sustainability and Society*. Routledge, 2020.

Reed, Maureen and Martin F. Price. eds. *UNESCO Biosphere Reserves: Supporting Biocultural Diversity, Sustainability and Society*. Routledge, 2020.

Robertson, Iain J. M. 'Hardscrabble Heritage: The Ruined Blackhouse and Crofting Landscape as Heritage from Below.' *Landscape Research* 40, no. 8 (2015): 8. https://doi.org/10.1080/01426397.2015.1074986.

Robertson, Iain J. M. 'Introduction: Heritage from Below.' In *Heritage from Below*, edited by Iain J. M Robertson. Routledge, 2016.

Robertson, Iain J. M. 'Afterword.' In *After Heritage: Critical Perspectives From Below*, edited by H. Muzzaini and C. Minca. Elgar, 2018.

Rohde, Rick. 'Written on the Surface of the Soil: West Highland Crofting Landscapes During the 20th Century.' In *Repeat Photography: Methods and Applications in the Geological and Ecological Sciences*, edited by R. H. Webb, D. E. Boyer and R. Turner. Island Press, 2010.

Rollo, Maria F. 'Interconnected Nature and People: Biosphere Reserves and the Power of Memory and Oral Histories as Biocultural Heritage for a Sustainable Future.' *Sustainability* 17, no. 9 (2025): 1–33. https://doi.org/10.3390/su17094030.

Ross, Andrea. 'The Future Scotland Wants – Is It Really All about Sustainable Economic Growth?' *Edinburgh Law Review* 19, no. 1 (2015): 66–100. https://doi.org/10.3366/elr.2015.0251.

Ross, Andrea. 'The Evolution of Sustainable Development in Scotland – A Case Study of Community Right-to-Buy Law and Policy 2003–2018.' *Sustainability* 11, no. 1 (2019): 1–18. https://doi.org/10.3390/su11010130.

Russell, Zoe. 'Common Sense Discourses of Nature: A Gramscian Analysis of Conservation Designations in the Scottish Highlands.' In *Heritage and Environment*. 5th Central European Heritage Forum. ICC, 2021.

Russell, Zoe. 'The Isle of Man Biosphere Reserve: An Entire Nation Approach to Sustainable Development.' *Journal of Environmental Policy and Planning* 25, no. 3 (2023): 273–86. https://doi.org/10.1080/1523908X.2022.2099366.

Russell, Zoe. 'An Anarchist Imagination for Critical Heritage Studies: Prefiguring Equitable and Sustainable Futures in Crofting and Beyond.' In *The Routledge International Handbook of Heritage and Politics*, edited by Gönül Bozoğlu, Gary Campbell, Laurajane Smith and Christopher Whitehead. Routledge, 2024. https://doi.org/10.4324/9781003300984-16.

Russell, Zoe, Lucy Beattie and David Heaney. 'Spaces of Well-Being: Social Crofting in Rural Scotland.' *Journal of Rural Studies* 86 (August 2021): 145–54. https://doi.org/10.1016/j.jrurstud.2021.05.007.

Savransky, Martin. 'Ecological Uncivilisation: Precarious World-Making after Progress.' *Sociological Review*, 15 March 2022, 003802612210847. https://doi.org/10.1177/00380261221084782.

Sayre, Matthew, Tammy Stenner and Alejandro Argumedo. 'You Can't Grow Potatoes in the Sky: Building Resilience in the Face of Climate Change in the Potato Park of Cuzco, Peru.' *Culture, Agriculture, Food and Environment* 39, no. 2 (2017): 100–8. https://doi.org/10.1111/cuag.12100.

Scarano, Fabio Rubio. 'Deep Sustainability Utopia.' In *Regenerative Dialogues for Sustainable Futures: Integrating Science, Arts, Spirituality and Ancestral Knowledge for Planetary Wellbeing*, edited by Fabio Scarano. Springer International Publishing, 2024. https://doi.org/10.1007/978-3-031-51841-6_18.

Schmid, Benedikt, Thomas S. J. Smith and Gerald Taylor Aiken. 'Governing through Community: Transformative Geographies from the Bottom Up.' *Environmental Policy and Governance* 31, no. 3 (2021): 155–8. https://doi.org/10.1002/eet.1928.

Schüttler, Elke, Roy Mackenzie and Lucas Muñoz-Petersen. 'Biocultural Conservation in Biosphere Reserves in Temperate Regions of Chile, Estonia, Germany, and Sweden.' In *Field Environmental Philosophy*. Springer, 2023. https://doi.org/10.1007/978-3-031-23368-5_29.

Scottish Government. Crofting: National Development Plan, 2021. https://www.gov.scot/publications/national-development-plan-crofting/.

Scottish Government. Community Ownership in Scotland 2022. Accessed 11 June 2025, https://www.gov.scot/publications/community-ownership-in-scotland-2022/.

Scottish Government. Scotland's Third Land Use Strategy 2021–2026. Getting the Best from our Land: Strategy 2021 to 2026. https://www.gov.scot/publications/scotlands-third-land-use-strategy-2021-2026-getting-best-land/pages/4/.

Scottish Government. Urban-Rural Classification 2020. Accessed 11 June 2025, https://www.gov.scot/publications/scottish-government-urban-rural-classification-2020/pages/2/.

Scottish Land Commission, Community Ownership, 2022. Accessed 11 June 2025, https://www.landcommission.gov.scot/our-work/ownership/community-ownership.

Shantz, Jeff. *Commonist Tendencies: Mutual Aid beyond Communism*. 2013. https://www.oapen.org/download?type=document&docid=1004518.

Shucksmith, Mark. 'Disintegrated Rural Development? Neo-Endogenous Rural Development, Planning and Place-Shaping in Diffused Power Contexts.' *Sociologia Ruralis* 50, no. 1 (2010): 1–14. https://doi.org/10.1111/j.1467-9523.2009.00497.x.

Shucksmith, Mark. 'Class, Power and Inequality in Rural Areas: Beyond Social Exclusion?: C lass, power and inequality in rural areas.' *Sociologia Ruralis* 52, no. 4 (2012): 377-97. https://doi.org/10.1111/j.1467-9523.2012.00570.x.

Shucksmith, Mark. 'Re-Imagining the Rural: From Rural Idyll to Good Countryside.' *Journal of Rural Studies* 59 (April 2018): 163–72. https://doi.org/10.1016/j.jrurstud.2016.07.019.

Shucksmith, Mark, and Katrina Rønningen. 'The Uplands after Neoliberalism? – The Role of the Small Farm in Rural Sustainability.' *Journal of Rural Studies* 27, no. 3 (2011): 3. https://doi.org/10.1016/j.jrurstud.2011.03.003.

Smith, Laura-Jane. *Uses of Heritage*. Routledge, 2006.

Springer, Simon, Jennifer Mateer, Martin Locret-Collet and Maleea Acker. *Undoing Human Supremacy: Anarchist Political Ecology in the Face of Anthroparchy*. Rowman and Littlefield, 2021.

Staddon, Sam. 'Conservation's All about Having a Blether and Getting People on Board: Exploring Cooperation for Conservation in Scotland.' *Conservation and Society*, 2021. https://doi.org/10.4103/cs.cs_20_58.

Sterling, Colin and Rodney Harrison. 'Introduction: of Territories and Temporalities.' In *Deterritorializing the Future: Heritage in, of and after the Anthropocene*. Open Humanities Press, 2020.

Stewart, Edward. 'Wicked Wild Wastes? Challenging Wildness through Repopulating Approaches to Archaeological Narratives in Scottish Highland Landscapes.' *Scottish Historical Review* 104, no. 2 (2025): 249–77. https://doi.org/10.3366/shr.2025.0721.

Stoll-Kleeman, Susanne, and Tim O'Riordan. 'The Challenges of the Anthropocene for Biosphere Reserves.' *PARKS* 23, no. 1 (2017): 89–100. https://doi.org/10.2305/IUCN.CH.2017.PARKS-23-1SS-K.en.

Stoll-Kleemann, Susanne, Anne Cristina De La Vega-Leinert and Lisen Schultz. 'The Role of Community Participation in the Effectiveness of UNESCO Biosphere Reserve Management: Evidence and Reflections from Two Parallel Global Surveys.' *Environmental Conservation* 37, no. 3 (2010): 227–38. https://doi.org/10.1017/S037689291000038X.

Stuart, Diana, and Ryan Gunderson. 'Human–Animal Relations in the Capitalocene: Environmental Impacts and Alternatives.' *Environmental Sociology* 6, no. 1 (2020): 68–81. https://doi.org/10.1080/23251042.2019.1666784.

Swiderska, Kystyna. 'Protecting Traditional Knowledge: A Holistic Approach Based on Customary Laws and Bio-Cultural Heritage.' In *Conserving and Valuing Ecosystem Services and Biodiversity: Economic, Institutional and Social Challenges*, edited by K. N. Ninan. Earthscan, 2009.

Swiderska, Krystyna, and Alejandro Argumedo. 'What is Biocultural Heritage?' International Institute for Environment and Development, 2017, https://pubs.iied.org/g04151.

Swiderska, Krystyna, Alejandro Argumedo and Michel Pimbert. *Biocultural Heritage Territories: Key to Halting Biodiversity Loss*. International Institute for Environment and Development, 2020. https://www.jstor.org/stable/resrep29050.

Swiderska, Krystyna, Alejandro Argumedo, Chemuku Wekesa et al. 'Indigenous Peoples' Food Systems and Biocultural Heritage: Addressing Indigenous Priorities Using Decolonial and Interdisciplinary Research Approaches.' *Sustainability* 14, no. 18 (2022): 18. https://doi.org/10.3390/su141811311.

Těšitel, Jan, and Drahomíra Kušová. 'The More Institutional Models, The More Challenges: Biosphere Reserves in the Czech Republic.' In *UNESCO Biosphere Reserves: Supporting Biocultural Diversity, Sustainability and Society*, edited by Maureen Reed and Martin F. Price. Routledge, 2020.

Thomas, Jim. *Doing Critical Ethnography*. Qualitative Research Methods, volume 26. Sage Publications, 1993.

Toogood, Mark. 'Decolonizing Highland Conservation.' In *Decolonizing Nature: Strategies for Conservation in a Post-Colonial Era*, edited by William M. Adams and Martin Mulligan. Earthscan from Routledge, 2003.

Torralba, Mario, Maria Garcia-Martin, Cristina Quintas-Soriano, Franziska Wolpert and Tobias Plieninger. 'Implementation of Social-Ecological Management

Approaches in Biosphere Reserves in the Mediterranean Basin.' In *UNESCO Biosphere Reserves: Supporting Biocultural Diversity, Sustainability and Society*, edited by Maureen Reed and Martin F. Price. Routledge, 2020.

Ullapool Community Trust, Community Growth Plan 2017–2027. https://ullapoolcommunity.org/wp-content/uploads/2019/12/CGP-2017_Executive-Summary.pdf.

UNESCO, 'A New Roadmap for the Man and the Biosphere (MAB) Programme and its World Network of Biosphere Reserves.' United Nations Educational, Scientific and Cultural Organization, 2017. https://unesdoc.unesco.org/ark:/48223/pf0000247418.

UNESCO, 'About the Man and the Biosphere (MAB) Programme.' Accessed 11 June 2025, https://www.unesco.org/en/mab/about?hub=66369.

UNESCO, 'What are Biosphere Reserves?' Accessed 11 June 2025, https://en.unesco.org/biosphere/about.

Vancouver Island University, 'Mount Arrowsmith Biosphere Region Research Institute.' Last accessed 5 September 2025, https://research.viu.ca/mount-arrowsmith-biosphere-region-research-institute.

Vasseur, Liette. 'Embracing Cultures in Ecosystem Governance in Biosphere Reserves: Slowing Down the Pace.' In *UNESCO Biosphere Reserves: Supporting Biocultural Diversity, Sustainability and Society*, edited by Maureen Reed and Martin F. Price. Routledge, 2020.

Vidal, Fernando, and Nélia Dias. *Endangerment, Biodiversity and Culture*. Routledge, 2014.

Walk, Heike, Vera Luthhardt and Benjamin Nolting. 'Participatory Learning for Transdisciplinary Science in Biosphere Reserves: A Modified Role for Universities.' In *UNESCO Biosphere Reserves: Supporting Biocultural Diversity, Sustainability and Society*, edited by Maureen Reed and Martin F. Price. Routledge, 2020.

Walsh, Cormac. 'Landscape Imaginaries and the Protection of Dynamic Nature at the Wadden Sea.' *Rural Landscapes: Society, Environment, History* 7, no. 1 (2020): 1–20.

Warburton, Theresa. 'What Looks like a Grave: Native and Anarchist Place-Making in New England.' *Studies in American Indian Literatures* 32, nos. 1–2 (2020): 1–2. https://doi.org/10.5250/studamerindilite.32.1-2.0075.

Weaver, John C. *Great Land Rush and the Making of the Modern World, 1650–1900*. McGill-Queen's University Press, 2003.

White, Eleanor, Rianne van Melik and James Bendle. 'Perceived Impacts of Tourism on Community Identity: Perspectives of Two Scottish Highland Communities.' *Tourism Planning and Development* 21, no. 6 (2024): 917–39. https://doi.org/10.1080/21568316.2024.2398465.

Whyte, Kyle. 'Indigenous Climate Change Studies: Indigenizing Futures, Decolonizing the Anthropocene.' *English Language Notes* 55, nos. 1–2 (2017): 153–62. https://doi.org/10.1215/00138282-55.1-2.153.

Wichterich, Christa. 'Contesting Green Growth: Connecting Care, Commons and Enough.' In *Practising Feminist Political Ecologies: Moving Beyond the Green Economy*, edited by Wendy Harcourt and Ingrid Nelson. Zed Books, 2015.

Wigger, Angela. 'Anarchism as Emancipatory Theory and Praxis: Implications for Critical Marxist Research.' *Capital and Class* 40, no. 1 (2016): 129–45. https://doi.org/10.1177/0309816816628247.

Wightman, Andy 'Who Owns Scotland?' (2025), https://andywightman.scot/wp-content/uploads/2025/03/WOS_2024.pdf.

Wilkes, Johanna. 'Reconnecting with Nature through Good Governance: Inclusive Policy across Scales.' *Agriculture* 12, no. 3 (2022): 3. https://doi.org/10.3390/agriculture12030382.

Wilkinson, Tim. 'Biocultural Heritage Tourism – a Review of Literature and Experiences', 2019, https://www.bcht.eu/uploads/1/5/4/4/15448192/bcht_literature_review___appendixes.pdf.

Williams, Daniel R. 'Spacing Conservation Practice: Place-Making, Social Learning, and Adaptive Landscape Governance in Natural Resource Management.' In *The Sage Handbook of Nature*, edited by T. Marsden. Sage, 2018.

Willis, Douglas. 'Man and the Land: Physical Environment and Settlement in the North-West Highlands.' In *Peoples And Settlement in North-West Ross*, edited by J. Baldwin. Scottish Society for Northern Studies, 1994.

Winkel, Thierry, Lizbeth Núñez-Carrasco, Pablo José Cruz et al. 'Mobilising Common Biocultural Heritage for the Socioeconomic Inclusion of Small Farmers: Panarchy of Two Case Studies on Quinoa in Chile and Bolivia.' *Agriculture and Human Values* 37, no. 2 (2020): 2. https://doi.org/10.1007/s10460-019-09996-1.

Winkler, 'Klara Johanna. 'The Implementation of the Conceptual Shift in Conservation: Pathways of Three German UNESCO Biosphere Reserves,' *Ecosystems and People*, 15, no. 1 (2019): 173–80.

Winkler, Klara J., and Jennifer Hauck. 'Landscape Stewardship for a German UNESCO Biosphere Reserve: A Network Approach to Establishing Stewardship Governance.' *Ecology and Society* 24, no. 3 (2019): 3. https://www.jstor.org/stable/26796978.

Winter, Tim. 'Clarifying the Critical in Critical Heritage Studies.' *International Journal of Heritage Studies* 19, no. 6 (2013): 532–45. https://doi.org/10.1080/13527258.2012.720997.

Wolford, Wendy W., Ben White, Ian Scoones, Ruth Hall, Marc Edelman and Saturnino M. Borras. 'Global Land Deals: What Has Been Done, What Has Changed, and What's Next?' *Journal of Peasant Studies* 0, no. 0 (2024): 1–38. https://doi.org/10.1080/03066150.2024.2325685.

Womack, Peter. *Improvement and Romance*. Macmillan, 1989.

Zimmerer, Karl S. 'The Reworking of Conservation Geographies: Nonequilibrium Landscapes and Nature-Society Hybrids.' *Annals of the Association of American Geographers* 90, no. 2 (2000): 2. https://doi.org/10.1111/0004-5608.00199.

Index

EU Authorised Representative:
Easy Access System Europe Mustamäe tee 50, 10621 Tallinn, Estonia
gpsr.requests@easproject.com

Printed and bound by CPI Group (UK) Ltd, Croydon, CR0 4YY
07/08/2026
02189980-0001